DEIFICATION IN CHRIST

CONTEMPORARY GREEK THEOLOGIANS

NUMBER FIVE

EDITORIAL COMMITTEE

PROFESSOR CHRISTOS YANNARAS
BISHOP KALLISTOS OF DIOKLEIA
COSTA CARRAS

PANAYIOTIS NELLAS

DEIFICATION IN CHRIST

Orthodox Perspectives on the Nature of the Human Person

Translated from the Greek
by
NORMAN RUSSELL

with a foreword
by
Bishop KALLISTOS OF DIOKLEIA

ST VLADIMIR'S SEMINARY PRESS
CRESTWOOD, NEW YORK 10707
1987

Library of Congress Cataloging-in-Publication Data

Nellas, Panayiotis, 1936-1986
    Deification in Christ.

    (Contemporary Greek theologians; no. 5)
    Translation of: Zōon theoumenon.
    Bibliography: p.
    1. Man (Christian theology)—History of doctrines—Early church,
ca. 30-600. 2. Image of God—History of doctrines—Early church, ca.
30-600. 3. Salvation—History of doctrines—Early church, ca. 30-600.
4. Spirituality—Orthodox Eastern Church—History of doctrines—Middle
Ages, 600-1500. 5. Man (Christian theology)—History of doctrines—
Middle Ages, 600-1500. 6. Orthodox Eastern Church—Doctrtines—History. 7. Cabasilas, Nicolaus, 14th cent. I. Title. II. Series.

BT701.2.N4413 1987   233   86-31479
ISBN 0-88141-030-6

DEIFICATION IN CHRIST

© Copyright 1987

by

ST VLADIMIR'S SEMINARY PRESS

ISBN 0-88141-030-6

PRINTED IN THE UNITED STATES OF AMERICA
BY
ATHENS PRINTING COMPANY
New York, NY 10018

Contents

PART TWO

THE SPIRITUAL LIFE IN CHRIST

Foreword

On the walls of the temple at Delphi were written the words "Know yourself." To know oneself, said St Clement of Alexandria, is the greatest of all lessons. Yet such self-knowledge is not easily attained. What is my true self? Who am I? What am I? The answers are far from obvious. The boundaries of each person are exceedingly wide, overlapping as they do with those of other persons, ranging over space and time, reaching out of space into infinity, out of time into eternity. In an important sense we do not know exactly what is involved in being a person, what is the true fulfilment of our personalness, what are the possibilities as yet latent within it. There is, as Panayiotis Nellas points out at the start of this book, a specific reason for this mysterious, indefinable character of the person. It is because the human being is made in God's image and likeness; since God is beyond understanding, His icon within humanity is also incomprehensible. In our talk about humans as well as our talk about God, there needs to be an apophatic dimension. Our negative theology demands as counterpart a "negative anthropology."

The human person—free, unpredictable, self-transcending —is coming more and more to constitute the central theme of contemporary theology, both Orthodox and non-Orthodox. To this continuing discussion the present work makes an outstanding contribution. Sadly, the author died on 6 April 1986, while this English translation was in preparation. His death from heart failure, at the early age of fifty, was altogether unexpected. It is a tragic loss to Greek theology; for, along with Christos Yannaras, his contemporary and friend from student years, Panayiotis Nellas was perhaps the most gifted and original religious thinker of the "middle" generation at work in Greece today, and at the time of his sudden death he was at the height of his creative activity.

Born in 1936, Panayiotis studied theology at the University of Athens, later spending two years on postgraduate work in France, at Lille and Paris, followed by six months at Rome. From 1968 until his death he taught religious studies at a high school in Athens. During his youth, in common with many of his generation who have since come to play a leading part in Greek church life, he was connected with the Zoe movement; but, like others in the early 1960s, he parted from it and chose a somewhat different path. He was profoundly influenced by Dimitrios Koutroubis (1921-83), the "lay elder" or kosmokalogeros of Vouliagmeni, who in a discreet and hidden manner had such a transfiguring effect upon the development of Greek theology in the 1960s and the 1970s. Unmarried, never ordained, Panayiotis was a lay theologian, one of the many active in Greece today, where theology is taught more by the laity than the clergy. He had a deep love for monasticism, often staying on Mount Athos; much of the present book was written there at the monastery of Stavronikita, whose abbot Fr Vasileios, author of Hymn of Entry, was his personal friend.

Most of what Panayiotis Nellas wrote was devoted to the fourteenth-century Byzantine theologian Nicolas Kavasilas (or Cabasilas), recently proclaimed a saint. His Prolegomena to the Study of Nicolas Kavasilas appeared in 1969, and this was followed in 1974 by his doctoral thesis for the University of Athens, The Teaching of Nicolas Kavasilas on Justification: A Contribution to Orthodox Soteriology. The second part of the present book describes what Panayiotis calls the "Christocentric anthropology" of Kavasilas, and shortly before he died he completed a further study on Kavasilas, as yet unpublished.

In 1968 Panayiotis launched the series Epi tas Pigas, "To the Sources," a Greek equivalent to the French collection Sources chrétiennes, although on a far more modest scale. The first volume, containing three homilies by Kavasilas in honor of the Mother of God, was edited by Panayiotis him-

self. Later volumes in the series included the Marian homilies
of St John of Damascus, edited by the Serbian theologian Fr
Athanasy Jevtich, and two volumes of works by St Maximos
the Confessor, edited by the Romanian theologian Fr Dumitru
Staniloae. It was characteristic of Panayiotis that he should
enlist contributors from outside as well as from within the
Greek world, for he had a keen sense of the universality of
Orthodoxy. Each volume in the series contains the original
Greek text, accompanied by a translation into modern Greek,
together with introduction and notes. His aim in this, as in
almost all his theological work, was to relate Patristic thought
to the modern world, to render the Fathers intelligible and
relevant to reflective Christians of our own day who are not
specialists in theology, to make the Fathers speak as our
contemporaries. I do not recall whether Panayiotis himself
made use of Fr George Florovsky's phrase "neopatristic
synthesis," but it describes very appropriately what he was
seeking to do.

At the time of his death Panayiotis was working on a
book about St Maximos the Confessor. But in his last years,
from 1982 onwards, his energies were chiefly devoted to the
review *Synaxi,* of which he was the founder and editor. This
appeared quarterly, with some 112 pages in each number,
and he was preparing the eighteenth issue when he died.
Here, as in the series *Epi tas Pigas,* Panayiotis sought to
relate traditional Orthodox theology to the modern world.
The title of the journal means "meeting," "gathering," "assembly" (often for liturgical prayer); in the pages of *Synaxi*
he aimed to gather together his contemporaries for a meeting,
for a creative dialogue, with each other and with the past.
Greece today has various learned periodicals, edited by university professors of theology and severely academic in tone;
it has also a vast number of popular religious magazines. But
until recently there has been a dearth of theological journals
appealing to the "middle ground," to the intelligent non-
specialist, and dealing in a sympathetic, sophisticated manner
with Christian themes in art and literature, in politics and
culture, as well as with more narrowly ecclesiastical questions.
Synaxi, continuing the traditions of the earlier review *Synoro*

which ceased publication in 1967, has served in a remarkable way to fill this gap. The contributors are drawn from a wide circle—university teachers, Athonite abbots, Marxists, leading literary figures—and include foreigners along with Greeks. Special numbers have been devoted to such topics as faith and science, ecumenism, education, Greece and Europe, the human body, and ecology. By the beginning of 1986 the circulation had risen to 4,000, an impressive total for such a periodical in Greece. The untiring efforts that Panayiotis devoted to *Synaxi,* attending to all the smallest details, must surely have contributed to his early death.

Short, somewhat stout, with a moustache and wavy hair, Panayiotis Nellas was by character vivacious, warm and friendly. He was a generous man, eager to commend and encourage others, a good listener. He loved the Church, and was closely involved in its sacramental life; it was no coincidence that he should have chosen for special study St Nicolas Kavasilas, who is pre-eminently a liturgical, sacramental theologian. For Panayiotis theology was inseparable from prayer, and involved not the reasoning brain only but the total human person.

His vivacity and his love for the Church are apparent in the work translated here under the title *Deification in Christ: Orthodox Perspectives on the Nature of the Human Person.* The original title in Greek begins *Zōon theoumenon,* a phrase taken from St Gregory of Nazianzus, *Oration* 38, 11, meaning literally "a living creature that is being deified." For Nellas, as for Nazianzus, man is not merely a rational or a political animal, not merely an animal that laughs, but primarily an animal called to share consciously in the life and glory of God. The Greek text was published by "Epopteia" in Athens in 1979; a second edition followed in 1982. In the English version, with the author's agreement, some bibliographical references in the notes have been omitted. In the Greek original the notes appear in two separate sections, but here they have been combined into a single series, and a few of the longer notes have been incorporated into the main text.

Deification in Christ is a work of synthesis, yet without being rigidly systematic. This lack of system is deliberate, as the author explained to me at our last meeting over lunch in Athens during December 1985. The most closely argued and analytical section of the work is Part One, dealing with the divine image in man, and more specifically with the "garments of skin" (Gen 3:21), a basic symbol in the Patristic interpretation of the fall. It is a symbol often mentioned by modern scholars, but no one hitherto seems to have explored its detailed implications with the close attention that Nellas displays. He saw this as the most original part of the book. But it is also the most complex, and some readers may prefer to commence a first reading with Part Two. This is concerned with one particular witness from tradition, Nicolas Kavasilas. Nicolas constantly underlines a point already made by Nellas in Part One, that there is an integral connection between the doctrine of man and the doctrine of Christ. Jesus Christ is *the* man, the model of what it means for us to be human, the mirror in which we see reflected our own true face; all theology of the human person needs to be Christ-centered, and so in the end anthropology turns out to be an aspect of christology. In Part Three Nellas takes a text from the service books, the Great Canon of St Andrew of Crete (seventh-eighth century), used by the Orthodox Church during Lent. Here we see the theology of the human person in its liturgical dimension, worked out in practical, existential terms. Part Four presents a sequence of representative testimonies, from St Irenaios in the second century to St Nikodimos of the Holy Mountain in the eighteenth. It would have been possible for Nellas to incorporate Parts Two, Three and Four within the opening section, but he preferred not to do this. It is significant that in the book's title he speaks of "perspectives" in the plural—not one perspective but many. Rather than risk imposing upon the material a single scheme of ideas—his own—he wished to allow the tradition to speak directly for itself, in its true diversity.

While I was preparing with others a new English translation of the *Philokalia*, we were frequently at a loss how best to render Greek terms relating to the human person. The difficulty was not only linguistic. If it is hard to find the right words, this is because our modern understanding of the person has come to differ in subtle but significant ways from that of Christian writers in the past. This has led me to recognize how delicate is the question of the human person, and how central to all theology. Few if any works have opened up for me more lines of inquiry than *Deification in Christ* by Panayiotis Nellas, and few if any have helped me better to appreciate the Patristic approach—or rather the Patristic approaches, for there is more than one. I am delighted that such a sensitive and illuminating book should now be available in English, sad though I am that the author did not live to see the appearance of this translation.

—Bishop Kallistos of Diokleia

Preface

There are times when one feels oneself literally "cast down and abandoned in a corner of the universe yet obliged to go on living." But there are other times when a strange inspiration, which nevertheless comes from deep within oneself, seems to raise one up above necessity and grant one a taste of true freedom and joy. The Church Fathers speak at length about this inspiration. They gave it absolute priority within themselves, united with it all the functions of their existence, and were exalted to a state in which they exercised the permanent freedom of the sons of the universal King. Looking down from this eminence, they observed the nature of the human person. They understood and taught that the inspiration which I have mentioned, "the inclination towards God" as they call it, is due to the fact that man is an image of God, that is to say, that he is simultaneously earthly and heavenly, transient and eternal, visible and invisible, truly and in fact "a deified animal."

Participating as they did in the common search of mankind for the true nature and meaning of existent things, they accepted that man is "a rational animal" or "a political animal," and they would not have doubted that man is "what he eats" or "what he produces" or "what he feels"; but they added that his true greatness is to be found not in these things but in the fact that he is "called to be a god." They stressed that man realizes his true existence in the measure in which he is raised up towards God and is united with Him. "I call a human being someone who has journeyed far from mankind and has advanced towards God Himself."

At the same time they have described in depth and in

detail what man's nature is like when it maintains its bond
with God and what happens when it breaks this bond, how its
various psychosomatic functions work in either case, and what
perception of its existence it has when united with God or
separated from Him. The study of all these matters is the
theme of this book.

Patristic anthropology does not form a system. But the
rich material which the Fathers provide, consistent as it is
within itself, could lead the modern scholar to the easy solution of presenting the living truths of the Fathers as mere
concepts and of using them to build up a well-articulated
logical structure. I have tried to counter this danger—fear a
system, say the Fathers, as you would fear a lion—by giving
the book a five-fold structure. Accordingly, I approach the
same unified theme in five distinct ways. In the first part of
the book certain central themes of patristic anthropology are
examined synthetically but not systematically throughout the
whole range of patristic literature, and their significance is
determined for the crucial problem of our time, the relationship of the Church to the world. In the second part the same
theme is examined in a particular Father; and in the third, in
a Church service. In the fourth part a number of key patristic
passages are cited at length to give the reader an immediate
taste of the perception and witness of the Fathers. The fifth
approach consists in the provision of references and notes in
which the book's theses are further developed by the use of
the modern scientific theological method.

Another important methodological difficulty arises from
the language which the Fathers use. In expressing what they
have experienced they use the terms current in their age but
at the same time alter their content. By making the terms of
their own age translucent with the light of their personal
experience, they reveal the truth—along with the truth which
the terms on their own were able to contribute. Today, however, the terms have changed. If we had restricted ourselves
exclusively to the patristic terms, we would probably have had
before us words of impenetrable obscurity which could not
have been used except as historical concepts. For this reason I
have made an attempt, as hesitantly and as carefully as possi-

ble, to set these terms alongside more recent formulations, so that the life-giving word of the Fathers might reach us and the patristic texts might speak to us today. From this point of view, the present work is nothing but a simple modern transcription of certain central elements of our tradition and thus a contribution to the work which I am endeavoring to do in the series *Epi tas pigas* ("To the Sources").

A third difficulty, this time having to do with substance rather than method, will perhaps be created by what is said with regard to the assumption in the person of the divine Logos—for man's sake—of a human nature *free from the effects of the fall,* thereby bringing to fulfillment the eternal will of God concerning the incarnation or "entry of the first-born into the world." It will be explained how supremely important this teaching is for the correct apprehension and practice of the Christian faith and also why it surprises us today. It should perhaps be said, however, at the outset that already in the time of St Nikodimos of the Holy Mountain certain "students of theology" had condemned him for upholding this. And the saint in his "Apology"—the reader is recommended to begin the study of the present book with this text—, in a passage in which he anticipates probable objections, writes: "If some people . . . condemn me, they would be condemning rather the Godbearing Maximos, Gregory of Thessaloniki, Andrew the Great and the others, from whom I have drawn this teaching."

A large part of this book was written in the library of the monastery of Stavronikita. I offer it to the community as a further expression of my gratitude.

—PANAYIOTIS NELLAS

PART ONE

THE IMAGE OF GOD AND THE "GARMENTS OF SKIN"

A Study of Certain Central Aspects
of the Teaching of the Fathers on Man
and on the Relationship Between
the Church and the World

I

The Image of God

The theme of the "image" has a long history. It was a basic term in Greek philosophy, in Plato, the Stoics and later the Neoplatonists.[1] At the same time it lies at the heart of the anthropology of the Old Testament, especially in the book of Genesis and in the Wisdom literature.[2] Midway between these two traditions Philo also uses the term in a manner central to his work, adding to it his own special meaning.[3]

In the New Testament the term is further enriched with a christological content, a fact which endows anthropology with new dimensions. For St Paul the "image of the invisible God" is Christ. And man, as we shall see, is the image of the Image. But the Johannine christological term, "Logos of God," as is well known, also has a meaning similar if not identical to that of the Pauline term, "image of the invisible God."[4]

In the subsequent patristic literature, on which, from the point of view of methodology, the present study concentrates,

[1]See H. Willms, *Eikon*; G. Kittel, 386-7; P. Aubin, "L'image dans l'oeuvre de Plotin"; H. Merki, "Ebenbildlichkeit."

[2]Gen. 1:26-7; Wisd. 7:24-8. See K.L. Schmidt, "Homo Imago Dei"; L. Köhler, "Die Grundstelle der Imago-Dei-Lehre Gn. 1, 26"; H.H. Rowley, *The Faith of Israel* (London 1956), 74-98; J.J. Stamm, *Die Gottebenbildlichkeit des Menschen*; J. Jervell, *Imago Dei*; V. Vellas, *O anthropos kata tin P. Diathikin*; N. Bratsiotis, *Anthropologia tis P. Diathikis*.

[3]See H. Willms, *Eikon*; J. Giblet, "L'homme image de Dieu dans... Philon d'Alexandrie"; J.D. Karavidopoulos, *I...didaskalia Philonos tou Alexandreos*; S. Agourides, *Philon o Ioudaios*.

[4]John Chrysostom, *On Hebrews* 2, 2-3, *PG* 63, 22-3. Cf. G. Kittel, 393-6; F.W. Eltester, *Eikon in N.T.*; I.D. Karavidopoulos, "*Eikon Theou*."

the "image" theme serves as an axis around which not only Orthodox cosmology but also Orthodox anthropology and christology itself are organized.[5] Faced with this immense patristic wealth of dogmatic teaching, we shall restrict ourselves to examining only the anthropological aspect, to see how the phrase "in the image" can serve as the foundation of an Orthodox anthropology.[6]

St Gregory of Nyssa, in his explanation of why "the nature of man is not open to contemplation," writes that since God is incomprehensible it can only be that His image within man is also incomprehensible.[7] This is the reason why we cannot find in the Fathers a definitive formulation or a clear definition of the "image." Yet it is nonetheless revealing that, in their repeated attempts to find a satisfactory solution to the anthropological problem, the Fathers use as the central tool for their investigation the expression "in the image."

The term is thus enriched with the most varied meanings, corresponding each time with the problems which have to be faced. Sometimes, for example, the expression "in the image" refers to man's free will, or to his rational faculty, or to his characteristic of self-determination, sometimes to the soul along with the body, sometimes to the mind, sometimes to the distinction between nature and person, etc.,[8] and sometimes comprehensively to the whole man.[9]

It would be interesting if someone were to assemble all these meanings and to analyze them. Such a phenomenological

---

[5]See V. Lossky, *Mystical Theology*, 114-34; and *Image and Likeness*, 125-39.

[6]It is clear that the theme of the "image," however fundamental, cannot exhaust every aspect of Orthodox anthropology. There are further themes, e.g. those of "likeness," "kinship," "grace," "adoption" and "deification," that offer other dimensions which fill in and complete the Orthodox doctrine.

[7]Gregory of Nyssa, *On the Creation of Man* 11, PG 44, 153D-156B, esp. 156AB; cf. R. Leys, *L'image de Dieu*, 77-8.

[8]John of Damascus, *On the two wills in Christ* 30, PG 95, 168B; cf. H.C. Graef, "L'image de Dieu"; P. Camelot, "La théologie de l'image de Dieu"; G.W.H. Lampe, *A Patristic Greek Lexicon*, 410-16, esp. 413-14. Sometimes the Fathers use these terms in a mutually exclusive way. This is because they are countering a specific heresy. See for example Origen, *On Genesis*, PG 12, 96, where he attacks those who limit the expression "in the image" to the body, "among whom is Melito, who has written treatises asserting that God is corporeal" (PG 12, 93).

[9]Epiphanios of Salamis, *Panarion* 70, PG 42, 344B.

study, however, always runs the risk of superficiality. For in fact the lack of clear and definitive formulations of the sense of the phrase "in the image" in the teaching of the Fathers does not imply a corresponding lack of clear orientation.

This patristic orientation, common as it is to the most varied applications of the term, is precisely that which can illuminate the term from within and thus on the one hand reveal the origin, the structure and the destiny of man, illuminating as much as possible his very nature, and on the other give to contemporary theology, once it has assimilated and discerned this orientation, the power to help the modern world in an effective way.

1. MAN AS AN IMAGE OF THE ARCHETYPE: "IMAGE OF THE IMAGE"

The starting-point and core of the theology of the "image" is for the Fathers the teaching of St Paul. And it is a hermeneutical datum of modern biblical scholarship that for Paul the "image of God" is Christ.[10] The relevant teaching of the Apostle is summarized in the first chapter of the Letter to the Colossians, and it is most characteristic that it is expressed not as the personal thought of Paul but as a liturgical hymn of the early Christian community: "He is the image of the invisible God, the first-born of all creation; for in Him all things were created, in heaven and on earth, visible and invisible, whether thrones or dominions or principalities or authorities—all things were created through Him and for Him. He is before all things, and in Him all things hold together. He is the head of the body, the Church" (Col 1:15-18).[11]

The important point about this text is that it constitutes a teaching concerned not with the Trinity but with cosmology

[10]O. Cullman, *Die Christologie des Neuen Testament* (Tübingen 1958), 152.

[11]See I.D. Karavidopoulos, "Ermineftikon ipomnima eis tin pros Kolossaeis epistolin," who also gives a good modern bibliography on this text. On other basic texts relevant to this theme, such as Rom. 8:29, 2 Cor. 4:4, Heb. 1:3 and 1 John 3:2, see G. Kittel, 393-6.

and anthropology. That is to say, it is not so much the relationship of the Logos to the Father which is stressed in this text—a relationship of course which is presupposed and which Paul develops elsewhere—as the significance of Christ for man. This point is extremely important, for it highlights the christological dimension of Paul's anthropology. The same dimension of the term "image" also appears in the Apostle's fundamental teaching that man, to be made whole, must put on "the image of the heavenly" man, who is Christ (1 Cor 15:49), in order to attain "to the measure of the stature of the fullness of Christ" (Eph 4:13), and this "that we may no longer be children" (Eph 4:14). Man's growth to full stature coincides for Paul with his Christification.

Modern hermeneutics will perhaps judge this interpretation to be arbitrary. If, however, we attempt to understand Paul's teaching with the aid not only of scientific critical analysis but also of the criteria that the Apostle himself used, as the Fathers did who had the same spiritual experiences as he had—that is to say, if we approach Paul's teachings from within the Church and use faith as our basic method—, we will appreciate not only the legitimacy of this interpretation but also its deepest significance.

Indeed, the Fathers carry further this line of thought found in Paul and the Old Testament writers by uniting the Pauline theme of *Christ—image of God* with the Genesis theme of *man—in the image of God*. Already in, among others, Irenaios, Clement, Origen, Athanasios, Gregory of Nyssa—to restrict ourselves only to those who have been the subject of special monographs[12]—the distinction is clear that Christ constitutes the image of God and man the image of Christ; that is to say, that man is the image of the Image. "The first-

[12]For example, A. Orbe, *Antropologia de San Ireneo*; A. Maver, *Das Bild Gottes im Menschen nach Clemens von Alexandrien*; H. Crouzel, *Théologie de l'image de Dieu chez Origène*; P. Ch. Dimitropoulos, *I anthropologia tou M. Athanasiou*; R. Bernard, *L'image de Dieu d'après saint Athanase*; J. Roldanus, *Le Christ et l'homme dans la théologie d'Athanase d' Alexandrie*; I. Moutsoulas, *I sarkosis tou Logou kai i theosis tou anthropou kata tin didaskalian Grigoriou tou Nyssis*; J. Daniélou, *Platonisme et théologie mystique*, 48-60; R. Leys, *L'image de Dieu chez Saint Grégoire de Nysse*; H. Merki, *Omoiosis Theo, Von der platonischen Angleichung an Gott zur Gottähnlichkeit bei Gregor von Nyssa*.

born of all creation is the image of God . . . and man was made in the image of God," as Origen says.[13] And in the words of Chrysostom, "In the image of Christ; for this is in the image of the Creator."[14]

This patristic standpoint, even though more often than not it remains implicit, is clear and constant and of capital significance, because it can help us to define the three basic anthropological headings: the structure, destiny and origin of man.

(a) *The christological structure of man*

The above brief survey unifies first of all the various applications in different periods of the phrase "in the image,"[15] and enables us to see them not as mutually exclusive aspects but as complementary dimensions of an orthodox, that is to say healthy, structure of man, as the dimensions of an Orthodox anthropology. I shall try to give a few examples.

We frequently meet in the Fathers the statement that man is a rational being because he has been created in the image of God. The dogmatic manuals, in their attempt to localize the "in the image," teach that it has its seat in man's rational faculty.[16] It would, however, be more correct if we were to understand that man is rational because he was created in the image of Christ, who is the hypostatic Logos of the Father. Athanasios the Great, who makes a special study of this theme, formulates the point with clarity: "In His own image He made them, having also given to them a share in the power of His own Logos, so that cleaving to the Logos like a shadow and having become rational (*logikoi*), they might be able to remain in a state of blessedness."[17]

[13]Origen, *Against Celsus* vi, 63, PG 11, 1393.

[14]John Chrysostom, *On Colossians* viii, 2, PG 62, 353; cf. Athanasios, *Against the Greeks* 2, PG 25, 8.

[15]See P. Bratsiotis, "To Gen. 1:26 en ti orthodoxo theologia," esp. 361-4.

[16]See for example P.N. Trembelas, *Dogmatiki tis Orthodoxou Katholikis Ekklisias*, vol. 1 (Athens 1959), 487-94, esp. 487.

[17]Athanasios, *On the Incarnation of the Logos* 3, PG 25, 101B; cf. ibid. 4, PG 25, 104CD, and *Against the Greeks* 2, PG 25, 5C-8A; see R. Bernard, *L'image de Dieu d'après saint Athanase*, 21-56, 91-126.

In the same way we can understand that man is a creator
because he is the image of the Logos, the supreme Creator:
"In this way," says Clement of Alexandria, "man becomes an
image of God in that he co-operates with Him in the pro-
creation of man."[18]

He is sovereign because Christ, in whose image he was
created, is the almighty Lord and King: "The fact that our
nature is an image of the Nature which rules over all things,"
says Gregory of Nyssa, "means nothing else than this, that
from the start our nature was created sovereign."[19]

He is free because he is an image of absolute self-determination: "In the self-determination of free choice," says
Gregory of Nyssa, "he possessed the likeness of the Sovereign
of all, for he was not subject to any external necessity but
guided by his own will towards what is fitting and chose
independently what pleased him."[20]

He is responsible for the creation, the recapitulation and
consciousness of all that has been brought into being, because
his archetype, Christ, is the recapitulator and savior of all
men: "Last in order," says Theodore of Mopsuestia, "He
brought forth man in His own image, as if the whole of
creation were to appear to have been put together for the
use of man."[21]

Made up of soul and body, he stands at the midway point
of creation, uniting within himself matter and spirit, since
Christ through whom and "in whom" "he was created" is the
incomprehensible, hypostatic, indivisible but at the same

[18]Clement of Alexandria, *Paidagogos* ii, 10, PG 8, 497B; cf. Gen. 1:27-31.
[19]Gregory of Nyssa, *On the Creation of Man* 4, PG 44, 136BC; cf.
On Virginity 12, PG 46, 369BC; see R. Leys, *L'image de Dieu chez Saint
Grégoire de Nysse*, 71-2. Cf. John Chrysostom, *To Stageirios* i, 2, PG 47,
427, and Th. Zissis, *Anthropos kai kosmos en ti oikonomia tou Theou kata
ton ieron Chrysostomon*, 76-8. As regards the Antiochene tradition generally
on the significance of the expression "in the image" for the sovereignty of
man (e.g. Diodoros of Tarsus, *On Genesis* 1, 26, PG 33, 1564-5), see K.
Kornitseskou, *O anthropismos kata ton ieron Chrysostomon*, 49.
[20]Gregory of Nyssa, *On Virginity* 12, PG 46, 369C; see R. Leys, *L'image
de Dieu chez Saint Grégoire de Nysse*, 72-5, and J. Gaïth, *La conception de
la liberté chez Grégoire de Nysse*, 40-6. Cf. Maximos the Confessor, *Debate
with Pyrrhos*, PG 91, 304C, and John of Damascus, *On the Orthodox Faith*
ii, 12, PG 94, 920.
[21]Theodoret of Cyrus, *On Genesis* 20, PG 80, 109B, where the text
of Theodore of Mopsuestia is cited.

time unconfused union of uncreated divinity and created contingency. "For as His own divinity was operative . . . in a theandric manner," says Anastasios of Sinai, "so the soul, which is in the image and likeness of the invisible divine Logos, operates in a 'psychandric' manner, that is to say, in a psychosomatic way after the example of Christ who exists in a theandric way."[22]

He is simultaneously person and nature, or more accurately, person who reveals nature and makes it concrete, since he is an image of the Son, who constitutes a distinct personal hypostasis of the one indivisible substance common to the Father, the Son and the Spirit.[23]

Perhaps I should have dwelt on this line of inquiry and drawn it out. Certainly this work must be done one day. For the characteristic features of the expression "in the image," which I have so far been indicating briefly, if filled out and analyzed can clearly contribute in a decisive manner to the determining of the central dimensions of the structure of man as the Orthodox tradition understands it.

Indeed, these elements may be summarized as follows: man is at the same time both person and nature, characterized fundamentally by the mystery of love, which inwardly impels persons to a natural communion; he is conscious personal existence in time; he is an indissoluble psychosomatic unity with unfathomable psychic depths; he is free, sovereign, creative, rational, scientific, and so on. It is these things that reveal the true structure of man in a realistic way. It is also worth noting that these elements, while constituting the central dimension of the traditional teaching on the phrase "in the image," are at the same time not very distant from the most profound conclusions of modern anthropological research.[24]

[22]Anastasios of Sinai (?), *From the "in the image,"* PG 89, 1148D-1149A; cf. *PG* 89, 1161C. Gregory Palamas (?), *Prosopopoiiai,* PG 150, 1361BC; for the authorship of the *Prosopopoiiai,* which is now ascribed to Michael Akominatos, see J. Meyendorff, *Introduction à l'étude de Grégoire Palamas* (Paris, 1959), 335, note 17.

[23]This thesis, along with the most important supporting texts, is presented by V. Lossky, *Mystical Theology,* 114-34, as the core of the patristic doctrine on the "in the image."

[24]See for example J. Mouroux, *Sens chrétien de l'homme* (Paris 1947);

(b)   *The destiny of man in Christ*

Beyond this static or anatomical analysis, however, the reality presented by the "image" also reveals the dynamic impetus of man's being, his destiny. In fact man, having been created "in the image" of the infinite God, is called by his own nature—and this is precisely the sense of "in the image" from this point of view—to transcend the limited boundaries of creation and to become infinite. This relates to all the elements of his being from the most peripheral to the very core of his existence. At this point too I shall give some examples.

The wisdom of man, in view of the fact that it constitutes an image of the supreme wisdom of the Creator, itself has the power and the obligation to raise itself to the level of supreme wisdom. Athanasios the Great writes: "In order that what has come to be may not simply exist . . . God has been pleased to bring down His own Wisdom to creatures . . . so that what has come to be may also be wise. . . . For as our own reason (*logos*) is an image of the true Logos of the Son of God, so the wisdom that has been created in us, whereby we possess the power to know and to think, is likewise an image of His true Wisdom; and so by virtue of our human wisdom we are capable of receiving the Wisdom of the Creator."[25] In this way it becomes clear that the progress of man in scientific knowledge is not an arbitrary or fortuitous matter. Human knowledge develops because development is an intrinsic element of it. Human knowledge is driven by its own nature to raise itself up to the totality of knowledge.

The same is true with regard to the sovereignty of man over nature. The Fathers consider man a real governor and lord of the universe. And they understand this lordship to be

P. Teilhard de Chardin, *Le phénomène humain* (Paris 1955); M. Barthélemy-Madaule, *La personne et le drame humain chez Teilhard de Chardin* (Paris 1967); J.E. Jarque, *Foi en l'homme* (Paris 1970); Olivier Clément, *Questions sur l'homme* (Paris 1972); P.P. Grassé, *Toi, ce petit Dieu! Essai sur l'histoire naturelle de l'homme* (Paris 1971); B. Häring, *Perspective chrétienne pour une médecine humaine* (Paris 1975); C. Tresmontant, *La mystique chrétienne et l'avenir de l'homme* (Paris 1977).

[25]Athanasios, *Against the Arians* ii, 78, *PG* 26, 312BC.

one of the ways in which man expresses his royal character.[26] Thus for the believer, who sees things under a theological aspect, no technological progress or achievement causes surprise. Man, in organizing the world and discovering its mysteries, does nothing but fulfill one of the marks of his destiny, provided, of course, that his organization of the world proceeds in the direction of its becoming fully human.

The above approach can be extended to cover the whole range of human life and activity. The demand for justice and peace is also revealed in the Orthodox perspective as the reflection of the triadic archetype of humanity, and at the same time as the conscious or unconscious nostalgic attempt by humanity to attain the wonderful mode of life of that archetype, in the image of which it has been formed and in which alone it can find its peace and rest.[27] The whole man, soul and body, a personal existence in a natural relationship with all other human existence and in an organic union with the world, tends from his own structure to surpass his limitations, to become unbounded and immortal. "For the thirst of human souls requires some infinite water; how could this limited world suffice?"[28]

This truth, the confirmation of which is always astonishing scientists, is interpreted and completed by the notion of "in the image." For all our disparate human undertakings, which by themselves are blind and therefore full of naive conceit, are unified and led conclusively to their true end by this notion.

The Fathers, as we can see in their writings, do not hesitate to appropriate the wonder of the Greeks at man as a "microcosm,"[29] that is to say, at the fact that man recapitulates within himself the whole universe. And yet even this great fact is still too small for the Fathers. They hasten to complete

[26]See Gregory of Nazianzus, *Oration* 45, 7, *PG* 36, 632AB; Gregory of Nyssa, *On the Creation of Man* 4, *PG* 44, 136; John Chrysostom, *To Stageirios* i, 2, *PG* 47, 427.

[27]See John Chrysostom, *On Genesis* v, 4, *PG* 56, 475.

[28]Nicolas Kavasilas, *The Life in Christ* 2, *PG* 150, 560D-561A.

[29]See Gregory of Nyssa, *On the Creation of Man* 16, *PG* 44, 177D-180A. On the history of the term "microcosm" see R. Allers, "Microcosmus from Anaximandros to Paracelsus," *Traditio* 2 (1944), 319-407.

it by adding that the true greatness of man is not found in
his being the highest biological existence, a "rational" or
"political" animal, but in his being a "deified animal,"[30] in
the fact that he constitutes a created existence "which has
received the command to become a god."[31] His greatness does
not lie simply in his being a "microcosm" but in his being
called to become "a mystical Church,"[32] a vast new world
within the small old one. "For each of us is brought forth by
God as a second world, a vast one in this small visible one."[33]
"In what does human greatness lie?" asks Gregory of Nyssa.
And he replies: "Not in his likeness to the created world, but
in the fact that he is made in the image of the nature of the
Creator."[34] This signifies that the greatness of man lies in his
destiny, in his appointed end.

As the truth of the material creation and its potentialities
are revealed and realized in man, so too the truth of created
man and his potentialities are revealed and realized in the
uncreated God. With this it becomes evident that the reason
why man remains and will remain a mystery to science is the
fact that what lies at his core, by reason of his very structure,
is a theological being which falls outside the scope of science.

(c) *The origin of man in Christ*

This last assertion leads us to the subject of the origin
of man and obliges us to examine not only his analogical
relationships but also his ontology "in the image."

For man to resemble God and incline towards Him, it is
necessary that he should have within him an element of the
divine. But what exactly is this element? The question is
fundamental. Indeed it concerns the great question of all

[30]Gregory of Nazianzus, *Oration* 45, 7, *PG* 36, 632AB; see the whole
text translated below, pp. 203-5.

[31]The expression is that of Basil the Great; see Gregory of Nazianzus,
Funeral Oration on Basil the Great, PG 36, 560A.

[32]Maximos the Confessor, *Mystagogia* 4, *PG* 91, 672B; cf. ibid. 6,
91, 684A.

[33]Symeon the New Theologian, *Moral Oration* 4, in *Traités théologiques
et éthiques,* ed. J. Darrouzès (Sources chrétiennes 129, Paris 1967), 64.

[34]Gregory of Nyssa, *On the Creation of Man* 16, *PG* 44, 180A.

serious philosophies and theologies, that is, the relationship between God and man, Creator and creature.[35] It is well known that various theories were formulated for the solution of this problem: the theory of ideas (Plato), of the Logos (Philo), of emanations (Gnostics), of autonomy (atheists), and so on.

From the Orthodox point of view St John of Damascus summarizes the whole of the patristic tradition which preceded him when he teaches that "all things are distant from God not by place but by nature."[36] In his interpretation of this expression Georges Florovsky formulates the basic thesis that the essential gulf between divine and human nature "is under no circumstances removed, but is only in some way hidden through God's infinite love."[37] The essential gulf between created and uncreated nature is absolute and infinite. But the equally infinite goodness of God, without abolishing that essential gulf, has been pleased to bridge it in a real way from the beginning with the uncreated divine energies. The theological and cosmological theme of the uncreated energies of God and the anthropological theme of the expression "in the image" meet at this point. The energies of God, which support and conserve the created order, and have in relation to the world the aim of guiding it towards its perfection, acquire in man a specific created vehicle, which is the freedom of man, and a specific direction, which is the union of man with the divine Logos. This is the meaning of the expression "in the image."

Man was the first portion of creation—"dust of the earth" (Gen 2:7)—which was really and truly bound to God, thanks to the "in the image"; he was the first form of biological life —and manifestly the highest that existed on earth on the sixth day of creation[38]—which thanks to the breath of the

[35]For the earlier history of the problem see E. des Places, *Syggeneia. La parenté de l'homme à Dieu d'Homère à la patristique* (Paris 1964).

[36]John of Damascus, *On the Orthodox Faith* i, 13, PG 94, 853C.

[37]G. Florovsky, "Tvar i tvarnost," *Pravoslavnaya Mysl'* (journal of the Orthodox Theological Institute of St Sergius, 1928), 176-212, esp. 179-81. Cf. Athanasios, *Against the Arians* i, 20, PG 26, 53; i, 21, PG 26, 56; iii, 60, PG 26, 448; Makarios of Egypt, *Spiritual Homilies* xlix, 4, PG 34, 816.

[38]Gregory of Nyssa, *On the Creation of Man* 8, PG 44, 145B, 148BC;

Spirit was raised to spiritual life, that is, to a life really and truly theocentric. Created matter, the "dust of the earth," was thus organized for the first time theologically; the material creation acquired a form and structure in the image of God; life on earth became conscious, free and personal.

We should note at the same time that St Nikodimos of the Holy Mountain, following St John of Damascus[39] and St Gregory Palamas,[40] teaches that three modes of union and communion are observed to exist in God: that which is "according to substance," that which is "according to hypostasis," and that which is "according to energy."[41] Only the three persons of the most Holy Trinity are united "according to substance." The hypostatic union was effected by the Logos when He assumed flesh. And what I have said above shows that the union "according to energy" was granted to man with his creation "in the image." But this third union—and this point is of crucial significance for our theme—is clearly not complete because it does not abolish the gulf between the divine and the human natures; we would say that it simply bridges it. Its entire significance lies in the fact that it prepares for and leads to the hypostatic union, which is complete and perfect because, since the divine and the human natures possess in Christ the same person, it is impossible for any gulf to separate them. The common hypostasis "destroys the gulf between divinity and humanity since it is a term common to both natures and so could not be common to what is separated."[42]

The union of God and man "according to energy" which was granted to mankind with the creation of Adam "in the

cf. P. Christou, "To anthropino pliroma kata tin didaskalian Grigoriou tou Nyssis," *Kleronomia* 4 (1972), 41-42. Athanasios, *Against the Arians* ii, 19, *PG* 26, 188B; Nikodimos of the Holy Mountain, *Eortodromion* (Venice 1836), xx: "Just as God chose Abraham from the people of the Chaldaeans ... so likewise at the beginning He made Adam His own from the whole of creation."

[39]John of Damascus, *On the Holy Icons* iii, 26, *PG* 94, 1348AB.

[40]*Works of Gregory Palamas*, ed. P. Christou (Thessaloniki 1969), ii, 255, 356-7, 440.

[41]Nikodimos of the Holy Mountain, "Apology," in *Symvouleftikon encheiridion, itoi peri phylakis ton pente aisthiseon*, ed. S.N. Schoinas (Volos 1958), 207. This text is translated below, pp. 227-37.

[42]Nicolas Kavasilas, *The Life in Christ* 3, *PG* 150, 572B.

image" had as its aim the leading of human nature to hypostatic union with the divine Logos in Christ. This aim constituted the original destiny of Adam and remained permanent and immutable—"for the counsels of the Lord are not repented of"—even after the fall. It continued to constitute the essential purpose of the training of the Jewish people by God, the content and the aim not only of the prophets but of the whole of sacred history.

It thus becomes clear that the essence of man is not found in the matter from which he was created but in the archetype on the basis of which he was formed and towards which he tends. It is precisely for this reason that, in the patristic treatment of the theme of the origin of man, the theory of evolution does not create a problem—just as for the believer the form of the wood from which an icon has been made does not create a problem. Science may well have an obligation to study the "matter" from which man was formed, but every serious scientist knows that it is impossible for him to undertake a thorough investigation, using the objective scientific method, of the "archetype" on the basis of which man was formed. As the truth of an icon lies in the person it represents, so the truth of man lies in his archetype. And this is precisely because the archetype is that which organizes, seals and gives shape to matter, and which simultaneously attracts it towards itself. The archetype constitutes the ontological content of the phrase "in the image."

This last point indicates that the ontological truth of man does not lie in himself conceived as an autonomous being—in his natural characteristics, as materialist theories maintain; in the soul or in the intellect, the higher part of the soul, as many ancient philosophers believed; or exclusively in the person of man, as contemporary philosophical systems centered on the person accept. No: it lies in the Archetype. Since man is an image, his real *being* is not defined by the created element with which the image is constructed, in spite of the iconic character which created "matter" itself possesses, but by his uncreated Archetype. The category of biological existence does not exhaust man. Man is understood ontologically by the Fathers only as a theological being. His ontology is iconic.

The two elements by which the Archetype comes to be present and truly operative in man, and which constitute the essential reality of man, are lucidly set out in a characteristic passage of St Gregory of Nyssa: "Through the natural glow lying within it, the eye, attracted by the innate power of what is akin to it, comes to have communion with the light. Similarly, it was necessary for something akin to the divine to be mingled with human nature, so that through this correspondence it should have a desire for what is its own. . . . For this reason it has been endowed with life and reason and wisdom and every good thing befitting God, so that through each of these things it might have a desire for what is its own. . . . The account of creation indicates all this succinctly by a single phrase when it says that man was made in the image of God."[43]

In this passage two things are made plain: the theological structure of man ("for this reason it has been endowed with life and reason and wisdom and every good thing befitting God"), and the attraction which the Archetype exercises on him in an interior way ("attracted by the innate power of what is akin to it").

But what, more specifically, is this Archetype? The theme is of decisive importance and must be investigated.

2. THE ARCHETYPE OF MAN: THE INCARNATE LOGOS

It has already been mentioned that for Irenaios, Origen, Athanasios, Gregory of Nyssa and other Fathers, among them Maximos the Confessor and Gregory Palamas, the archetype of man is Christ. A passage from Nicolas Kavasilas does not permit any doubt on this point. It is very similar in character to the passage from Gregory of Nyssa which has been cited and at the same time interprets it in a decisive way: "It was for the new man that human nature was originally created;

[43]Gregory of Nyssa, *Catechetical Oration* 5, PG 45, 21CD.

it was for Him that intellect and desire were prepared. We received rationality that we might know Christ, desire that we might run towards Him. We possessed memory that we might bear Him in us, since He was the archetype for those who have been created. For the old Adam is not a model for the new, but the new a model for the old."[44]

Man's archetype is therefore not simply the Logos but the incarnate Logos. "Man hastens towards Christ not only on account of His divinity, which is the goal of all things, but also because of His human nature."[45]

The fact that Christ did not exist historically at the time of Adam's creation is of no significance. It is a fundamental biblical teaching that on the level of the supra-temporal reality of God Christ is "the first-born of all creation" (Col 1:15-17). If man, for whom all the material creation was brought into being, rose last of all creatures from the earth, it is surely logical that Christ, who is the goal of the whole of the material and spiritual creation, should be later than Adam, since all things are led from imperfection to perfection.[46] Christ, as the highest realization of man, naturally constitutes the goal of mankind's upward journey, the beginning but also the end of history.

Within the first truth lies a second which is equally significant. The fact that Adam was created in the image of Christ implies that it was his vocation to be raised up to the Archetype or, more precisely, to be purified and to love God so much that God would come to dwell within him, that the Logos would enter into a hypostatic union with man, and thus appear in history as the Christ, be manifested as the God-man. The "entry of the first-born into the world" (Heb 1:6) fulfils the eternal will of God, the highest mystery "hidden from the ages and from generations" (Col 1:26). Christ was "the counsel and will of the Father."[47] This was the destiny of man and in consequence his physiological path and his goal. In relation to Christ man "was made in the begin-

[44]Nicolas Kavasilas, *The Life in Christ* 6, PG 150, 680A.
[45]Ibid., 681AB.
[46]Ibid., 681A.
[47]John of Damascus, *On the Withered Fig Tree and the Parable of the Vineyard* 2, PG 96, 580B.

ning as if to a standard or pattern . . . so that he could receive God."[48] Man's straying from this path constituted the fall.

"Hence the original creation of man, formed in the image of God, was for the sake of Christ, so that man should be able one day to make room for the Archetype; and hence the law laid down by God in paradise was on His [Christ's] account," that is, to help man be guided towards Christ, writes St Gregory Palamas.[49]

And St Maximos comments: "This is the great hidden mystery. This is the blessed end for which all things were created. This is the preordained divine goal of the origin of beings, which we define as the preordained end for the sake of which all things exist, although this end itself depends on nothing. It was with a view to this end [Christ, the hypostatic union of divine and human nature] that God brought forth the essence of all beings."[50]

With even greater lucidity Kavasilas writes: "God created human nature with no other end in view . . . but this, that when He needed to be born He should receive His mother from that nature. And, having established human nature first as a necessary standard [in the person of the God-man, Christ], He then forms man in accordance with it."[51]

Consequently the fact that God formed man "in the image" means, in the last analysis, that He formed him in this way so that he might tend of his own nature, by the very fact that he is man, towards the Image. It means that He gave him as gifts in a realistic manner—in such a manner that these gifts should constitute man—the power and the aim of serving as the effective instrument of the incarnation of the Logos, who is the perfect and unique "Image of the Father." And in this way man, enhypostatized in the Logos, becomes capa-

[48]Nicolas Kavasilas, *The Life in Christ* 2, PG 150, 560D.

[49]Gregory Palamas, *Homily* 7, in *Grigoriou tou Palama Omiliai 22*, ed S. Oikonomos (Athens 1861), 259.

[50]Maximos the Confessor, *To Thalassios: On Various Questions* 60, PG 90, 621A.

[51]Nicolas Kavasilas, *I Theomitor. Treis theomitorikes omilies* ed. P. Nellas (Athens 1974), 150-2. See also the wealth of patristic evidence cited by Nikodimos of the Holy Mountain in his "Apology" translated below, pp. 227-37.

ble of being himself raised up into an "image," of being himself manifested as "image of God."

This makes plain the truth that the phrase "in the image" implies a gift within man but at the same time a goal set before him, a possession but also a destiny, since it really does constitute man's *being,* but only in potentiality. The "in the image" is a real power, a pledge which should lead to marriage, that is, to hypostatic union, the unconfused but real and fulfilling mixture and commingling of the divine and the human natures. Only then does the iconic or potential being of man become real *authentic* being. Man finds in the Archetype his true ontological meaning.

There are certain aspects of this fundamental truth which must be stressed.

1. Christ is not a mere event or happening in history. The incarnation of the divine Logos was not a simple consequence of the victory of the devil over man. Christ is not the result of an act of Satan. The union of the divine and the human natures took place because it fulfilled the eternal will of God. The manner in which this great mystery was realized changed,[52] but the fact remained the same. "For it is plainly evident to all that the mystery effected in Christ at the end of the age is without doubt a proof and fulfillment of what was set forth at the beginning of the age in our common ancestor."[53]

[52]See Maximos the Confessor, *Ambigua,* PG 91, 1097C.

[53]Maximos the Confessor, *Ambigua,* PG 91, 1097D; cf. 1092BC, 1280ABC, 1308C-1309A; cf. also *To Thalassios: On Various Questions* 22, PG 90, 317B-320C; 60, PG 90, 620C-621C. The thesis first formulated by Rupert of Deutz (12th century) and developed in a penetrating way by Duns Scotus (12th century), that the Logos would have become man independently of Adam's fall, is well known. Also well known are the long discussions which this thesis stimulated in the West (see the synoptic presentation of these discussions in G. Florovsky, *"Cur Deus Homo? The Motive for the Incarnation," Creation and Redemption* [Collected Works vol. 3, Belmont 1976], 163-171). After serious and valuable researches, however, many modern Western students of the Fathers (e.g. H. Urs von Balthasar, *Liturgie Cosmique. Maxime le Confesseur* [Paris 1947], 205) and Orthodox theologians (e.g. G. Florovsky, art. cit., 167-8; N. Nissiotis, *Prolegomena eis tin theologikin gnosiologian* [Athens 1965], 67; A. Theodorou, *Cur Deus Homo? Aproïpothetos i emproïpothetos enanthropisis tou Theiou Logou* [Athens 1974], appear to have failed in their attempt to relate the above thesis of Duns Scotus to the patristic teaching on the

2. Prior to the hypostatic union of the divine nature with the human, man even before the fall was anterior to Christ, a fact which means that even then, in spite of not having sinned, man had need of salvation, since he was an imperfect and incomplete "child." This teaching lies at the core of the theology of St Irenaios.[54] Human nature could not have been completed simply by its tendency; it had to attain union with the Archetype. Since Christ is "the head of the body, the Church" (Col 1:18), a fact which means in patristic thought that Christ is the head of true humanity, as long as human nature had not yet received the hypostasis of the Logos it was in some way without real hypostasis—it lacked real "subsistence."[55] It was like an unmarried woman—unfruitful and, as Paul says, "without a head" (1 Cor 11:3).[56] The realization of man as a truly completed, "saved" being took place with the birth of Christ. Real men "were born when Christ came into this life and was born."[57] For this reason Basil the Great calls the day of Christ's birth truly and not metaphorically "the birthday of mankind."[58]

3. The goal of the first man always remains the same. Every man created "in the image" of God is called to become an "image" in Christ. "Let us transform into the image that which is in the image," writes St Gregory the Theologian.[59]

eternal will of God that in the hypostasis of the Logos the human nature should be united with the divine. Finally, and within the climate created by the Western discussions, they accept that for the Orthodox tradition the matter has not been clarified but remains a "theologoumenon." In my opinion however, no real internal relationship exists between the question posed by Duns Scotus and the teaching of the Fathers. See also p. 94, note 217.

[54]See J. Romanides, *To propatorikon amartima*, 113-40; E. Peterson, "L'homme image de Dieu chez saint Irénée"; A. Benoit, *Saint Irénée*, 227-33; A. Orbe. *Antropologia de San Ireneo*; A. Theodorou, *I peri anakephalaioseos didaskalia tou Eirenaiou*; H. Lassiat, *Promotion de l'homme en Jésus-Christ d'après Irénée de Lyon*; H. Lassiat, "L'anthropologie d'Irénée." See also the representative passage of St Irenaios translated below, pp. 201-2.

[55]Nicolas Kavasilas, *The Life in Christ* 2, PG 150, 533D.

[56]The theology of 1 Cor. 11:1-16 is characteristic. The head of the wife is the husband, the head of the husband is Christ, and the head of Christ is God. The line is continuous. Should a division occur, an interruption of communion is created, a privation of fullness, a sterility.

[57]Nicolas Kavasilas, *The Life in Christ* 4, PG 150, 604A.

[58]Basil, *On the Nativity of Christ* 6, PG 31, 1473A.

[59]Gregory of Nazianzus, *Oration* 1, 4, PG 35, 397B.

Christ opened up the way to the realization of this goal. Indeed, the birth of the divine Logos and the dispensation of
the incarnation are not exhausted by redemption, by deliverance from the consequences of Adam's fault. The Lord redeemed man from slavery to sin, death and devil, but He also
put into effect the work which had not been effected by Adam.
He united him with God, granting him true "being" in God
and raising him to a new creation.[60] Christ accomplishes the
salvation of man not only in a negative way, liberating him
from the consequences of original sin, but also in a positive
way, completing his iconic, prelapsarian "being." His relationship with man is not only that of a healer. The salvation
of man is something much wider than redemption; it coincides with deification.

4. The real anthropological meaning of deification is
Christification. It is no accident that in his Letter to the
Colossians, where he hymns Christ as "the image of the
invisible God, the first-born of all creation" (Col 1:15), St
Paul calls on "every man" to become "mature in Christ" (Col
1:28), and adds that the faithful "have come to fullness of
life in Him" (Col 2:10). When he urges the faithful to show
that they are attaining "to mature manhood, to the measure
of the stature of the fullness of Christ" (Eph 4:13), and to
acquire "the mind of Christ" (1 Cor 2:16), the heart of
Christ (cf. Eph 3:17) and so on, St Paul does not do so for
reasons of external piety and sentiment; he speaks ontologically. He is not advocating an external imitation or a simple
ethical improvement but a real Christification. For, as St
Maximos says, "God the divine Logos wishes to effect the
mystery of His incarnation always and in all things."[61]

5. The Fathers described the Pauline "life in Christ" as
deification (*theosis*) mainly in order to safeguard the final
goal and the true meaning of life in Christ from the dangers
created by the christological heresies. Arianism, by teaching
that Christ is a creature, inevitably limited life in Christ to

---

[60]See Maximos the Confessor, *To Thalassios: On Various Questions* 63,
PG 90, 692B.

[61]Maximos the Confessor, *Ambigua*, PG 91, 1084D.

the created order.[62] Nestorianism, by teaching that the human
and the divine natures are contiguous but not really united,
ended up by maintaining that man can approach the infinite
but cannot penetrate it. On the other hand, Monophysitism
by regarding man's salvation as his absorption into God ended
up by preaching the annihilation rather than the salvation of
man. The struggle of the Fathers against the heresies had an
anthropological side to it. It was a struggle to safeguard man's
final goal and consequently his greatness. The Fathers never
omitted, however, to stress that the content and the way of
deification is union with Christ, because it is precisely union
with the Archetype which leads man to his fulfilment.[63]

6. In a later period—and this observation is necessary if
the reader who is surprised at the theses set out above is to
understand why he is surprised—and more specifically from
the twelfth century onwards, there comes to prevail in the
West a theological and anthropological, and by extension
soteriological and ecclesiological, understanding different from
that which has been outlined above. This understanding was
transmitted to Greece too in the nineteenth century, when
theology in the newly-founded University of Athens was
pursued and taught in relation not so much to the patristic
tradition as to the prevailing Western forms of theological
science. The result was a broad dissemination in Greece also
of the Western understanding of Christianity.

7. In the last few decades the theme of deification has
come to the surface again and is much studied. This fact is
auspicious, but I believe that a further step must be taken.
Deification must not remain a general spiritual category but
must acquire a specific anthropological content, which in the
language of the Fathers means a content at once anthropological and christological: that is to say, it must be understood
again as Christification. Understood in this way, the goal of
man and the means of realizing that goal—faith, keeping the
commandments, ascesis, the sacraments, the whole ecclesiastical and spiritual life—are illuminated internally and dis-

[62]Athanasios, *Against the Arians* ii, 67, PG 26, 289C, and ii, 70, PG
26, 296A.
[63]See I. Dalmais, "Divinisation, Patristique grecque."

cover their organic connections with themselves, with the world and with Christ, the beginning and the end of all things.

8. In the other sections of this book I shall attempt to present an understanding of these realities which is unfamiliar to us today but is nevertheless patristic. Here it is worth noting the liberation which this viewpoint wins for man.

First there is the liberation from evil and sin. However frightening evil may be, since it and not Christ constitutes an event or episode, it is shown in the last analysis to be puny. The understanding of man—of salavation, of the spiritual life, and so on—is detached from evil and united with Christ. Evil is made relative. Even the greatest depth of sin does not touch upon the origin and destiny of man. Man can remain a slave to sin but he can also detach himself from it. His deiform origin and his theocentric destiny make him broader than evil and sin, stronger than the devil.

Secondly, there is a liberation not only from the cyclic, and in the final analysis static, understanding of history, but also from the opposite point of view which sees history as a biological or dialectical evolutionary process. Since the ontological origin of man is not found in his biological being but in his being in Christ, and the realization of his being in Christ constitutes a journey from the "in the image" to the image itself, or from the iconic to that which truly exists, history can be understood precisely as the realization of this journey. As such, it has its beginning and its end in Christ. And since Christ is not only He "who was and who is" but also He "who is to come," it is not only the present and the past which move and determine history but also the future, when we regard as future not the fulfilment of natural laws to which the necessary biological or dialectical evolution of creation leads, but the advent, at the end of the age, of Christ the recapitulator of all things, that is, of the Logos together with His body, the transformed world. Thus the development or evolution of humanity and of creation in general is illuminated inwardly. Our understanding of humanity is not determined simply by the processes of change which are observed in the matter of the image, but, without this first aspect being over-looked, our viewpoint is extended and understood primarily in terms of an evolution or raising up of the image to the Archetype. The evolution of the image thus surpasses the bounds of creation—bounds which those who see only the matter of the image find themselves obliged to set since they are ignorant of the image itself—and reaches infinity. Evolution in this way is understood in all its dimensions—not only in those which are determined by scientific observation—and is given its true and full value.

9. These theses lead us to the kernel of the anthropo-logical problem as we encounter it today. The truth which they contain is the most vital of the anthropological truths, painful but at the same time offering salvation to modern man. It is painful because it eradicates even the slightest tendency towards the vindication of autonomy. It offers salvation because of a real and truly human activity and development.

Of course in saying that this truth crushes autonomy I do not mean that it justifies "heteronomy," in the philosophical sense of the term. These terms have been tragically misunder-stood in the last few centuries and lie essentially outside the Orthodox setting of the problem. The attempt I am making here is to show that for man God is not an external "prin-ciple" (*archi*) on which man depends, but truly and in reality his ontological origin (*archi*) and consummation. Having been made in the image of God, man has a theological struc-ture. And to be a true man he must at every moment exist and live theocentrically. When he denies God he denies him-self and destroys himself. When he lives theocentrically he realizes himself by reaching out into infinity; he attains his true fulfilment by extending into eternity. We shall return to this point.

II

The "Garments of Skin"

I mentioned at the beginning of this study that its aim is on the one hand to illuminate the origin, structure, destiny, and in general the nature of man, and on the other to establish a basis for Orthodox theology such as will enable it to be of effective help to the modern world.

What I have said about the meaning of "in the image" answers to the first point; it indicates the natural state of man. It does not, however, provide a complete answer, since experience proves that the historical reality of man is different from that which we have seen to be defined by the phrase "in the image." In the Christian perception of things this is to be ascribed to the fact that the historical reality develops within the unnatural situation in which man has found himself since the fall. We must now study this situation.

What I have already said is also of partial help with regard to the second point, because it justifies fundamentally the central quests of modern man for knowledge, development, justice, freedom and the rest, vindicating them as quests for his iconic nature, and shedding light on them in a positive way. Experience, however, proves again that humanity does not find today what it seeks. This, in the Christian view of things, is not because it is impossible for humanity to find these things, or because they do not belong to it, but because it begins from a false strating-point and a mistaken orientation. The false starting-point is the failure to appreciate the unnatural condition in which we find ourselves, and the mistaken orientation is that we are searching for something which is natural in the midst of what is unnatural. What is naturally good for man can be found if it is sought at its real source, and if man in order to find it makes full use of his natural powers.

The teaching of the Fathers on human nature contains two fundamental theses. It forms, as it were, a bridge with two piers, the first pier being the understanding of what is "in the image," the second the deeply significant notion of "garments of skin," which makes possible an interpretation of the postlapsarian state of man. But the "garments of skin" have a wider meaning than this: their purpose is not merely to ensure man's survival within the unnatural state which he has acquired in one way or another and his return to what is "in the image," but also to bring to fulfilment the inherent impetus of the latter, whereby man attains to the image itself. Such are the true implications of the second fundamental thesis in the revealed teaching of the Bible on the creation of man, namely, that after the fall of the first human beings God in His compassion, in order to enable them to survive, "clothed them . . . in garments of skin" (Gen 3:21). It is clear that to complete our study we now need to take a close look at this patristic teaching.[64]

1. THE GENERAL ANTHROPOLOGICAL CONTENT

First it must be stressed that the "garments of skin," as the Genesis narrative clearly shows, were put on man after

[64]To my knowledge the patristic teaching on the "garments of skin" has not been fully studied. The following works (in chronological order) deal with the subject in part: E. Stephanou, "La coexistence initiale du corps et d l'âme"; J.W. McGarry, "St Gregory of Nyssa and Adam's Body"; J. Quasten, "A Pythagorean idea in Jerome"; J. Quasten, "Theodore of Mopsuestia on the Exorcism of the Cilicium"; E. Peterson, *Pour une théologie du vêtement*; W. Burghardt, "Cyril of Alexandria on Wool and Linen"; J. Daniélou, *Platonisme et théologie mystique*, 48-60; G. Ladner, "The Philosophical Anthropology of Saint Gregory of Nyssa," esp. 88-9; I. Moutsoulas, *I sarkosis tou Logou kai i theosis tou anthropou*, 87-96; L. Thunberg, *Microcosm and Mediator*, 159-64; J. Daniélou, "Les tuniques de peau chez Grégoire de Nysse"; K. Skouteris, *Synepeiai tis ptoseos kai loutron palingenesias*, 61-8; M. Orphanos, *I psychi kai to soma tou anthropou kata Didymon Alexandrea*, 94-102; A. Radsalievits, *To mystirion tis sotirias kata ton aghion Maximon*, 59-60; C. Bernard, *Théologie symbolique* (Paris 1978), 207-10.

the fall and do not form one of his natural constituent elements.[65] That which empirical observation calls "human nature" is in biblical and patristic teaching a later nature, a state which came about after the fall, and not the original, and therefore true, human nature. "For the life which has been made similar to the divine nature is that which is proper to men and in accordance with nature."[66] Consequently, if modern man wishes to understand fully the nature of his existence, the good elements as well as the bad ones which scourge him, he needs to broaden his horizon, to ask himself whether what he considers "natural" is in reality so very self-evident. And we should note the encouraging fact that in recent years this question has been raised in the field of the anthropological sciences.[67] At any rate for the student of biblical and patristic anthropology this distinction is of fundamental importance and should constantly be borne in mind.

The second point which needs to be noted at the outset is that the garments of skin are not to be identified with the human body. The Fathers found themselves compelled to stress this at an early date,[68] so as to counter the gnostic heresies which depreciated the human body.[69] It is not surprising that Origen, influenced by his mistaken concept of the pre-existence of souls, should have been in some doubt as to whether or not the scriptural expression "garments of skin" should be understood as signifying the body.[70] With regard to such doubt the Fathers were strongly critical,[71] their

[65]Gen. 2:25 - 3:24; cf. Gregory of Nyssa, *Catechetical Oration* 8, *PG* 45, 33C; *On The Lord's Prayer* 5, *PG* 44, 1184B. The significance of this fact is analyzed by J. Daniélou, *Platonisme et théologie mystique*, 58-9.

[66]Gregory of Nyssa, *On Ecclesiastes* 1, *PG* 44, 624B.

[67]See H.F. Ellenberger, *A la découverte de l'Inconscient* (Villeurbanne 1974); C. Tresmontant, *Sciences de l'univers et problèmes métaphysiques* (Paris 1976). See also p. 27, note 24.

[68]See e.g. Methodios of Olympus, *On the Resurrection of the Dead* i, 39, *GCS* 27 (ed. Bonwetsch, 1917) 282-4.

[69]See J. Daniélou, "Les tuniques de peau chez Grégoire de Nysse," 355; K. Skouteris, *Synepeiai tis ptoseos kai loutron palingenesias*, 62; M. Orphanos, *I psychi kai to soma tou anthropou kata Didymon Alexandrea*, 94, note 1, with references.

[70]Origen, *On Genesis* iii, 2, *PG* 12, 101A.

[71]See Methodios of Olympus, *On the Resurrection of the Dead* i, 39, gcs 27, 282-4, (the same text is found verbatim also in Epiphanios of Salamis, *Panarion* 64, 23, *PG* 41, 1105C-1109A; Epiphanios of Salamis,

criticism arising from their concern not simply to underline
the positive value of the body, but to stress the central Christian truth that the body and the soul together "constitute"
the "natural" man. "The natural man is correctly said to be
neither soul without body nor conversely body without soul,
but the single form of beauty constituted from the combination of soul and body."[72] This truth is not only central to the
patristic tradition but also clearly expressed. And so we do
not need to analyze it here or dwell on the evidence for it.

What, then, are the "garments of skin?" I mentioned
above the important teaching of the Fathers on this theme.
The patristic teaching is indeed weighty but it is not systematic. Just as the Fathers used the phrase "in the image" to
express the reality of the natural man without constructing a
system around this truth, so they were frequently helped by
the concept of "garments of skin" to describe and interpret
the post-lapsarian state of man. It was in this way that they
expressed many truths relating to the garments of skin and
made numerous applications of the term.

The chief point that all these applications share in common is that the garments of skin express the mortality which
man put on as his second nature after the fall. Methodios,
for example, says: "God made the garments of skin for this
reason, as if clothing man in mortality."[73] And Gregory of

Panarion 64, 4, PG 41, 1077; Jerome, Against John of Jerusalem 7, PL
23, 360BC. For further information see A. Guillaumont, Les "Kephalaia
gnostica" d' Evagre le Pontique et l'histoire de l'Origenisme chez les Grecs
et chez les Syriens (Patristica Sorbonensia 5, Paris 1962), 89-90. These
Fathers clearly attribute to Origen the heretical belief that the garments of
skin are to be regarded as the body. But at the same time they mention
certain points in Origen which imply that the garments of skin are not the
body: thus Origen observes that Adam says before the fall, "This at last is
bone of my bones and flesh of my flesh" (On Genesis iii, 2, PG 12, 101A);
he also takes the view that the garments of skin are the "mortality" that
followed the fall (ibid. 101B). Perhaps on this point Origen fell victim
to his other heretical views. His precise understanding of the "garments of
skin" has still to be investigated. See A. Guillaumont, op. cit. 109, note
131, and L. Thunberg, Microcosm and Mediator, 159.

[72]Epiphanios of Salamis, Panarion 64, 18, PG 41, 1097D. Cf. Gregory
of Nazianzus, Oration 45, PG 36, 632; Gregory of Nyssa, On the Creation
of Man 29, PG 44, 233D. See also p. 27, note 22.

[73]Methodios of Olympus, On the Resurrection of the Dead i, 39, GCS 27,
281, 13-14.

Nyssa says that, whereas before the fall man was "naked of the covering of dead skins," afterwards "he was clothed with dead skins."[74] "Therefore mortality, derived from the nature of beings lacking intelligence, was by God's dispensation imposed on a nature created for immortality."[75]

In these passages, and in others which I have not cited,[76] it is characteristic that the discussion is not about death but about mortality, about a new state in which man finds himself, about a "life in death."[77] The change is great and constitutes a complete reversal of the situation. Man no longer has life in the way that he did previously, as a characteristic proper to his being. There is now no grace in the life welling up naturally within him. Life continues only so long as death is postponed. That which exists now in the proper sense is death: "life" has been transmuted into "survival."

St Maximos the Confessor in an inspired "study of the way in which the transgression of Adam took place" sees the first human being hastening to create within himself in a counterfeit manner the attributes of God, so as to create autonomously "without God and before God and not in accordance with God" that which is the exclusive characteristic of God, namely, self-subsistent life. Thus he abandoned the divine food which accorded with his nature,[78] and in order to establish his independent life chose as food the fruit

---

[74]Gregory of Nyssa, *On Virginity* 12, *PG* 46, 373C, 376A. See K. Skouteris, *Synepeiai tis ptoseos kai loutron palingenesias*, 61.

[75]Gregory of Nyssa, *Catechetical Oration* 8, *PG* 45, 33CD.

[76]See Athanasios, *On the Passion*, *PG* 28, 221A (on the genuine Athanasian authorship of the homily, see J. Quasten, *Patrology* iii [Utrecht 1960], 50); Gregory of Nazianzus, *Oration* 38, 12, *PG* 36, 324CD; Neilos, *Letter to Sosandros the First Secretary* i, 241, *PG* 79, 172A; Gregory Palamas, *Homily* 31, *PG* 151, 388C.

[77]See Gregory of Nyssa, *Commentary on the Song of Songs* 12, *PG* 44, 1021D.

[78]A passing remark of St Maximos in the passage presented here is remarkable for the alternative understanding of time which it presupposes. It is of special interest for the theme of the first part of this study. Maximos implies that, *even before the fall,* the Word was the "bread that came down from heaven": "The food of that blessed life is the bread which came down from heaven and gave life to the world, as the Word who does not lie declared about Himself in the Gospels. Since the first man refused to be nourished with this Word, he was rightly excluded from divine life and received another life productive of death." *Ambigua, PG* 91, 1157A.

of the forbidden tree, in spite of having already been taught
that it was the fruit of death, that is, the fruit of constant
flux, mutation and change. Thus, in conformity with the fruit
that he chose, he also made his life subject to decay and
created a living death within him. For, as St Maximos explains, death exists as the corruption of that which is being
all the time created, and the body with the intake and excretion of food constantly decays in a natural manner; and so
it is clear that the very things with which Adam thought life
was created have in fact created death within him and within
us, and have kept it flourishing ever since. Thus Adam
handed over the whole of nature as food for death. And
"death lives throughout this whole space of time, having
made us its food, but we never truly live, for we are always
devoured by death through decay."[79] That is why a little
further on he calls "the termination of this present life not
death but deliverance from death."[80]

Mortality, then—the absence of life which is experienced
by the sensitive souls of every period as the absence of meaning—or the "moist and slackened life,"[81] or the "chilled
life,"[82] is the primary significance of the garments of skin.

This mortality is characteristic of a nature which is not
endowed with intelligence. That man clothed himself with
mortality coincides with the fact that he clothed himself with
irrational nature, with the fact that henceforth he lives the
life of such a nature and is characterized by its attributes. St
Gregory of Nyssa speaks of "that dead and ugly garment in
which we are clothed, formed from the skins of unintelligent
beings." He goes on to explain, "When I hear the word
'skin' it conveys to me the form of irrational nature, with
which, having become familiar with passion, we have been
clothed." And he defines it with even greater clarity: "It is
those things which [man] took in addition from irrational
skin: sexual union, conception, birth, pollution, the nipple,

[79]Maximos the Confessor, *Ambigua*, PG 91, 1156C-1157A.

[80]Maximos the Confessor, *Ambigua*, PG 91, 1157C.

[81]John Chrysostom, *On 2 Corinthians* 1, 4, PG 61, 387. The phrase is
also found in *On Genesis* 18, PG 53, 150, in a close relationship with
mortality and the "garments of skin."

[82]Gregory of Nyssa, *On the Soul and Resurrection*, PG 46, 148C-149A.

food, excretion, gradual growth to full stature, adult life, old age, sickness, death,"[83] that is, what we call today biological life.

It would be a mistake to think that this text is concerned exclusively with the body and that the garments of skin are restricted to the body. "Sexual union," "birth," "the nipple" and the other stages of man's development are not restricted to bodily activities; they also imply activities or functions of the soul, which likewise dress themselves in the "irrational form"—it is characteristic that he does not say "irrational body"—, losing their freedom and intelligence and degenerating into instincts. The whole psychosomatic human organism suffered with the fall a kind of stunting; it has been constricted within the boundaries of the "irrational form."

The result of this constriction is a life which is non-rational or irrational. The deiform characteristics and tendencies of the "in the image" have fallen away from their natural state, from their orientation and function which harmonized with their inner principle or innate reason; they have been perverted; they have submitted to the non-rational nature and have clothed man in the attributes of this nature as if in non-rational garments. Carnivorous animals are maintained by their incensive aspect, writes St Gregory, and prolific breeders by their love of pleasure. Cowardice saves the weak, and fear those which are the prey of others. These characteristics and others similar to them "through an animal-like mode of generation entered man's composite being."[84] Thus "the attributes of non-rational nature were commingled with man."[85] We shall see below in greater detail how man came to be united with the attributes of non-rational nature, which appear and operate in him as passions.[86] Here it is sufficient to note that it constitutes an element of the garments of skin.

But the life with which the garments of skin clothe man is dead or biological or non-rational because in the last analysis it is material. The "garments of skin" are identified by St

[83]Gregory of Nyssa, *On the Soul and Resurrection*, PG 46, 148C-149A.
[84]Gregory of Nyssa, *On the Creation of Man* 18, PG 44, 192BC.
[85]Gregory of Nyssa, *On Those who have Fallen Asleep*, PG 46, 524D.
[86]See Gregory of Nyssa, *On the Creation of Man* 18, PG 44, 192B.

Gregory of Nyssa with the "transient leaves of this material life, which, when we had been stripped of our proper radiant garments, we sewed together for ourselves in an evil way."[87] This materiality embraces the whole of the psychosomatic human organism; it does not refer—it is worth noting again— exclusively to the body. St Gregory in the same passage defines the "leaves of the material life" as the "delight and glories and transient honors and fading satisfactions of the flesh,"[88] and elsewhere as "sensual pleasure and anger and gluttony and insatiate greed and the like."[89] Glory, honor and anger are not characteristics of the body. St John Chrysostom, commenting on the Pauline text, "Those who are in the flesh cannot please God" (Rom 8:8), writes: "He says 'flesh' and therefore not 'body,' or the substance of the body, but the life of the flesh, or of the world, full of self-indulgence and profligacy, which makes man entirely flesh."[90]

The body has certainly dressed itself in garments of skin. It has become "coarse and solid";[91] it is characterized by "this gross and heavy composition,"[92] although at the resurrection, when it will recover its prelapsarian nature in a perfected form, it will be "respun" "into something lighter and more aerial"; it will be re-established "in a better and more attractive beauty."[93]

The functions of the soul, however, have also become

[87]Gregory of Nyssa, *On the Lord's Prayer* 5, PG 44, 1184B.
[88]Ibid.
[89]Gregory of Nyssa, *On Those who have Fallen Asleep*, PG 46, 524D.
[90]John Chrysostom, *Commentary on Romans* 13, 7, PG 60, 517.
[91]Gregory of Nyssa, *On Those who have Fallen Asleep*, PG 46, 532C.
[92]Gregory of Nyssa, *On the Soul and Resurrection*, PG 46, 108A. These and other similar phrases lead almost all the students of St Gregory, if not to identify the "garments of skin" with the postlapsarian human body, then at least to link them with it in a one-sided manner. They overlook the fact that by the term "garments of skin" St Gregory is referring to the entire postlapsarian psychosomatic clothing of the human person. See e.g. G.B. Ladner, *The Philosophical Anthropology of Saint Gregory of Nyssa*, 88, who, while clearly expressing the bodily aspect of the "garments of skin," entirely overlooks the psychic aspect.
[93]Gregory of Nyssa, *On the Soul and Resurrection*, PG 46, 108A; cf. *On Those who have Fallen Asleep*, PG 46, 532C; *Funeral Oration on Meletios*, PG 46, 861B. See K. Skouteris, *Synepeiai tis ptoseos kai loutron palingenesias*, 67.

"corporeal" along with those of the body.[94] According to St Gregory of Nyssa they form together with the body "the veil of the heart . . . the fleshy covering of the old man."[95] "When he says 'flesh' he defines with greater exactitude the old man, whom the divine Apostle orders to be stripped off and put away,"[96] that is, the man that the Apostle calls "carnal" or "natural" as opposed to "spiritual."[97] In a succinct formulation of St Gregory, the garments of skin are "the will of the flesh."[98]

The heart of the matter, then, is a general association of man with materiality, with the perpetual flux of the elements which constitute the material world, with the constant movement and change which make him impassioned and in his totality "carnal." Thus we understand why for St Gregory the "honors" which man finds in this dead, biological, non-rational, material carnality are inescapably "transient," and

[94]Gregory of Nyssa, *On the Life of Moses*, PG 44, 388D. He who "intends to be ordained a priest by God" is called in this text "to refine . . . by purity of life all the artificialities of human life" and "to subdue this corporeal nature" (i.e. the whole nature of man which became corporeal; he does not say "the body"). A corresponding sense of the refashioning of the human person is found in the hymnology of the Orthodox Church, particularly when referring to martyrs and monastic saints. See e.g. the *Doxastikon* for the Feast of St Euphemia, 11 July.

[95]Gregory of Nyssa, *Commentary on the Song of Songs* 11, PG 44, 1005A. Here St Gregory describes how the Bride of the Song, having previously shed "that garment of skin which she put on after sin," "the fleshly covering of the old man," dresses herself in "the garment created in accordance with God, in holiness and righteousness." This new garment, explains St Gregory, is "the garment of the Lord, as bright as the sun . . . which He manifested in the transfiguration on the mountain." This text has been discussed at length by K. Skouteris, *Synepeiai tis ptoseos kai loutron palingenesias*, 34, 64. Scholars regard "the garment of the Lord, as bright as the sun" as His body, although we should rather take this expression to refer to the uncreated glory of the divinity which radiated from within the Lord. This is also clear in the hymnology of the Feast of the Transfiguration. See the eighth canticle: Christ "puts on light and glory as a garment." There has also been some discussion about the dependence of the term "bright as the sun" (*ilioeidis*) on a corresponding term in Plato which is also used by Plotinos. St Gregory of course knows Plato and uses him, but here he is more likely to have in mind the Gospel narrative of the Transfiguration.

[96]Gregory of Nyssa, *Commentary on the Song of Songs* 11, PG 44, 1004D-1005A.

[97]1 Cor. 2:14, 3:3; Eph. 4:22; Rom. 8:8. See John Chrysostom, *On Romans* 13, 7, PG 60, 517, where he interprets Rom. 8:8.

[98]Gregory of Nyssa, *On Virginity* 12, PG 46, 376B.

why the "satisfactions," that is, the props or assurances of
the "flesh," are "fading," that is, mortal and therefore death-
bringing.

Before he dressed himself in the garments of skin man
wore a "divinely woven"[99] attire, his psychosomatic dress
which had been woven with grace, with the light and glory
of God. Our first parents "were clothed in glory from above
. . . the heavenly glory covered them better than any garment
could do."[100] This refers to the attire of the "in the image,"
the prelapsarian human nature formed by the breath of God
and endowed with a deiform structure. This attire shone with
"the likeness to the divine" which was constituted, not by
a "shape" or a "color," but by "dispassion," "blessedness"
and "incorruption," the characteristics by which "the divine
is contemplated as beauty."[101]

The first man, according to the succinct expression of
St Gregory the Theologian, was "naked by virtue of his
simplicity."[102] This means, as St Maximos explains, that his
body did not contain within it the mutually contradictory
"qualities" which now pull it in different directions, scourge
it with corruption and make it decay, but it possessed "another
temperament which befitted it, a temperament maintained by
simple qualities compatible with each other." It was "without
flux or wastage," free from "constant change depending on
which quality was predominant," and for this reason was not
bereft "of immortality by grace."[103] If we understand the
"nakedness" as transparency, we can say that the body of
Adam was so simple that it was in reality transparent, open to
the material creation without resisting it in any way, and

[99]This is the usual characteristic which hymnology attributes to the
prelapsarian human attire: "Thou hast dressed me in a divinely woven
attire, O Savior" (canticle 6, troparion 1, *Canon of the Sunday of Cheesefare*).
Cf. Romanos Melodos, *Kontakion on Epiphany, Oikos* 2. See also the study
of the Great Canon below, pp. 173-4. For the general condition of the first
human beings before the fall according to Gregory of Nyssa, see J. Gaïth,
La conception de liberté chez Grégoire de Nysse, 52 ff.

[100]John Chrysostom, *On Genesis* 15, 4, PG 53, 123, and 16, 5, PG 53,
131. Cf. E. Peterson, *Pour une théologie du vêtement,* 5-9, who also gives
references to Irenaios, Ambrose and Augustine.

[101]Gregory of Nyssa, *On Those who have Fallen Asleep,* PG 46, 521D.
[102]Gregory of Nazianzus, *Oration* 45, 8, PG 36, 632C.
[103]Maximos the Confessor, *Ambigua, PG* 91, 1353AB.

without the world offering any resistance to the body—the world had been surrendered to it. The human body, while maintaining its own peculiar constitution and separate identity with regard to the world, was nevertheless not divided from it at all.

Moreover, the human soul was open to the angelic powers and to God. It offered no resistance and communicated with ease alike with the angelic spiritual world and with the Spirit of God. There then existed, writes St Gregory of Nyssa, a unified choir of intelligent nature, both angelic and human, "gazing towards the one Head of the choir and singing in harmony with the Head." But sin "dissolved that inspired harmony of the choir," opening out below the feet of the first human beings, "who had their place in the choir of the angelic powers," the slippery slope of illusion; and so man fell and was mixed with the mire, he deserted to the serpent, dressed himself in dead skins and became a "corpse." Thus "man's union with the angels was shattered."[104] In a similar way man's union with the material creation was also shattered.

With this we arrive at the second stage of our study. We shall now examine in a more analytical way how the above rupture and the corresponding union with the "non-rational form" took place. That is to say, we shall investigate in greater detail how the prelapsarian deiform and divinely-woven attire of man was transformed into garments of skin. In this way perhaps more light can be shed on the original question concerning the true anthropological content of the garments of skin.

2. THE TRANSFORMATION OF THE PRELAPSARIAN POWERS OF THAT WHICH IS "IN THE IMAGE" INTO "GARMENTS OF SKIN"

At this stage our guide will be St Maximos. In his view

[104]Gregory of Nyssa, *On the Titles of the Psalms* 2, 6, *PG* 44, 508BC. I have inserted the phrase "was mixed with the mire, deserted to the serpent" from another text of St Gregory; see *On the Lord's Prayer* 5, *PG* 44, 1184C.

the central characteristic of man in his natural state is a relative, or more precisely, a potential unity. Man is called, "through the right use of his natural faculties,"[105] to transform this potential unity into a full unity of himself and the world in God realized in actuality.

He explains that this potential unity already exists between the material world and the human body, between the body and the soul, between the soul and God. We recognize, he writes, "that the soul lies midway between God and matter and has faculties that unite it with both."[106] It was Adam's vocation to effect, through the correct use of these unifying faculties, the actual realization of the potential unity, unifying and thus abolishing the four great divisions of the universe: the division of mankind into male and female, the division of the earth into paradise and the inhabited land, the division of sensible nature into earth and sky, the division of created nature into spiritual and sensible, and finally the fifth, highest and ineffable division between creation and Creator.[107]

In another very dense text[108] St Maximos describes in greater detail the original, natural, potential unity and clarifies more specifically the way in which it is brought to fulfilment. He teaches that there is a "natural" correspondence between the faculties of the soul and the senses of the body, between, for example, the noetic faculty of the soul, the intellect, and the sense of vision, between the appetitive faculty and the sense of taste, between the life-preserving faculty and the sense of touch, and so on. It is upon these bodily senses, which are manifested externally through their corresponding sense organs, that the soul "depends through

[105]Maximos the Confessor, *Ambigua, PG* 91, 1097C.

[106]Maximos the Confessor, *Ambigua, PG* 91, 1193D.

[107]Maximos the Confessor, *Ambigua, PG* 91, 1304D-1308C. The work which Adam did not do was accomplished by Christ. See the continuation of the text, 1308C-1312B, which is translated in its entirety below, pp. 211-16. Cf. *To Thalassios: On Various Questions* 48, *PG* 90, 436AB. A synoptic view of St. Maximos' teaching on the five divisions and their transcendence is given by V. Lossky, *Mystical Theology,* 136-8. For a full analysis of this teaching in conjunction with other relevant points of St Maximos's doctrine, see L. Thunberg, *Microcosm and Mediator,* 351-459.

[108]Maximos the Confessor, *Ambigua, PG* 91, 1248A-1249C. This text is translated below, pp. 216-18.

its own faculties" in an organic way, and it is through the intermediary of the bodily senses that the faculties of the soul are "conveyed" to the sensible material world. Thus not only can the soul, if it uses the senses correctly, "through its own proper faculties" organize and govern the world, while at the same time keeping the world external to itself, but, and this is fundamental, it also has the power to convey "wisely to itself everything visible in which God is concealed and proclaimed in silence."

In this manner the four cardinal virtues are created, which are not simply properties of the soul but, so to speak, actualized embodied states, since they are created by the conjunction, or more accurately the interweaving (*sym-ploki*), of the faculties of the soul with the corresponding senses and sense organs of the body, and with the operations of the senses by means of which the soul embraces sensible things. The first virtue is moral judgment, which comes into being through the interweaving of the rational and intellective faculties of the soul not only with the bodily senses of sight and hearing but also with the corresponding operations or energies—the cognitive, which is the operation of the cognitive faculty, and the epistemic, which is the operation of the intellective faculty. Through moral judgment the soul concentrates within it the inner principles (*logoi*) of sensible things and thus unites them with itself. In a similar way the other three cardinal virtues, justice, courage and self-restraint, are also brought into being.

As a consequence of the conjunction of the first two virtues, moral judgment and justice—each of which, as we have seen, already contains interwoven with it the relevant faculties of the soul, the corresponding bodily senses and the operations of the senses on things—, the more general virtue of wisdom is brought into being. This is composed of all the cognitive faculties and senses—I would say, of the cognitive psychosomatic functions of man—together with the operations of these faculties or with the fruits which are engendered by the meeting of the cognitive functions with things, these fruits being termed cognitions. And through the interweaving of the other two general virtues, courage and self-restraint, the more general virtue of gentleness is brought into being. This, because it effects the harmonization and combination of all the active faculties of the soul, and likewise of the corresponding bodily senses and the operations of the senses, is also called dispassion, because it is nothing other than "the total cessation of the movement of the incensive and appetitive aspects of the soul towards things contrary to nature."

These two more general virtues, which could also be called "pneumatohylic" states or psychosomatic functions of man, are united—with all that we have seen them to contain in a real sense—"in the virtue which is the most general of all, namely, love." Love, as the "unifying" virtue which it is, draws together all things, that is, not only the fundamental elements (soul and the soul's faculties, body and the bodily senses, the action of the senses on things and the inner essences of those same things) but also the movement of these towards their goal (the cardinal and more general virtues which we have seen to be actualized states) ; and it brings them to a unified synthesis, a final and simple unity which takes place in God. Love does this because it is a virtue which is "ecstatic . . . and unlike the others capable of deifying."

Thus the soul, St Maximos recapitulates, by using the senses "as intelligent vehicles of its faculties," apprehends sensible objects through them and makes their inward principles its own. And it unites its own faculties, along with all that these now contain, with the virtues and the deiform principles hidden within them; for the virtues are not simply human states—they are theanthropic states. And the spiritual intelligence which lies in the deiform principles urges on the soul in the midst of all this and "presents it wholly to the whole of God. And God embraces it wholly together with the body natural to it and makes it like Himself in an appropriate manner."[109]

In this way the multiplicity of created things, "drawing

[109]Maximos the Confessor, *Ambigua, PG* 91, 1248A-1249C. This splendid text has not received the attention it deserves, even from L. Thunberg, although it is central to his theme. Cf. *Ambigua, PG* 91, 1193C-1196B; 1113C.

together around the one nature of man," can be gathered together into one, and the Creator of all things is manifested as one, "reigning over created beings proportionately through the human race"; and so "God Himself becomes all in all, embracing all things and giving subsistence to them in Himself."[110]

This is man's natural state in the image of God; this is his natural function, his natural work and goal. When he turns aside from this orientation he falls into what is contrary to nature.

That is what happened in Adam's case. The first man did not move towards God, the Archetype, his natural principle (*archi*), but in the opposite direction. This was something which naturally reversed the way in which his psychosomatic organism functioned. Since man's point of reference or attraction was displaced, the faculties of the soul no longer used the operations of the senses but were used by them. The soul, instead of using the senses to concentrate and unite in itself, and consequently in God, all the things that are separated by their nature, was drawn away by sensible things and through these things was made utterly captive by means of the senses. Thus fragmentation prevailed. Man, who was "like some workshop holding all things together in the closest way,"[111] who was "like some natural bond"[112] uniting all things, by his withdrawal from his natural work and by his unnatural submission to the sensible world also shattered the relative or potential unity which his existence as an image of God created, as we have seen, within the universe. "Having abused the natural power given to him for the union of what was divided," he brought about instead "the division of what was united."[113]

But when the soul is taken captive by sensible things, then the operations of the senses, the senses themselves, and within them the corresponding faculties of the soul, put on the form of sensible things, seeing that they submit to them and are

---

[110]Maximos the Confessor, *Ambigua*, PG 91, 1092C.
[111]Ibid., 1305A.
[112]Ibid., 1305B.
[113]Ibid., 1308C.

shaped in conformity with them. "When the soul is moved towards matter by means of the flesh in a way contrary to nature, it puts on the earthly form."[114] That is what was termed above, in our analysis of St Gregory of Nyssa, union with the "non-rational form." The result of this union is the non-rational life, which is characterized by the passions, as St Gregory has already taught us. St Maximos explains in addition how the passions are brought into being.

When the intellect, he writes, denies its natural movement towards God, since there is no other direction in which it can move, it gives itself over to the senses, and these delude it ceaselessly, deceiving it by the superficial aspects of sensible things "through which [the soul] grows forgetful of natural goods and perverts[115] the whole of its activity with regard to sensible things, becoming subject to unseemly fits of anger, desires and pleasures through what I have mentioned." For pleasure is nothing other than a "mode of sensory operation constituted by irrational desire." Irrational desire, when it gains a hold on sensation, transforms it into pleasure, adding to it a "non-rational form." Moreover, when sensation, moving in accordance with irrational desire, attaches itself to the sensible object it creates pleasure.[116]

And in another text he says with direct reference to Adam: "Thus, having become a transgressor [having changed direction] and having become ignorant of God, and having closely mingled the whole of his intellective faculty with the whole of sensation, he embraced the knowledge of sensible things, which is composite and destructive and oriented towards passion. So he came to resemble the dumb beasts, doing, seek-

[114]Ibid., 1112C.

[115]"This verb 'perverts' (*katastrephei*) signifies a movement contrary to nature, an upset like that of a wagon overturning and lying with its wheels in the air, and therefore a degeneration, a disaster. The soul, misusing its whole capacity to act in regard to nature, that is, to visible things, distorts this capacity and so becomes filled wih rancours, desires and pleasures contrary to nature. These are forms of movement which have degenerated and become violent." A note by D. Staniloae in Maximos the Confessor, *Philosophika kai theologika erotimata* (Epi tas pigas 4, Athens 1978), 249. This book is an edition of the text of the *Ambigua* with a parallel modern Greek translation, introduction and notes.

[116]Maximos the Confessor, *Ambigua*, PG 91, 1112ABC.

ing and desiring the same things as they do in every way and, moreover, cleaving to irrationality."[117]

At this point the reader will perhaps permit me to add a personal note. It has not been at all easy to penetrate the above texts of St Maximos. Indeed, it has proved impossible to master their content thoroughly and to set it adequately within the argument of this essay, even though the argument clearly emanates from these very texts. The difficulty arises from the fact that St Maximus' thought is so dense and so rich in different layers of meaning that it seems as if every word is pulling one simultaneously in two or three directions and is demanding that one move at the same time on two or three levels. I therefore ask the reader not to rely totally on my presentation of St Maximos' thought but to study the texts themselves, at least in the translations set out at the end of the book. He will see in these that the cosmology of Plato and the anthropology of Aristotle, both of which have left clear traces, have been thoroughly assimilated and broken down as systems, and that the true elements which they contain have been unified and used to illuminate the real relationship that exists between sensible things and their inner principles, between matter and form, and so on. It is precisely these elements that are used by St Maximos as categories or, more accurately, as realities, so as to construct out them, stone by stone, a bridge uniting the created with the uncreated. And this bridge, St Maximos makes clear, is in potentiality and may become in actuality the human person. I have myself not met a more exact description of the bond uniting man with God and the world, or a higher evaluation and more exalted understanding of human nature.

These texts are persuasive in their realism. At the same time they illuminate many other matters. The bond, for example, uniting the faculty of the human will with the sense of smell, on which I have touched above, shows why in the technique of inner prayer, and also in the ascetic techniques of other traditions, such attention is given to the control of breathing. St Maximos offers an anthropological foundation

[117]Maximos the Confessor, *To Thalassios: On Various Questions*, PG 90, 253CD.

for inner prayer. There are many such aspects of the saint's thought which the reader will find in the texts.

3. THE TWO-FOLD CHARACTER OF THE "GARMENTS OF SKIN"

The texts quoted in the last section, I believe, provide us with a satisfactory reply to the question I have posed, namely, how the union of man with the form of non-rationality took place, how the natural iconic powers and potentialities of man were transformed into "garments of skin."

Earlier I cited some passages in which God is represented actively clothing our first ancestors in the garments of skin. And this is not simply a manner of speaking, since the express wording of Scripture itself says categorically, "And the Lord God made for Adam and for his wife garments of skin, and clothed them" (Gen 3:21). However, if the garments of skin are the result of the natural process through which the sinner comes to be united with the non-rational form and in consequence to be dressed in dead skins, how can it be that it is God who dresses fallen humanity in these skins? In this apparent contradiction is hidden a great truth which deserves examination.

We have seen that the central content of the "garments of skin" is mortality, the transformation of life into survival. This is indeed a physiological consequence of sin; it is not a creation of God. God does not create evil.[118] But He tolerates (that is, accepts by consent, holds and supports) within His infinitive love even this new situation and transforms it into a blessing. He changes that which is the result of denial and therefore is negative into something relatively positive, if we take into account its final metamorphosis. "For God acts in a loving way even towards those who have become evil, so as to bring about our correction."[119] Evil, which by itself is "not

---

[118]On this central doctrine of the patristic tradition, see Basil, *That God is not the Source of Evil*, PG 31, 329A-353A.

[119]Maximos the Confessor, *Scholia on the Divine Names*, 4, 33, PG 4, 305D.

even a being," much less "productive of beings," can, under the dissolving and reconstituting love of Him who is Good, become in the striking phase of St Dionysios the Areopagite "both a being and a good productive of goods."[120]

Thus almighty God uses the new situation as one of the many paths which, His compassionate and multifaceted wisdom recognizes, can lead humanity to the greatest good, which is Christ, who will realize in us in a new manner, a manner more paradoxical and more befitting God, the original destiny which Adam by misusing his natural powers failed to attain.[121] And He offers this relatively positive condition of the "garments of skin" as a second blessing to a self-exiled humanity. He adds it like a second nature to the existing human nature, so that by using it correctly humanity can survive and realize its original goal in Christ. "For the garment is something put on us from the outside, lending itself for use by the body for a time but not becoming part of its nature. Therefore from the nature of irrational things mortality was providentially put on a nature which was created for immortality."[122]

The reality of the fall, besides the natural character which we have studied above, also has a moral content. Sin is rebellion and "hubris" against the righteousness of God. In the teaching of the Fathers, as summarized by Nicolas Kavasilas in the fourteenth century, the righteousness of God is "the supreme compassion and goodness of God towards the human race . . . the bestowal of His blessings upon all in abundance and the sharing of His blessedness."[123] According to Kavasilas the Love which is God (1 John 4:8) created contingent being freely *ex nihilo*. The same act of creation, being good, had as its result a world (*cosmos*), that is, an order and harmony, which constitutes the righteousness of creation. Consequently, between the righteousness-goodness of the Creator and the righteousness-order-harmony of creation there exists a genuine interior iconic relationship. Thus the rebellion or "hubris" of

[120]Dionysios the Areopagite, *On the Divine Names*, 4, 20, *PG* 3, 717C.
[121]Maximos the Confessor, *Ambigua*, *PG* 91, 1097CD.
[122]Gregory of Nyssa, *Catechetical Oration* 8, *PG* 45, 33CD.
[123]Nicolas Kavasilas, *The Life in Christ* 1, *PG* 150, 508A.

man against God, unable to touch the righteousness of God—
how is it possible for the infinite to be wounded or in any
way touched by the contingent?—in fact wounds the image
of divine righteousness within creation, shattering and throw-
ing into disarray the iconic psychosomatic constitution and
liturgical character of man and the order and harmony of
creation. The "hubris" is in reality a "trauma."[124]

But since the fall constitutes a real "hubris," there must
also be a real and corresponding "penalty." "For it was necessary that sin should be abolished by some penalty and that
we by suffering a proportionate punishment should be freed
from the offences we have committed against God."[125] The
penalty, however, which is naturally inflicted on the perpe-
trator of "hubris" comes not from the righteousness of God,
which was neither wounded nor seeks satisfaction, but from
the righteousness of creation. The laws of the latter continue
to operate, but now in a disorganized and disordered way, and
they involve man too in this disordered operation with the
result that they draw him into misery and anguish.

From this point of view, then, the union of man with the
form of non-rationality, and the transformation of his natural
functions into passions, that is, the "garments of skin," constitute the "penalty" which the very righteousness of creation
imposes on man. It is for this reason that man finds pain
while searching for pleasure, and death while searching for
life. In our study of St Maximos we saw *how* this took
place; Kavasilas explains *why*.[126]

The penalty which the implacable righteousness of creation imposes on man would have been eternal, Kavasilas

---

[124]Ibid., 516BC; cf. Basil, *On Envy* 3, *PG* 31, 376AB.

[125]Nicolas Kavasilas, *The Life in Christ* 1, *PG* 150, 516B.

[126]Kavasilas developed this doctrine—underlining the elements which
existed in the earlier patristic tradition and presenting them as an organic
whole—as a result of the soteriological systems which were propounded
from the 11th to the 14th centuries in the West, and particularly as a
result of Anselm's theory of satisfaction. That which previously circulated
in a disjointed form as a life-giving element in the patristic tradition now
needed to be formulated by Kavasilas as a doctrine. For an analysis of this
doctrine and how it took shape, and also for an account of its relationship
with the theory of satisfaction, see P. Nellas, *I peri dikaioseos tou anthropou
didaskalia Nikolaou tou Kavasila*.

teaches, if the righteousness-goodness of God had not intervened to correct the righteousness of nature, transforming in a compassionate and interior manner the "penalty" into a "remedy," and thus healing the "trauma" and punishing or abolishing[127] the "hubris" which is sin. "Wound and pain and death were from the beginning devised against sin. . . . For this reason after the sin God immediately permitted death and pain, not inflicting a penalty on the sinner but rather applying a remedy to the patient."[128]

The above makes clear, and this point is of vital and decisive importance to our theme, that in the single and unique reality of the "garments of skin" we are to discern two aspects. I would describe this reality as biform, like those pictures with two views printed on them, which when moved show now one and now the other, one view stimulating fear and the other joy.[129] To the repulsive form which man created when he acted with "hubris" towards God and traumatized himself, to this "ugly mask," as St Gregory of Nyssa calls it,[130] God, using the same material, adds a second form, and thus creates the positive aspect of the garments of skin. On the one hand, then, the garments of skin are the physiological result of sin, constituting an obscuring of the image, a fall from what is according to nature, and introducing "hubris," "penalty" and "trauma"; on the other they constitute a "remedy" and blessing, introducing a new potentiality which God gives to man, enabling him, since he has forfeited life, to survive in death and even to survive in the right way so as to reach the point of finding again the fullness of life and the beauty of form that belongs to his nature in Christ.

---

[127]The expression is that of Kavasilas, *The Life in Christ* 1, *PG* 150, 516B.

[128]Nicolas Kavasilas, *The Life in Christ* 1, *PG* 150, 513C. The same is taught, though without the analytical detail found in Kavasilas, by John Chrysostom, *On Greeting Priscilla*, 1, 5, *PG* 51, 194. For an anthropological analysis of how the results of the wounded righteousness of creation are used by God pedagogically for the healing of mankind, see Maximos the Confessor, *Ambigua*, *PG* 91, 1104A-1105A.

[129]In order to express another truth St Gregory of Nyssa uses the image of "diglyph sculptures": "The sculptors of such works contrive to surprise those who chance upon them by carving two forms on a single head" (*On the Creation of Man* 18, *PG* 44, 192C).

[130]Gregory of Nyssa, *On the Creation of Man* 18, *PG* 44, 193C.

When contemplating a specific instance of this ineffable mystery of divine compassion, St Paul is lost in ecstatic worship: "O the depth of the riches and wisdom and knowledge of God! How unsearchable are His judgments and how inscrutable His ways!" (Rom 11:33).

4. THE ANTHROPOLOGICAL AND COSMOLOGICAL DIMENSIONS OF THE TWO-FOLD REALITY OF THE "GARMENTS OF SKIN"

A few examples will allow the truth of this two-fold reality of the "garments of skin" to the expressed in a more concrete manner. At the same time the essential content of the notion of the "garments of skin" will become clearer and more specific.

(a) Death

The final physical result of the fall and its greatest penalty is, as we have seen, death. As soon, however, as death appeared in history, God, to whom every initiative ultimately belongs, used it as He Himself wished, and as a result of His different use of it fundamentally changed its nature. By allowing man to dress himself in biological life, the fruit of sin, He redirected death, which was also the fruit of sin, against biological life, and thus by death is put to death not man but the corruption which clothes him. Death destroys the prison of life-in-corruption, and man, by abandoning to corruption what he received from it, is liberated through death.[131]

In this way the great marvel of the wisdom, love and power of God is revealed. The devil lures man and casts him into the abyss of corruption, where he keeps him bound by

---

[131]Cf. Methodios of Olympus, *On the Resurrection of the Dead* i, 38-41, *GCS* 27, 280-7; Methodios of Olympus, *Banquet of the Ten Virgins* 2, *GCS* 27, 15 ff; Irenaios, *Against Heresies* iii, 23, 5-6, *PG* 7, 963-4; Gregory of Nyssa, *Commentary on the Song of Songs* 12, *PG* 44, 1020B.

death. God allows death to exist but turns it against corruption and its cause, sin, and sets a boundary both to corruption and to sin. Thus He restricts evil and relativizes the fall. His original plan for man's eternal and blessed life in Him remains intact. Commenting on this mystery of infinite divine compassion, the Fathers teach that God tolerated death and permitted it to exist "that evil might not become immortal."[132] And gazing down at death from this eminence, they mock it: "Let us therefore stand firm, pouring scorn on death."[133]

The devil in addition contrived to subordinate man through the fall to the material creation. And he succeeded by dressing him in the form of non-rational matter. Furthermore, it was his plan to obliterate man through death, dissolving him in matter. And to all appearances he succeeded, since after burial the body surrenders to the earth the constituent elements which it received from it and is dissolved into it.[134] "This was contrived by the sower of sin . . . to make the works of God disappear and to dissolve the elements that hold them together in being."[135]

The wisdom of God, however, intervenes at this point with great discernment, enriching the passive movement to the grave with an element which may be called "active," and thus transforming it. Death becomes the means by which the human body penetrates into the interior of the earth, reaching the inmost parts of creation. With death, man touches the boundaries of the universe, becomes air, water and fire, matter and energy, an element of space. "The dust returns to the earth as it was," says Ecclesiastes (12:7). But this "dust" is no longer only matter. It carries in actual fact the "principle" and the "form" of man, as St Maximos would have said. Thus the material creation which, as we have seen, clothed man in its corruption in an organic way, is now dressed, it could be

---

[132]Gregory of Nazianzus, *Oration* 45, 8, *PG* 36, 633A. Cf. Maximos the Confessor, *To Thalassios: On Various Questions* 61, *PG* 90, 633D; John Chrysostom, *On the Statues* 5, 4, *PG* 49, 75.

[133]John Chrysostom, *On Hebrews* 4, *PG* 63, 42. Cf. J. Romanides, *To propatorikon amartima*, 145-55.

[134]Gregory of Nyssa, *Catechetical Oration* 8, *PG* 45, 33D.

[135]Maximos the Confessor, *To Thalassios: On Various Questions* 61, *PG* 90, 633BC; cf. ibid., scholion 1, *PG* 90, 641B.

said, from within, once more in an organic way; thanks to the other aspect of the two-fold reality which death itself constitutes, it is dressed with a new element which, as the human body, is receptive of incorruption. For this reason, along with the final resurrection of bodies which He will bring about at His second coming, Christ will also bring about the transformation of the universe into a "new earth" and a "new heaven." Creation "will then be manifested to us with an incorrupt beauty, since we will receive incorrupt bodies, and will finally be transformed into something better."[136] "And heaven and earth and the whole of creation will be changed along with our own bodies."[137]

The eschatological transformation of the universe cannot be realized in a magical or mechanical way through the simple operation of an external power—since God does not realize anything in this way—but only from within, organically and naturally, within the human person.[138]

(b) Law

I mentioned above that St Gregory of Nyssa's carnal or biological man—man united with the "non-rational form"—is what St Paul calls the "old man,"[139] and that St Gregory discusses the "garments of skin" in terms of the "will of the flesh."[140] St Paul sees this "will" as dominating the old carnal man, "sold under sin" (Rom 7:14). He sees it as the "law of

[136]John Chrysostom, *To Theodore* 1, 11, *PG* 47, 291.

[137]John Chrysostom, *On Galatians* 6, 3, *PG* 61, 679; cf. *On Romans* 14, 5, *PG* 60, 530.

[138]Apart from what has been said above, the teaching of St Maximos the Confessor on man as the "natural link" and "the comprehensive workshop of all things" within whom the five divisions are transcended also, in my opinion, leads to this thesis. Cf. Mark Evgenikos, *On the Resurrection,* ed. A. Schmemann, *Theologia* 22 (1951), 53-60, esp. 56-7; Nicolas Kavasilas, *Prayer to Our Lord Jesus Christ,* in P. Nellas, *Prolegomena eis tin meletin Nikolaou tou Kavasila,* 58-9; J. Daniélou, *La Résurrection* (Paris 1969), 95-8; K. Rahner, *Le chrétien et la mort* (Paris 1966), 20-1, 37-8, 71-2. The reader interested in this theme should not fail to study Gregory of Nyssa, *On the Creation of Man* 27, *PG* 44, 225A-229A.

[139]See above, p. 51.

[140]See above, p. 51 and note 98.

sin," as existing in the "members" of the old man, as holding
him captive like a second nature from which he cannot be
delivered. "Who will deliver me from this body of death?"
(Rom 7:24).[141]

St Paul of course does not use the phrase from Genesis
about the "garments of skin," but the teaching of the Fathers
on the content of this expression is merely a development of
Paul's teaching on the postlapsarian state of man. The "garments of skin," the irrational, impassioned, dead "life," are
truly the "will of the flesh" (cf. Rom 8:5-8), the life "according to the flesh" which leads to death (Rom 8:12-13), "the
law of sin and death" from which "the law of the spirit of life
in Christ Jesus" liberates us (Rom 8:2).[142]

The law of the Spirit came with Christ; the law of sin
originated in the fall and is put into practice, according to
St John of Damascus, "by the non-rational part of the soul."[143]
Between them stands the Jewish law, which St Paul, as is well
known, found himself obliged to discuss extensively.

St Paul distinguishes the Jewish law as much from the
law of sin as from the law of the Spirit. He calls the Jewish

---

[141]In his interpretation of this passage St John Chrysostom stresses that
the Apostle does not speak about the body in general but about "the body
of death, that is, the mortal body which has been mastered by death . . .
[concerning] the mortal body he hinted at that which he has often said,
namely that through having become subject to the passions it has also
come to be easily attacked by sin" (John Chrysostom, *On Romans* 13, 3,
PG 60, 512). On this subject generally, see the whole of *On Romans* 13,
PG 60, 507-524, esp. 512-3, 515-7.

[142]"Here he calls the 'will of the flesh,' " explains St John Chrysostom,
"thought which is earthly, gross and excited about worldly things and evil
deeds" (John Chrysostom, *On Romans* 13, 6, PG 60, 516). In this study I
have not attempted to use the scientific analytical method to demonstrate
the harmony which exists among the Fathers who use the term "garments of
skin" and those who speak only about its content—mortality, passion, irrationality, subjection to materiality, etc.—without using the term. In my
opinion such a method would not have furthered the aim of this study—
and of the book generally—which is to bring the patristic teaching to life
and transpose it to our own times rather than to analyze it historically and
linguistically. This is also true with regard to the specific point of the relationship of the Pauline expression "will of the flesh" to the term "garments
of skin." Apart from the clear formulation of St Gregory of Nyssa and
the less direct but equally clear interpretation of St John Chrysostom, I think
that anyone who reads with Orthodox criteria will not find any difficulty
in discerning the identity of doctrine under the different terms.

[143]John of Damascus, *On the Orthodox Faith* 4, 22, PG 94, 1200B.

law "spiritual" (Rom 7:14). "Here he refers to the law of
the Spirit as Spirit," explains St John Chrysostom. "For just
as he refers to the law of sin as sin, so he refers to the law of
the Spirit as Spirit. Furthermore, he also refers to the law of
Moses in the same way, saying, 'We know that the law is
spiritual.' What then is the difference? A great and infinite
one, for the latter is spiritual, the former the law of the Spirit
. . . the latter was merely given by the Spirit, the former sup-
plies the Spirit Himself in abundance to those who receive
Him."[144]

Going more deeply into the question, the Apostle asks,
"Why then the law?" and replies very concisely, "It was
added because of transgressions, till the offspring should come
to whom the promise had been made" (Gal 3:19). The
phrase "it was added" points to its later character; it was not
originally present. The expression "because of transgressions"
should not be difficult to understand if we regard as "transgressions" the many postlapsarian sins or even original sin
itself. At this point, however, a question arises which is much
more vital to our theme, namely, whether a relationship exists
between the law which was given—"added"—to the Jews and
the "law of sin" which was created as a state in man after the
fall.

It is not easy to reply. Some indication of the answer is
given in the passage which closes the long discussion of the
resurrection of the dead in the First Letter to the Corinthians
(15:35-58). Paul begins with the question, "But one will ask,
'How are the dead raised? With what kind of body do they
come?'" He explains in what follows that "it is sown a
physical body" and "is raised a spiritual body." He appeals
to creation and re-creation: "The first man Adam became a
living being; the last Adam became a life-giving Spirit." He
asserts that with the resurrection will be realized "the saying
that is written, 'Death is swallowed up in victory. O death,
where is thy sting? O hades, where is thy victory?'" And he
ends with the passage which interests us: "The sting of death
is sin, and the power of sin is the law." Here surely he is

---

[144]John Chrysostom, *On Romans* 13, 4, *PG* 60, 513; cf. *On 2 Corinthians*
6, 2, *PG* 61, 438.

speaking of the Jewish law. But how does the law which God gave come to constitute the power of sin? Perhaps the position of the passage, its connection with death and resurrection, with the first Adam from whom death came and with the second who abolishes the "sting" of death which is sin, can illuminate the sense of the passage. Perhaps the law constitutes the power of sin because in some way it has its roots in sin, because it is given to man when in a state of sin, and is related to this state precisely in order to be able to correct it.

When the law which is "added" after the fall as a "condescension"[145] is viewed in this way, it may be said to constitute another aspect, a positive aspect, of the law of sin, which is the sorry state to which man has been reduced and has a purely negative quality. "What then shall we say? That the law is sin? By no means! Yet if it had not been for the law, I should not have known sin" (Rom 7:7). The second, positive aspect of this reality, the law which was "added" by God, illuminates the first, the "law of sin," and shows it to be negative so that it can thus be corrected.[146] The law which was "added" by God could not have corrected the law of sin justly if it did not have an internal relationship with it, if it did not have its roots within it. Without such an internal relationship the law which God gave would have been unjust; it would have operated externally or of necessity, and God never acts unjustly.

Within this perspective we can understand St Paul's struggle, so well expressed in his letters to the Romans and the Galatians, to show the two aspects of this reality simultaneously. The law is "holy" (Rom 7:12), but it is also a "curse" (Gal 3:13). We have been freed from the law (cf Gal 4:5)[147]—but it should not be thought that by faith in Christ

---

[145] John Chrysostom, *On Romans* 13, 4, *PG* 60, 512. Cf. *On Virginity* 16, *PG* 48, 545; Gregory of Nazianzus, *Oration* 45, 12, *PG* 36, 640B.

[146] Of course this also brings about a reawakening of sin and its consequent punishment. These are aspects on which the Apostle dwells, but they are not studied here as they are not directly relevant to our theme. On the law, see P. Nellas, "I en Christo dikaiosis tou anthropou kata ton Apostolon Pavlon" in *Charistiria eis timin tou Mitropolitou Gerontos Chalkidonos Melitonos* (Thessaloniki 1977), 379-400.

[147] Cf. "Thou hast redeemed us from the curse of the law by Thy precious blood" (*Triodion,* Office of the Holy Passion).

we abolish the law: "By no means! On the contrary, we uphold the law" (Rom 3:31). The law exists "till the offspring should come to whom the promise had been made" (Gal 3:19), but the love which the promised Savior brings is not an abolition but a "fulfilling of the law" (Rom 13:10). "We know that the law is good," but "the law is not laid down for the just but for the lawless and disobedient, for the ungodly and sinners . . ." (1 Tim 1:8-9), that is to say, it is designed for those in whom the law of sin is operative. It is certain that the goal of the law is Christ, "for Christ is the end of the law" (Rom 10:4); therefore its character is purely preparatory: "So that the law was our custodian until Christ came" (Gal 3:24).[148]

It would be fair to say then that the law is given—"added" —so that each person individually and society as a whole can survive morally in the situation created by the fall.[149] Its content is useful and positive, since it balances the law of sin, and of course holy, since it leads to Christ. But finally the Jewish law will be transcended, together with the law of sin, in Christ, or more precisely, while the law of sin will be abolished, the other law will be "fulfilled," will be transformed by the love which is the new life in Christ.

Since love, as "the fulfilment of the law" (Rom 13:10), exceeds the limits of the law, it leads man to the place of freedom, where there is no boundary and no limit except for the limit implied by the concept of freedom itself. Freedom, moreover, which as complete personal harmony and concord with God, mankind and the world is the opposite to individual independence, has love as its precise content and actually functions as love. Freedom and love are human functions and states with an identical content. Love is freedom. For this reason freedom does not fight the law but regards it with love;[150] it broadens the law with love, clarifying its limits and transforming it. "Truth does not destroy types but makes

[148]See John Chrysostom, *On Galatians* 3, 5, PG 61, 655.

[149]It is like a doctor's prescription which prescribes for the patient not the full diet of a healthy person but that which allows him to survive and recover his health. See John Chrysostom *On Virginity* 16, PG 48, 545-6.

[150]John Chrysostom, *On Romans* 12, 6, PG 60, 503.

them clearer."[151] The moral content of freedom is defined by the bonds of love.

Consequently, the law as a "garment of skin" is good and precious and constitutes a gift given by God to man. But love exercised in freedom is superior to the law. "Love alone, properly speaking, represents true humanity in the image of the Creator . . . for it persuades the will to advance in accordance with nature, in no way rebelling against the inward principle of its nature."[152]

(c) *Marriage*

We have seen above that in his prelapsarian life in accordance with nature man's aim was to concentrate all sensible things within himself and offer them to God in order to unite creation with its Creator. This would have brought about a universal integration in God also of man himself in all his dimensions, including the dimension of sexual differentiation, since among the divisions which according to St Maximos had to be transcended, and which were transcended definitively in Christ, is included the division into male and female.

We have seen, moreover, how by reversing the natural movement of his psychosomatic functions man became enslaved to unnatural pleasure, and how the righteousness of nature in man's ceaseless quest for pleasure continually requites him with pain in a just manner. St Maximos speaks at length about the vicious circle created in this way in which the sinner is imprisoned. It is an irrational and deadly circle because the more intently one seeks pleasure the more bitterly will one taste pain, which finally reaches its climax in death. "Therefore through pleasure, which was introduced into nature in a manner contrary to reason, pain, which is in accordance with reason, entered in its turn."[153] Realizing that every pleasure is followed by pain, man "acquired an impulse

151Cyril of Alexandria, *On Romans*, PG 74, 780D; cf. 801B-804A.
152Maximos the Confessor, *Letter* 2, *To John the Cubicularius*, PG 91, 396C.
153Maximos the Confessor, *To Thalassios: On Various Questions* 61, PG 90, 628B.

towards pleasure as a whole and an aversion to pain as a whole. He fought with all his strength to attain the one and struggled with all his might to avoid the other, thinking that in this way he could keep the two apart from each other, and that he could possess only the pleasure that is linked to self-love and be entirely without experience of pain, which was impossible. For he did not realize . . . that pleasure can never be received without pain; the distress caused by pain is contained within pleasure."[154]

This new reality created by sin, that is, the sinful union of pleasure with pain, was used by God compassionately after the fall to grant the human race biological survival—just as with the law He granted it morality. In one and the same act He limited both pleasure and pain decisively and neutralized them completely in Christ.

Before, however, we examine this compassionate intervention of God in more detail, we must first recall briefly the clear and unanimous teaching of the Fathers that before the fall there was no use of marriage, *as we understand it today,* for the purpose of reproduction.

St John Chrysostom writes: "When he was created, Adam remained in paradise, and there was no question of marriage. He needed a helper and a helper was provided for him. But even then marriage did not seem to be necessary. . . . Desire for sexual intercourse and conception and pangs and childbirth and every form of corruption were alien to their soul."[155]

This text is reminiscent, even verbally, of the one in which St Gregory of Nyssa, as we have seen, defines "sexual union," "conception," "birth" and the like, as aspects of the "garments of skin." The teaching of the two Fathers coincides, and explains why in speaking about marriage just now I stressed the phrase "as we understand it today." In my opinion, the main emphasis in these passages falls in fact on the sexual intercourse, conception, pangs, childbirth and remaining forms of corruption which were added to man as "garments of skin" after the fall. Precisely what the phrase "he shall cleave to

---

[154]Maximos the Confessor, *To Thalassios: On Various Questions,* PG 90, 256A; cf. 61, 629D-632A.

[155]John Chrysostom, *On Virginity* 14, PG 48, 543.

his wife and the two shall become one flesh" (Gen 2:24) implied before the fall, to what form and quality of union or marriage it led, we do not know, since we do not know precisely what the human body was like before the fall.

The body existed, and male and female existed separately, each with his or her special psychosomatic make-up. There is, however, no doubt that St John Chrysostom—to stay with the same Father—asserts in many of his texts that the first human beings "were not subject to bodily needs";[156] although they had bodies they had need of "nothing bodily."[157] "Thus they lived in paradise like angels, neither set on fire by desire nor besieged by other passions."[158] For the same reason we do not know how the prelapsarian "increase and multiply" (Gen 1:28) was realized. St Maximos speaks in a general manner about the "spiritual increase" of the human race.[159]

The holy Fathers confine themselves to stating that the "forms of corruption"—pleasurable attraction, sexual union and biological birth—did not exist before the fall. Since, however, their intention is not to provide an answer to a purely speculative question, they refuse to give positive support to any specific view about the prelapsarian state. We have here an application of the apophatic method to anthropology. The aim of the Fathers is through constant negations to create a dynamic state which will not permit man to stop at any point short of God, but will push him ceaselessly towards his final end.

Within this perspective some light is shed, I believe, on two difficult points concerning the creation of man which have been discussed at length by modern theologians. I refer to the view which St Gregory of Nyssa expresses relating (a) to the so-called "primeval man," that is, to the "first creation" of man in which there was no division into sexes, and (b) to the so-called "second creation," in which, as St Gregory expresses it,[160] the division into sexes was already "devised" (*epetechnithi*) by God before the fall, with a view to making

156John Chrysostom, *On Genesis* 18, 4, *PG* 53, 153; cf. 16, 1, *PG* 53, 126.
157John Chrysostom, *On Genesis* 16, 4, *PG* 53, 130.
158John Chrysostom, *On Genesis* 15, 4, *PG* 53, 123.
159Maximos the Confessor, *Ambigua*, *PG* 91, 1341C.
160Gregory of Nyssa, *On the Creation of Man* 16, *PG* 44, 185A.

possible the multiplication of the human race after the fall, which God had foreseen, whereas without the fall the human race would have multiplied "in the same way as the angels increased in number."[161]

It would be useful to broaden the discussion by taking into consideration the opinions of other Fathers too, such as the view of Methodios of Olympus, who argues that it is not possible for the body to constitute the "garments of skin" because the expression "male and female" (Gen 1:27) and the verse "he shall cleave to his wife and the two shall become one flesh" (Gen 2:24) refer to the situation before the fall,[162] and also the view of St John Chrysostom that after the fall God "refashioned" the human body, which was "originally superior to what it is now," so that it would be useful to us in our new situation.[163] It is characteristic that Chrysostom does not speak of a second creation either before or after the fall but of a "refashioning," and that in his description of the workings of the eye in the same homily he writes that tears are a postlapsarian function,[164] something of course with parallels in respect of other organs too. I alluded above to the physical aspects of this refashioning when discussing the teaching of St Maximos the Confessor. One could perhaps argue that in the perspective of St. Maximos the whole functioning of the psychosomatic human organism was real before the fall but spiritual, and in particular devoid of the pleasure which disorientates, cripples and finally reverses—and in this sense refashions—the psychosomatic functioning of man.[165]

---

[161]Gregory of Nyssa, *On the Creation of Man* 17, *PG* 44, 189CD. On these themes, see I. Moutsoulas, *I sarkosis tou Logou kai i theosis tou anthropou*, 63-96; E. Corsini, "Plérôme humain et plérôme cosmique chez Grégoire de Nysse"; P. Christou, "To anthropinon pliroma kata tin didaskalian tou Grigoriou Nyssis"; L. Thunberg, *Microcosm and Mediator*, 155-63 (for the history of the "double creation"); F. Floeri, "Le sens de la 'division des sexes' chez Grégoire de Nysse."

[162]Methodios of Olympus, *On the Resurrection of the Dead* i, 38, *GCS* 27, 280.

[163]John Chrysostom, *On the Statues* 11, 4, *PG* 49, 125.

[164]John Chrysostom, *On the Statues* 11, 3, *PG* 49, 122.

[165]It would be useful, moreover, if the patristic interpretations of Gal. 3:28 were to be taken into consideration, that is, of the division of the human race into male and female and its transcendence in Christ. See p. 81, note 187.

All the above opinions, however,—and this point seems to me the most basic of all and properly determinative for the understanding of patristic thought—do not constitute cataphatic positions for the Fathers, but rather hints which in the last analysis are denials of any clear and final position whatsoever. This is because any positive position in this field would be in danger of interpreting man, who is by nature a theological being, simply in terms of biological categories. In the Fathers, however, man is always understood iconically, a fact which signifies that for the views mentioned above to be understood rightly they should be situated in the context of what I have called anthropological apophaticism. The sure general framework which was believed everywhere at all times and by everyone, and within which the Fathers always conducted their investigations, is summed up in epigrammatic form by St John of Damascus: "But since God, who knows all things before they come into being, knew in His foreknowledge that humans would transgress and be condemned to death, He made them male and female in anticipation and ordered them to increase and multiply."[166]

The above suffice, I think, to shed light on the diffcult passages of St Gregory of Nyssa to which I have referred.[167] Moreover, St Gregory takes up the same apophatic position with regard to the last item in the sequence creation—fall—salvation in the Church—last things, since, as is well known, he touches on the theme of apocatastasis, though without pronouncing a final verdict.[168] While giving full explanations of the intermediate stages, he offers only apophatic hints,

---

[166]John of Damascus, *On the Orthodox Faith* 4, 24, PG 94, 1208D.

[167]E. Corsini, "Plérôme humain et plérôme cosmique chez Grégoire de Nysse," describes St Gregory's view of the "primeval man" and the "second creation" as "enigmatic" and observes that its understanding and its harmonious integration with the other aspects of St Gregory's teaching constitutes a problem for all who have hitherto studied his philosophy, theology and mystical teaching. This observation is correct. The cause of the problem, in my opinion, may be traced to the fact that the view which we are discussing constitutes the reply not to a speculative difficulty but to a mystical one, that is to say, it is by its nature an apophatic intuition with a soteriological content, which in the last analysis aims at escaping the danger of imprisonment in any given cataphatic and therefore partial position.

[168]See J. Daniélou, "L'apocatastase chez saint Grégoire de Nysse"; A.J. Phillips, *The Eschatology of St Gregory of Nyssa.*

which are nonetheless very helpful to the spiritual life, about the two ends of the sequence. That which joins the beginning to the end, as we saw in the first part of this study, is Christ, who constitutes the Image of the Father and the final realization of man as image.[169]

To return to St John Chrysostom, his comments on the role of marriage deserve to be quoted at length: "Since they disobeyed God and became earth and dust, after losing that blessed way of life they lost the beauty of virginity too. . . . For when they had become prisoners, they put off this royal dress, and rejected the heavenly world, and accepted the corruption and the curse and the pain and the life of toil that come from death. Then marriage entered in with these things. . . . Do you see from where marriage took its origin, the reason why it seemed necessary? . . . For where there is death, there too is marriage; if there had not been the one, the other would not have followed. . . . Tell me, what kind of marriage gave birth to Adam? What kind of pains produced Eve? . . . Ten thousand times ten thousand angels serve God . . . and none of them came into being by arising from one that came before, nor by births and pains and conception. Therefore He would much rather have made men without marriage. . . . And now it is not the power of marriage that keeps our race in being but the word of the Lord, who said at the beginning, 'Increase and multiply and fill the earth' (Gen 1:28)." To the question, how would the human race have multiplied except by creative acts like those of Adam and Eve, he replies characteristically, "Whether in this way or in another I am unable to say; what should be observed now is that marriage was not necessary to God in order to multiply men on earth."[170] And interpreting the verse in Genesis, "And Adam knew Eve his wife" (Gen 4:1), he writes, "Observe when this took place—after the act of disobedience, after the fall from paradise; that is when

---

[169]For this reason, among all the attempts which have been made until now to interpret the "primeval man" and the "second creation" in St Gregory of Nyssa, the most successful, in my opinion, is that of J. Daniélou, who gives a Christological interpretation to this point of St Gregory's teaching, even though he does not insist on it as much as he should. See *Platonisme et théologie mystique*, 52-3, 56 ff, 167 ff.

[170]John Chrysostom, *On Virginity* 14-17, PG 48, 544-6.

he began to cohabit with Eve. For before the act of disobedience they imitated the angelic life and there was no question
of sexual union."[171]

We have quoted at length from St John Chrysostom, one
of the most philanthropic and socially-minded of saints, so as
to make clear the positive character of the patristic attitude
to marriage.[172] For the teaching that marriage as we understand
it today is a postlapsarian phenomenon, that it constitutes an
element of the two-fold reality of the "garments of skin,"
does not at all imply any contempt for it, not even the slightest
depreciation of it, since that which is from one point of view
truly the result of sin, is from another turned by God into a
blessing, into "a great mystery," which according to St Paul
manifests the union of Christ with the Church, a union which
the prelapsarian relationship between Adam and Eve also
prefigured. "This is a great mystery, and I take it to mean
Christ and the Church" (Eph 5:32).

This Pauline affirmation, which is expressed in an enor-
mous variety of ways in patristic literature,[173] forms the basis
of the marriage service.[174] In the celebration of this joyful
sacrament the Church lavishly administers all her blessings
and prays for all the graces of this world and of the world
to come upon the newly married couple: "Bless them, O Lord
our God, as Thou hast blessed Abraham and Sarah. . . . Give
them the fruit of the womb, fair offspring, harmony of souls
and bodies. Raise them up like the cedars of Lebanon, like

[171]John Chrysostom, *On Genesis* 18, 4, *PG* 53, 153; cf. ibid. 15, 4,
PG 53, 123-4.

[172]St John Chrysostom has been described felicitously as "the defender
of marriage and the apostle of virginity": J. Moulard, *Saint Jean Chrysostome,
le défenseur du marriage et l'apôtre de la virginité* (Paris 1923). The patristic
tradition on this point is well summarized by St John of Damascus, *On the
Orthodox Faith* 4, 24, *PG* 94, 1208B. See also D.S. Bailey, *The Man-Woman
Relation in Christian Thought* (London 1959), esp. 19-102; P. Evdokimov,
Sacrement de l'amour (Paris 1962); Ch. Vantsos, *O gamos kai i proetoimasia
avtou ex epopseos orthodoxou poimantikis* (Athens 1977), esp. 33-107.

[173]See e.g. John Chrysostom, *On Colossians* 12, 5, *PG* 62, 387; ibid. 12,
6-7, *PG* 62, 389-90; *On Ephesians* 20, *PG* 62, 135-50. Cf. Th. Zissis,
Anthropos kai kosmos, 144-5.

[174]"The eternal God, who unites what has been separated . . . who out of
the nations has from the beginning betrothed the Church to Himself . . ."
(*Euchologion*).

a spreading vine. Grant them ears of grain, that enjoying all
sufficiency they may have enough to spare for every work
that is good and pleasing to Thee, and that they may see their
children's children like new shoots of the olive round their
table. And having been pleasing in Thy sight may they shine
as lights in heaven, in Thee, our Lord."

Conversely, in the same unanimous and positive manner
in which they express the above teaching on marriage, the
holy Fathers describe as heretics those who condemn marriage
as a sin and excommunicate them, that is, cut them off from
the Church, regarding them as members which have freely
and deliberately placed themselves on the side of the devil.[175]
It was the devil who originally deceived man and alienated him
from God, as a consequence of which man was stripped of
the bright garment of virginity. Now the devil changes tactics
and with the heretical teaching that marriage is a sin seeks to
deprive him also of the sacred garment of marriage, with
which God in His compassion had subsequently dressed him.

It is not without relevance to dwell briefly on the fact that
the Fathers expressed themselves eloquently on the theme of
the man-woman relationship, not only on the dogmatic and
ontological level, but also on the practical pastoral level, thus
demonstrating that they were well aware of all the dimensions of the subject. Here as an example is an excerpt from a
text of St John Chrysostom in which the saint, with a deep
understanding of humanity and of the delicate nature of family
relationships, advises the husband how to conduct himself
and with what words to address his wife:

"Speak to her words of love. . . . 'Of all things I value
your love most and nothing is so painful to me or so displeas-
ing as to find myself in dispute with you at any time. Even if
I must lose everything and become poorer than Iros, even if
I find myself in the last extremities of danger, whatever
happens to me, everything is bearable and tolerable as long
as all is well between us. And my children are dearly beloved

---

[175]See the *Apostolic Canon* 51; cf. canons, 1, 4, 9, 10 and 14 of the
Council of Gangra. See G. Kapsanis, *I poimantiki diakonia kata tous ierous
kanonas* (Peiraeus 1976), 175-84; cf. Ch. Vantsos, *O gamos kai i proetoimasia
avtou*, 35-41.

to me, provided that you are affectionate towards us. . . .'
Perhaps sometimes she will say, 'How is it that up to now I
have not spent any of your property? I still dress myself with
my own money which my parents gave me.' Then tell her,
'What are you saying, my love? That you still dress yourself
with your own money? What complaint could be worse than
this? You no longer possess your own body, yet you possess
your own money? We are not two bodies after marriage but
have become one, and yet our properties are two rather than
one? . . . All things are yours . . . and I am yours, my little
one. This is what Paul advises men when he says, "the husband
does not rule over his own body but the wife does" (1 Cor
7:4). And if I have no authority over my body but you do,
how much more does this apply to my property . . .' Never
speak to her in a rough manner but with courtesy, with
respect, with much love. Respect her and she will not need
to seek respect from others; she will not need to seek praise
from others if she enjoys praise from you. In all things prefer
her to all others, for her beauty, for her modesty, and keep
praising her. In this way you will persuade her not to prefer
any stranger but to spurn all other men."[176]

After these various clarifications we can now return to
the vicious circles of pleasure and pain. By intervening precisely in this circle God in His compassion redirected pleasure
towards the goal of the reproduction of the human race, and
thus limited it and tamed it and even gave it the power to
transcend itself by transforming it from an end to a means.
There are indeed examples in which pleasure is transcended,
as in the case of the blessed couple Joachim and Anna, whose
child was not the fruit of pleasure but of prayer.

Moreover, pleasure, a product of self-love, is transcended
within marriage by being transformed into spiritual pleasure
and joy in those cases where self-love gives way to love. "You
have a wife," writes St John Chrysostom, "you have children;
what is equal to this pleasure? . . . Tell me, what is sweeter
than children? Or what is more delightful than a wife for a
man who desires to be chaste? . . . Nothing is sweeter than

[176]John Chrysostom, *On Ephesians* 20, 8-9, *PG* 62, 146-8.

children and a wife, if you wish to live with reverence."[177]
The Lord clothed pleasure in the positive dress of joy, and
it is not without significance that it was precisely at a marriage
that He performed His first miracle, changing water into wine
that human joy might not be curtailed.

In the same act of compassion God also moderated the
pain which is created by corruption and death, since the
bearing of children is "our greatest consolation in the face
of death."[178] For truly "death is an inconsolable evil," writes
Chrysostom.[179] "And for this reason," he adds, "God in His
compassion swiftly and at the outset . . . stripped off the fear-
ful mask of death and granted to men children to take their
place, giving a glimpse in this life of the image of the resurrection, as one might say, and making provision for others to
rise up in place of those who have fallen."[180]

So that both pleasure and pain could be destroyed in their
entirety by the birth of the Lord, this took place not only without pleasure and pangs of childbirth, but with a radical
renewal of the laws to which sin had subjected nature; for it
took place through a conception "without seed" and a birth
"without corruption,"[181] without the destruction of His
mother's virginity.[182]

Since the Lord had a generation, an entry into life, which
was radically different from the familiar biological generation
which we call birth, He was of course free from all postlapsarian biological laws and certainly also from death. When
He accepted them voluntarily, together with His actual birth—
which was nevertheless free and outside the postlapsarian law
of generation,[183] that is, outside "the conception through seed
and the birth through corruption which nature embraced after

[177]John Chrysostom, *On Matthew* 38, 6, *PG* 57, 428.
[178]John Chrysostom, *On Matthew* 48, 3, *PG* 58, 490; cf. Gregory of
Nyssa, *On Virginity* 12, *PG* 46, 376A.
[179]John Chrysostom, *On Matthew* 48, 3, *PG* 58, 490.
[180]John Chrysostom, *On Genesis* 18, 4, *PG* 53, 154; see the analysis of
this thesis, ibid. 17, 7, *PG* 53, 143-4.
[181]Maximos the Confessor, *Ambigua, PG* 91, 1341C-1349A.
[182]Maximos the Confessor, *Ambigua, PG* 91, 1276A.
[183]See the description and deep analysis of this law in Maximos the
Confessor, *To Thalassios: On Various Questions* 21, *PG* 90, 312C-313A. Cf.
ibid. 61, 633B; *Ambigua, PG* 91, 1276ABC, 1316A-1417C, 1345D-1348A.

the transgression"[184]—He did this in order to destroy them. "The generation from Adam in pleasure," whereby the human race increases and multiplies, so St Maximos explains, ruled tyranically over nature, providing it with the "food of death" which it deserved. But "the birth of the Lord in the flesh, which was the result of His compassion for men, brought about the destruction of both, namely, of the pleasure that derives from Adam and of the death that has come through Adam, wiping out the penalty imposed on Adam together with the sin committed by him."[185] In this way the vicious circle of pleasure and pain was broken and human nature was liberated.

More generally, with this new method of His generation the Lord not only brought human nature back to its pre-lapsarian state, but also rendered it complete. Adam's goal was to "shake off" the division into male and female "from the whole of nature through a relationship with divine virtue utterly free from passion."[186] This was brought to pass by the Lord: He realized and manifested the true essence (*logos*) of human nature, free from the characteristics of male and female, at its deepest and most unified level, which is common to both sexes.[187]

Moreover, by becoming truly man the Lord endowed human nature with a fresh start, with "the beginning of a second form of generation,"[188] that is, with spiritual birth

[184]Maximos the Confessor, *Ambigua*, PG 91, 1341C; cf. *To Thalassios: On Various Questions* 61, PG 90, 632B.

[185]Maximos the Confessor, *To Thalassios: On Various Questions* 61, PG 90, 632D; cf. ibid. 61, PG 90, 644B, and ibid. 21, PG 90, 313BC.

[186]Maximos the Confessor, *Ambigua*, PG 91, 1305CD.

[187]Maximos the Confessor, *To Thalassios: On Various Questions* 48, PG 90, 436A. Cf. *Ambigua*, PG 91, 1309AB; *On the Lord's Prayer*, PG 90, 889C-892A—an important passage. On this last, see I.H. Dalmais, "Une traité de théologie contemplative: Le commentaire du Pater Noster de saint Maxime le Confesseur," *Revue d'Ascétique et de Mystique* 29 (1953), 132-9 and 159, where a bibliography is given. Cf. Gregory of Nazianzus, *Oration* 7, 23, PG 35, 785C; Evagrios, *Gnostic Chapters* 1, 63, PG 40, 1237B; Clement of Alexandria, *Stromateis* 3, 13, *VEPES* 8, 44, and 6, 12, *VEPES* 8, 215-6. See also F. Quatemberg, *Die christliche Lebenshaltung des Klemens von Alexandrien nach seinen Paedagogus* (Vienna 1946), 137-40; D.S. Bailey, *The Man-Woman Relation in Christian Thought*, 33 ff.

[188]Maximos the Confessor, *To Thalassios: On Various Questions* 61, PG 90, 632A.

through baptism,[189] which is not only a deliverance from the consequences of original sin but is also for each believer a realization of the work which Adam failed to achieve. Our first ancestor was made in the image of God, explains St Maximos, in order that through the Spirit he might be born in God by his own free will, that "the same man" might thus be "on the one hand a creature of God by nature, and on the other a son of God and a god through the Spirit by grace."[190] It was not, however, possible for this to be brought about except by his being born through the Spirit, himself cooperating freely with the "self-moving and autonomous power" which in a natural manner existed within him.

But the first man exchanged this "deifying and divine and incorporeal birth"[191] for a "bodily birth which is involuntary, material . . . impassioned, servile and subject to necessity." This bodily birth, "in which existed the power of our condemnation," was accepted by Him who alone is free and sinless, "because He is good and compassionate"—with the sole exception, as we have seen, of "seed" and "corruption"[192] —and thus, loosing the bonds within Himself for our sake, "He gave us who believe in His name authority through the birth which is spiritual and freely chosen to become children of God instead of children of flesh and blood."[193]

Only a few of the positions argued by St Maximos have been presented above. In his texts he advances to much deeper analyses and expresses much higher truths, relating not only to the human state before the fall which we have discussed, but also to the biological reality of man's life after the fall and to the new human nature recreated in Christ in which, as the Apostle declares and as St Maximos expounds at length, "there is neither male nor female" (Gal 3:28). But

[189]Maximos the Confessor, *To Thalassios: On Various Questions* 61, PG 90, 632D.

[190]Maximos the Confessor, *Ambigua*, PG 1345D-1348C. This passage is translated in its entirety below, pp. 218-21.

[191]". . . through his preferring what is pleasant and manifest to the senses to the blessings hitherto intellectual and invisible," St Maximos adds (*Ambigua*, PG 91, 1345D).

[192]My own parenthesis.

[193]Maximos the Confessor, *Ambigua*, PG 91, 1345D-1348C.

these truths are beyond my powers, and therefore I confine myself here simply to indicating where the reader may find them.[194]

At any rate it is clear from what I have said that the holy Fathers, within the very broad natural dimensions wherein they set man as a theological being by virtue of his god-like beginning and his theocentric end, do not hesitate to proclaim unambiguously what is the greatest stumbling-block to the rational viewpoint of biological man; they repudiate the most fundamental sign of self-determination which he possesses, his biological birth. The disintegration and dissolution—the "putting off"[195]—of the "garments of skin," or more precisely of one aspect of them, the one which was created by sin, is in fact the first indispensable step which a person must take in order to be led to a life which will not be subject to decay, but will bear within it even now the signs of resurrection.[196]

In particular, biological birth in this perspective is not condemned but becomes intelligible and thus acceptable in the way God intends it to be, that is, as the great gift of generation, entry into existence. On the basis of this gift, and with the proper use of it, man can once again be led to the true spiritual birth, can clothe his biological being in the blessed and eternal being which is found in Christ,[197] so that

[194]See PG 90, 253C-256B, 312B-313D, 628A-645C; PG 91, 1195D-1196B, 1273D-1276D, 1304D-1305A, 1308D-1309A, 1313CD, 1316A-1321D, 1340B-1341C, 1345C-1349A. The most systematic aid to the understanding of St Maximos's texts is still L. Thunberg's *Microcosm and Mediator.* For the passages indicated here, see pp. 396-405. It is important, however, that one should not rely wholly on Thunberg's insights but study the texts themselves. The best theological introduction to the thought of St Maximos and the most faithful presentation of his teaching is to be found in D. Staniloae's extensive introduction and notes in the following publications: Maximos the Confessor, *Mystagogia* (Epi tas pigas 1, Athens 1973), and Maximos the Confessor, *Philosophika kai theologika erotimata* [*Ambigua*] (Epi tas pigas 4, Athens 1978).

[195]The relation to biblical teaching is clear: "seeing that you have put off the old nature" (Col 3:9).

[196]"...and have put on the new nature, which is being renewed in knowledge after the image of its Creator. Here there cannot be Greek and Jew, circumcised and uncircumcised, barbarian, Scythian, slave, free man, but Christ is all, and in all" (Col 3:10-11).

[197]"For as many of you as were baptized into Christ have put on Christ" (Gal 3:27).

every person may become of his own free will that which
Adam refused to become, "on the one hand a creature of
God by nature, and on the other a son of God and a god
through the Spirit by grace." Thus sin can be transcended in
an ocean of divine love, thereby proving that in reality the
great tragedy of the fall is only a small incident in time.

The difficulty which the teaching of the Fathers on biological birth creates in our minds, imprisoned as they are in
postlapsarian habits of thought, is greater than that caused
by the doctrine of the resurrection of the body. It is easier
to accept the resurrection, because we can transfer it to the
future rather than attempt to realize it here and now, putting
to death within ourselves the negative aspects of our biological existence—putting to death the earthly members, as St
Paul says (cf. Col 3:5-8)—and raising up the positive aspects,
that is, transforming them through the Spirit in Christ. But
without such an attempt we cannot be liberated.

That is why the holy Fathers, who knew the power of the
resurrection and had experienced the freedom of the children
of God, out of their love for men do not hesitate to insist
on this teaching about the possibility of the resurrection here
and now, however hard such teaching might appear to be at
first sight. They do so to show man his real nature and his true
majesty in God, while at the same time indicating the paths
which lead to it. For this teaching also manifests the fundamental *ontological* significance which baptism and the whole
of the sacramental, ascetic and spiritual life of the Church
has for humankind. All these things do not constitute elements which are added to the nature of man, which one may
or may not have according to preference; they form and maintain the essence of man's natural being.

Since this is their character, they are able to effect a transformation, as we shall see in greater detail in the second part
of this book, in man's biological being, in his biological birth,
in all the dimensions and functions of his biological life, with
that of marriage as the first and best.[198] In the sacrament of

_____

[198]In reading this section the reader might be tempted to ask, "Is
marriage then abolished?" The reply is clear: by no means. Far from
abolishing marriage, I am setting it on its true foundations. Indeed, the

marriage the love which makes two people decide to live together is crowned with the love which unites the three persons of the holy Trinity,[199] and thus the family which is created is not simply a biological reality, a social institution, a psychological or at least erotic existential union, but infinitely more, a cell of the Church, that is, a truly and genuinely living and holy member of the sacred Body of Christ.

(d) Functions of Life

The disruption which sin created in man brought with it the disruption of the cosmos. In creating man in the image of the King of the ages, God made him, according to Nikitas Stithatos, "king of creation" and enabled him "to possess within himself the inward essences, the natures and the knowledge of all beings."[200] It was therefore unavoidable that the disruption of man should have brought about the disruption of the "essences" and the "natures" of beings, that is, the disruption also of creation.

This comprehensive change which was effected within creation, in the anthropological aspect which interests us here, is described by St Gregory Palamas with the very expressive phrase, "we have changed our abode": "For through this sin we have put on the garments of skin . . . and changed our abode to this transient and perishable world, and we have condemned ourselves to live a life full of passions and many misfortunes."[201]

In this passage there is a clear hint of the cosmological

institution of marriage is passing through a grave crisis in our time precisely because these foundations are being neglected. On the solution within this perspective of the delicate moral problems connected with marriage, such as the conception of children and the purpose of sexual relations, see the following passages of St John Chrysostom: *On the words "Because of the Temptation to Immorality"* 3, PG 51, 213; *On Virginity* 19, 1, PG 48, 547; *On Romans* 13, 1, PG 60, 508.

[199]Cf. the words of the Orthodox marriage service: "The servant [handmaid] of God . . . is crowned in the name of the Father and of the Son and of the Holy Spirit."

[200]Nikitas Stithatos, *Century* 3, 10, PG 120, 957D-980A.

[201]Gregory Palamas, *Homily* 31, PG 151, 388C.

dimension of the "garments of skin." The world before the
fall was, as we have seen, relatively unified within man.
Through man the movement of matter naturally followed its
course towards the End. And through man this movement too
was to a certain extent spiritual. But the transgression of Adam
also made the movement of matter to run off course. Since the
relationship of matter with the human body, and therefore
with the soul and with God, has been overturned, matter has
become enclosed within itself; its movement has become blind
and futile. Materiality is that state in which matter is characterized exclusively by its own elements, in which it is deprived of its development or movement towards spirit. Within
the fall there thus exists a fall also of matter itself. So the
imprisonment of man in materiality transformed a world that
was "very good" into one that was "perishable," and man who
has dressed himself in materiality—because of this materiality,
that is, because of the "garments of skin"—lives "a life
full of passions and many misfortunes." The phrase "we
have changed our abode" consequently does not mean a
change of place—since in any case even before the fall man
was not outside the world—but a change of relationships, a
concept which we today, who recognize that "position" is
always the product of a network of relationships, can understand very well.

In other Fathers this aspect of the "garments of skin" is
expressed with greater clarity. St John Chrysostom teaches
that before the fall man had no need either for "cities," or for
"arts and skills," or for "the covering of clothing." "These
were then superfluous," he continues, "but afterwards they
became necessary because of our infirmity; and not only these
things but everything else . . . the whole throng of remaining
necessities. And death entered with all these, dragging all of
them in along with itself."[202] The "garments of skin" are the
clothing in which man confronts death. We can understand
them as the new organization of human life, the new methods
—like another suit of clothing, we could say—which are appro-

[202]John Chrysostom, *On Virginity* 15, *PG* 48, 545. *When the King had
Come* 1, *PG* 63, 474B; *On 1 Corinthians* 17, 3, *PG* 61, 143; *On Virginity*
14, *PG* 48, 544; *On Genesis* 16, 1-5, *PG* 53, 126-31.

priate and indispensable for us if we are to grapple with all
the other circumstances which have affected our planet after
the fall. There are, however, other texts in which St John
Chrysostom speaks about a certain work which Adam did and
certain skills which he practised in paradise even before the
fall.[203]

In order to describe man's imprisonment in the futile and
corrupt cycle of materiality, St Gregory of Nyssa uses the
image of "animals turning the mill." "With our eyes blind-
folded we walk round the mill of life, always treading the
same circular path and returning to the same things. Let me
spell out this circular path: appetite, satiety, sleep, waking up,
emptiness, fullness. From the former of each pair we constantly pass to the latter, and back again to the former, and
then back again to the latter, and we never cease to go round
in a circle." And, passing from the biological to the existential
level of perception: "Solomon well describes this life as a
leaking pitcher and an alien house (cf. Eccles 12:6). . . . Do
you see how men draw up for themselves honors, power,
fame and all such things? But what is put in flows out again
below and does not remain in the container. We are always
consumed with anxious concern for fame and power and
honor, but the pitcher of desire remains unfilled."[204]

With his characteristic density of expression St Gregory
the Theologian writes that before the fall man enjoyed "a
life without artifice, without any kind of cover or shelter, for
such was it fitting that he should be from the beginning."[205]
In his analysis of the above passage of St Gregory, the
philosopher St Maximos the Confessor illuminates our theme
with even greater clarity. Our first ancestor lived without
artifice, without arts and skills, he writes, because "the natural
well-being with which he was endowed in his essential nature"
was not dissipated, and thus he was not troubled by those

[203]See e.g. *On the Statues* 19, 1, *PG* 49, 188; *On 2 Corinthians* 15, 3,
PG 61, 506. To my knowledge the best study of this apparent contradiction
is J. Lappas, *I peri ergasias didaskalia Ioannou tou Chrysostomou* (Thessalonike 1980), ch. 3. See also my own attempt to resolve the paradox
below, p. 90.
[204]Gregory of Nyssa, *Funeral Oration on Placilla*, *PG* 46, 888D-889A.
[205]Gregory of Nazianzus, *Oration* 45, 8, *PG* 36, 632C.

needs which today have to be met through human arts and skills. "And he was without need of covering" because of the dispassion he possessed which kept him from feeling shame, and also because he was not then subject to extremes of cold or hot weather, to combat which men invented houses and clothing. Besides, Maximos continues, human life revolves today either around the deceptive impressions which the irrational passions create of the external world for the sake of sensual pleasure, or around the arts and skills in order to satisfy the necessities of life, or around the natural principles of created things for the sake of learning. None of these things, however, influenced man before the fall, because he was above them all. Our first ancestor, being "dispassionate by grace," had no contact with the delusory fantasies created by the passions for the sake of sensual pleasure. Being "self-sufficient," he was free from the obligation to use arts and skills in order to satisfy his needs. And being "wise," he was superior to the study of created things, whose investigation demands scholarship and learning. Between man and God nothing interposed itself which man needed to investigate, which impeded his free movement in love towards God and his advance towards the kinship with God which this movement created. That is why, insists St Maximos, man was called by St Gregory "naked by virtue of simplicity," because he was above every natural need. He lived a life without arts and skills, "lacking every artifice because his life was pure." He had no covering and no protection against anything, because he was free from the impassioned interweaving of the senses with sensible things. He was justly made subject to these things "later on, when he had suffered loss, and had passed of his own free will from the fullness of being to total emptiness, and had become inferior to those things to which he had naturally been made superior."[206]

In this text the familiar central functions of life, that is to say, those which relate to the search for satisfactions, learning and professional effectiveness, are plainly defined as postlapsarian phenomena, that is, as the content of the "garments of skin." The functions mentioned and those that flow

[206]Maximos the Confessor, *Ambigua*, PG 91, 1352B-1356A.

from them are a result of the disruption which original sin has brought to the order and harmony of creation.

Learning and work, in particular, constitute a coarsening, so to speak, of the original natural properties of wisdom and lordship over nature which man possessed as an image of God. They constitute an expression and function of these properties in material dress. Their aim when properly used was to lead man, and with him the world, towards God. But with sin they became imprisoned in the corrupt biological cycle, and they were coarsened and transformed into "garments of skin."

The same is true, to mention one more example, with regard to the deep and natural communion between persons which existed before the fall. (We have seen that a fundamental dimension of man's being "in the image" is that he constitutes at the same time both person and nature.) With the decline of man into individuality this communion was corrupted and shattered, and consequently in order to survive socially human beings needed some external organization, that is to say, they needed the city and, by extension, political life.[207]

The laborious cultivation of the soil, then, the professions, the sciences, the arts, politics, all the operations and functions by which man lives in this world, make up the content of the "garments of skin" and bear the two-fold character which we have discussed above. On the one hand they are a consequence of sin and constitute a misuse of various aspects of our creation "in the image."[208] On the other they are a result of the wise and compassionate intervention of God and constitute the new clothing thanks to which human beings are able to live under the new conditions created by the fall.

God did not in fact permit the characteristics belonging to man's creation "in the image" to be destroyed or to perish in their entirety.[209] Intervening in the process of decay, He changed these characteristics into "garments of skin" and

207The division of the humanity into separate races and nations is a similar phenomenon. See Gregory of Nazianzus, *Oration* 7, 23, *PG* 35, 785C. Cf. Evagrios, *Gnostic Chapters* 1, 63, *PG* 40, 1237.

208Gregory of Nyssa, *On the Beatitudes* 3, *PG* 44, 1228AB.

209Epiphanios of Salamis, *Panarion* 70, *PG* 42, 344B. Cf. Gregory of Nyssa, *On the Beatitudes*, *PG* 44, 1272A; *On Virginity* 12, *PG* 46, 373C.

thus made them into the very things which enable man to
survive. St John Chrysostom, who with great emphasis ascribes
to God the difference after the fall in man's state and conditions of life, teaches that God did not deprive man of all the
authority which he had over the world but only "subtracted
a little" from it.[210] He left him authority over those animals
which were indispensable for his sustenance, and also a certain authority over the rest, and over the earth generally,
through the skills which he has developed thanks to the reason
which God gave him originally and did not withdraw totally
after the fall. Through these skills, which have been developed
progressively in the passage of time since the fall, "the constitution of the world is providentially ordered."[211]

It seems to me that within this perspective the apparent
contradiction which may be observed in Chrysostom in relation
to the development of the arts[212] finds its solution. The "garments of skin" are not unrelated to the iconic faculties of man
before the fall. They constitute a functioning of these prelapsarian faculties as they are now, rendered coarse and
dressed in materiality. In paradise man had a task to accomplish—we have seen an analytical description of it in St
Maximos—and the accomplishment of this task involved a
kind of art or skill, one of course which was of a different
quality and was practised on another level and for another
purpose. It is significant that Chrysostom speaks of this task
and this art which existed before the fall mainly in reference
to monks,[213] whose aim, as is well known, is to retrace the
path of Adam in reverse, to cleanse the "garments of skin"
and to raise the functions of their existence to the level of
the natural iconic functions which existed before the fall.

Yet this is not all. God's intervention is more positive
and goes so far as to enable the attributes of that which is "in
the image"—the attributes which were transformed into the

[210]John Chrysostom, On the Eighth Psalm 7, PG 55, 118; cf. On the
Statues 11, 4-5, PG 49, 124-6.
[211]John Chrysostom, On Genesis 29, 3, PG 53, 264-5; cf. 20, 2, PG
53, 168.
[212]See above p. 86, note 202.
[213]John Chrysostom, On the Statues 19, 1, PG 49, 188; On Matthew 68,
3, PG 58, 643.

"garments of skin" without being changed in essence—to be useful to man not only in his struggle for mere survival but also as a means of making the new journey towards God. The desire for satisfactions and the search for them, by failing to find fulfilment in the world, lead the intelligent person once again to the search for the permanent good. "More than anything else," writes St Gregory the Theologian, "this too has been admirably devised by the Logos and Wisdom, the supreme artificer who surpasses every intellect: that we should be teased by visible things, which change in a variety of ways and effect changes, which go up and down and twist and slide and escape. . . . In this way we perceive their instability and disorder and advance towards that which belongs to the age to come."[214] The same sinful search for sensual pleasure— which is the negative expression of the original God-given "potentiality for pleasure, namely, the natural desire of the intellect for God"[215]—continues to swamp the original positive element, and it depends on man to turn its movement again towards the real good, to make not a negative but a positive use of it.

This applies even more strongly to learning, work, science, the arts and politics. These functions can and should be used as the new means by which man will exercise his dominion over the world, and, living by the grace of God, will channel this grace into the world. In this way he will transform the conditions of life, and grafting himself, the conditions of life and the world onto Christ he will not only correct the disruptions which sin has created on all levels, but will bring about in practice within the historical process that union of the prelapsarian divisions which Christ realized within Himself for the sake of the whole world. This is the great task, beyond the simple ensuring of survival, which human knowledge, work, art, politics and all the other postlapsarian functions of life are called to serve.

---

[214]Gregory of Nazianzus, *Oration* 14, 20, *PG* 35, 884AB. Cf. Gregory of Nyssa, *To Those Who Mourn*, *PG* 46, 524BCD, and the excellent analysis of this text in J. Daniélou, "Les tuniques de peau," 359-62.

[215]Maximos the Confessor, *To Thalassios: On Various Questions* 61, *PG* 90, 628A.

III

Consequences of the Theology of the Image and of the "Garments of Skin" for the Relationship Between the Church and the World

1. THE CHURCH JUDGES THE WORLD

The patristic teaching on the image and the "garments of skin" which we have been examining up to now offers, I believe, not only an Orthodox understanding of man but also a foundation upon which Orthodox theology can be based in order to give effective help to the modern world. The position of Orthodox theology *vis-à-vis* the world, as defined by this teaching, is at the same time both radically critical and radically positive.

Orthodox theology is called in the first place to judge autonomy on all its levels and in all its forms and to condemn it relentlessly. In our study of the anthropological dimension of sin we have seen how autonomy is the source and the content of sin, since it constitutes a counterfeit of the truth about man, his mutilation and his restriction to the biological level of existence. This crime becomes even greater when man, dressed in the "garments of skin," as a consequence treats even these as autonomous. Under such conditions the "garments of skin" appear in their negative aspect alone; they function as the will of the flesh and, according to Paul, lead inescapably to death. This means for us today that the making autonomous of the law, of sexuality, of technology, of politics and so on, is in danger of leading humanity to ultimate self-destruction on the moral, political and even biological levels. Christian theology has the duty to proclaim this truth most emphatically because we are in genuine reality living at the eleventh hour.

But in order to carry out this task contemporary Christian theology must recover its authentic evangelical and patristic voice. It is impossible for its message to be heard by any reasonable modern person at all when it presents sin as disobedience to a set of external rules, or even worse, as disobedience to an enshrined social or political establishment.

An even greater problem, however, is created by the basic distortion of the biblical and patristic teaching about man by Christian theology, initially in the West. This has had painful consequences. The opinion that Adam's original nature lay in his biological constitution, to which grace was added by God as a supernatural gift, has led serious inquirers into the authentic nature of man to reject God's existence altogether (in the context, of course, of more general circumstances and also under other influences).[216]

Similar consequences followed also from Augustine's axiom that "if man had not perished, the Son of Man would not have come."[217] This trapped Christ, and by extension the

[216]See J. Daniélou, *Platonisme et théologie mystique*, 50, 58-9.

[217]Augustine, *Enchiridion* viii, 27-ix, 29. See J. Rivière, *Le dogme de la Rédemption chez saint Augustin* (Paris 1933); T.J. van Bavel, *Recherches sur la Christologie de saint Augustin* (Fribourg [Suisse] 1954); P. Bergauer, *Des Jacobus-brief beim Augustinus und die damit verbundenen Probleme der Rechtfertigungslehre* (Vienna 1962). It is clear that Duns Scotus' thesis (see above, p. 37, note 53) lies at the opposite pole to this thesis of Augustine. I shall not enter here into the discussion of how far Scotus' thesis is the inevitable historical consequence of that of Augustine. In both, however, I believe that there is the same fundamental error of attributing to God an aim which derives from the world. This error leads either to the undervaluing of the world (the world as radically powerless finds itself one-sidely at the exclusive and absolute disposition of God) or to its overvaluing (the world is regarded as having the power to impose the incarnation on God). In the rest of this section I show very briefly the consequences of undervaluing the world. The inevitable result of overvaluing it, in my opinion, is an understanding of the incarnation and also of God Himself which is rooted within this world. For the fruits of this latter understanding, see e.g. G. Vahanian, *The Death of God. The Culture of Our Post-Christian Era* (New York 1961); P.M. van Buren, *The Secular Meaning of the Gospel* (New York 1963); J.A.T. Robinson, *Honest to God*

Christian life and the realities of the Church, the sacraments, faith and the rest, within the bounds defined by sin. Christ in this perspective is not so much the creator and recapitulator of all things, the Alpha and Omega as Scripture says, but simply the redeemer from sin. The Christian life is regarded not so much as the realization of Adam's original destiny, as a dynamic transformation of man and the world and as union with God, but as a simple escape from sin. The sacraments are not realizations here and now of the kingdom of God and manifestations of it, but mere religious duties and means of acquiring grace. The same is true with regard to good works and faith. The boundaries are thus narrowed in an asphyxiating manner. The Church forgets her ontological bond with the world. And the world, seeing that its positive aspects are not appreciated within the Church, feels a sense of alienation and breaks off relations with it.

The theology of the image and of the garments of skin overcomes these difficulties and others like them and can offer the world real help. By seeing man and the world as an image, it honors the image and the matter which makes up the image. When the matter desires to become autonomous, to neglect not the archetype but itself, this theology does not hesitate to proclaim that by such an action the matter destroys itself. The theology of the image condemns the action of seeking autonomy in a radical way, but it also continues to love the matter, wounded and corrupt as it is, because God accepted it and in His love gave it the new powers and functions of the "garments of skin." It honors the "garments of skin," marriage, science, politics, art and the rest, without however hesitating to testify to mankind that when these are made autonomous they bring about the final consolidation of sin and the destruction of man. With this simultaneous judgment and appreciation of the world Orthodox theology remains faithful to the biblical and patristic teaching on the two-fold nature of the "garments of skin."

This strand of our tradition has a special significance for the modern world. It shows from one point of view that for

(London 1963) ; T.J.J. Altizer, *The Gospel of Christian Atheism* (Philadelphia 1966) ; T.J.J. Altizer, *Toward a New Christianity* (New York 1967).

a man to place his hope exclusively in the "garments of skin," whatever the form they may take, is not only an empty labor or a utopian quest but a tragic mistake.[218] For if they are made autonomous the "garments of skin" work in a contrary direction. Indeed, it is not accidental but natural and unavoidable in this perverted order of things that revolutions undertaken sincerely for the sake of freedom should lead as soon as they succeed to enslavement, that an improved development in production should lead to inflation, that the maintenance of peace should demand an increase in armaments, that is, preparation for war. Enlightened sociologists have been led by the accurate study of these phenomena to suggest that the great problem mankind faces in our day is one of morality, great economists that it is one of self-restraint in consumption, distinguished philosophers that it is one of ontology. They are right, but all these theses are still insufficient. For Holy Scripture and the Orthodox Fathers the core of the problem is faith in God, that is, whether the goal of human endeavor is situated in God or not.

If man's goal is situated in creation, whether on a lower level (of material prosperity) or on a higher one (of the moral order), or worse, if man's being is understood in purely this-worldly terms, an unavoidable impasse is created since the movement or development towards the uncreated is interrupted, and man, who by nature is godlike, is mutilated by being confined to the categories of this world. In such a situation the powers which move both man and the world are disorientated, come into conflict with one another, and neutralize themselves. For this reason, that is, out of love for humanity, Orthodox theology feels an obligation to be radical and resolute in its condemnation of autonomy.

---

[218]St John Chrysostom was severe on those Christians who ignored spiritual works and placed all their hope on the activities of this world, putting their whole effort into them: *On John* 30, 3, *PG* 59, 175. I shall rely heavily on Chrysostom in the rest of this discussion to demonstrate the positive aspects of the garments of skin (technical skills, work, etc.). It is essential, however, that the reader should bear in mind Chrysostom's fundamental hierarchy of values.

2. THE CHURCH SAYS "YES"
TO THE WORLD

From another point of view, however, the same love makes Orthodox theology take up a positive attitude towards the world, again with the same resolute radicality. For the world is a creation of God and the "garments of skin" themselves, under their second positive aspect, are a blessing and a gift from God.

On this theme St John Chrysostom is characteristically clear and insistent. Speaking specifically on the subject of technical skills, as already mentioned, he teaches that these skills were developed on earth in a gradual manner after the fall.[219] He sees the power with which God endowed human nature as functioning and developing on the social and scientific levels in what we would today call a positive evolutionary process. "Consider for a moment, my friend, how the constitution of the world is providentially ordered. And each person became an inventor of some art originally by virtue of the wisdom of God hidden in nature, and thus introduced into human life the practice of technical skills. First one man discovered the cultivation of the land, another after him the art of shepherding flocks, another that of raising cattle, and another music, another the working of copper, and Noah invented viticulture through the teaching hidden in nature."[220]

In another of his homilies he regards man's natural ability to subjugate and use the powers of non-rational nature as a gift and blessing from God. The horse, he says, is faster than man. But however fast it is it cannot cover more than twenty-five miles a day. Man, however, by changing mounts can cover more than 250 miles. "Therefore," he concludes, "what speed is to the one, reason is to the other; and so technical skill has enabled man to achieve far more than any animal. . . . Of the non-rational animals not one," he continues, "is able to harness another to its own use, but man is

---

[219]More precisely I should say: the technical skills as we understand them today. See above, p. 86.

[220]John Chrysostom, *On Genesis* 29, 3, *PG* 53, 264; cf. 20, 2, *PG* 53, 168.

set over all things and through the varied skills given to him
by God subjugates each of the animals for the use most
convenient to him."[221] In the spirit of this teaching we can
also claim today that, by virtue of the technical skill given
to him by God, man harnesses the energy of steam, of elec-
tricity, or of the atom, "for the use most convenient to him."

We often feel fear in the face of the achievements of
modern science, for example in the field of atomic energy,
just as many Christians in the time of Galileo felt fear because
they saw that a certain world-view in which they felt secure
was changing. But the saints are not afraid, for they do not
place their hope in any world-view or in any specific form
of civilization. On the contrary, they rejoice and glorify God
for the new technical skills with which men in the midst
of the new needs of every age exercise stewardship over their
world.[222]

St John Chrysostom, moreover, in his commentary on the
Book of Genesis, writes that God "proved the greatness of
His love for men" by the fact that "He communicated to
fallen man many other innumerable kinds of blessings."[223]
He refers here to the new functions with which God endowed
man after he had sinned, to the positive aspect of the "garments of skin." "Look," he insists elsewhere—that is, open
your eyes and see—"the Master has made subject to you
through your technical skill even the creatures that swim in
the depths of the waters and those that fly high in the air";
and, we might add today, the forces that exist on land, in the
sea, under the sea and throughout the cosmos. All these are
causes for praising the Creator: "Let us, then, continue speaking of these same things," he adds, giving the reason for his
insistence, "marvelling at His solicitude, astonished at His
wisdom, His compassion and His providential care for us."[224]

Here surely the problem of the use of the "garments of
skin" is set forth with critical acuteness. For the same reality,

221John Chrysostom, *On the Statues* 11, 4, *PG* 49, 124.
222See John Chrysostom, *On Genesis* 29, 3, *PG* 53, 264; cf. *On Matthew*
49, 4, *PG* 58, 501.
223John Chrysostom, *On Genesis* 27, 1, *PG* 53, 240. Chrysostom dwells
at length on this point. See Th. Zissis, *Anthropos kai kosmos*, 133-88.
224John Chrysostom, *On the Eighth Psalm* 8, *PG* 55, 119.

our biological nature in all its dimensions and with all its functions, can through the exercise of our free will present at any given moment either its negative abhorrent aspect or its positive aspect.

But even when they present their negative aspect the "garments of skin" are not themselves to blame; it is rather our exercise of free will which is at fault. Chrysostom, in the continuation of the passage on technical skills to which we have referred, asserts that Noah "planted a vine and drank from the wine and became drunk. Thus, since the medicine against despondency, the bringer of health, was through ignorance used without moderation, it was not only of no benefit but inflicted indignities on his condition." And he poses the crucial question: "But perhaps one would say, 'And for whose sake was a plant full of such evils brought into being?'" He replies: "Do not simply talk about the events that follow. For the plant is not evil, nor is the wine vicious, but its abuse. . . . So, when you see wine being drunk, do not ascribe everything to the wine, but ascribe it rather to the corrupt use of free will and to assent to evil. Besides, think how useful wine has become and tremble. For the work of our salvation . . . is accomplished through it, as those who have been initiated know."[225]

The saint is categorical in his declaration—many applications of which could surely be found also in our times—that viticulture and its product are good things, and that the danger of evil resulting from their use is not intrinsic to them but arises from man's freedom of choice. This common and fundamental viewpoint of the Fathers is expressed with the same categorical emphasis by St John of Damascus: "Do not blame matter, for it is not dishonorable. Nothing is dishonorable which was brought into being by God. That is the opinion of the Manichees. The only thing that is dishonorable is that which did not have its origin from God, but is our own invention through a movement of the will and a voluntary decline from what is according to nature to what is contrary to nature, that is to say, through sin."[226]

[225]John Chrysostom, *On Genesis* 29, 3, PG 53, 264-5.
[226]John of Damascus, *On the Holy Icons* 1, 16, PG 94, 1245C. Cf. Maximos the Confessor, *Centuries on Love* 3, 4, PG 90, 1017CD.

But Chrysostom in the passage quoted above goes even deeper. The wine which "inflicted indignities on Noah's condition" is not only "the medicine against despondency" and "the bringer of health"; much more, it is the means through which is accomplished "the work of our salvation," the divine eucharist. It is not irrelevant to our theme to underline that on the basis of this majestic patristic principle, namely, that the world constitutes a means of our union with God, the entire liturgical life of the Church has been constructed. In the *Hagiasmatarion* we find services for sowing, for harvesting grapes, for setting out on a task, for all the joys and sorrows of human life. All the functions of life are taken up by the Church, and after being sanctified they operate correctly. They assist human life in the fullest possible way. They transcend the boundaries of specific time and place and initiate man into the infinite, that is to say, they are raised up to the level of sacraments.

It would be useful for us to study this correct and full use of the "garment of skin" at length and in great detail. But such a discussion would lead us far from our specific theme. I shall limit myself here to mentioning that in the patristic perspective the correct use of the "garments of skin" is defined basically by the principle of moderation. "That which is beyond your needs is superfluous and useless; to put on a shoe bigger than your foot hinders you from walking," writes Chrysostom.[227]

The full development of the "garments of skin" takes place through their elevation into spiritual senses, that is to say, through their transformation into functions of the body of Christ. The themes of the "spiritual senses" and the "indwelling of Christ," neglected by modern theology, constitute the central axes of patristic teaching. From Origen, the Cappadocians and Makarios of Egypt they are taken up and developed by Maximos the Confessor, John of Damascus, Symeon the New Theologian, Gregory Palamas, Nicolas Kavasilas, and eventually by Nikodimos of the Holy Mountain. According to this teaching Christ, dwelling within man,

[227]John Chrysostom, *On the Statues* 2, 5, *PG* 49, 42; cf. *On 2 Corinthians* 19, 3, *PG* 61, 534. See Th. Zissis, *O anthropos kai o kosmos*, 151-61.

unites the various psychosomatic senses and functions of man with the senses and functions of His own body, and thus the former become senses and functions of the risen body of Christ, that is to say, spiritual and immortal.[228] For this reason Gregory of Nyssa, who has so much to say about the post-lapsarian clothing of the "garments of skin," comes to the conclusion that in the new reality which Christ creates He Himself finally becomes and constitutes the new clothing of the human race: "It is said that Jesus is the clothing."[229]

Turning again to our specific theme, we are in a position now to sum up and conclude. The patristic teaching on the image and the "garments of skin" can provide a means of contact between Orthodoxy and the modern world, since it permits or, more strongly, obliges theological thought to be set squarely before man and his culture. The achievements of modern science, the discoveries of psychology, the triumphs of technology, the researches of philosophy are not evil or even simply tolerable; they are positively good and valuable. But the vain striving for a lawless autonomy nearly always

[228]The natural course of the investigation I have been making in this essay would have been to follow the first and second sections (on the image of God and the garments of skin) with a study of the restoration of the garments of skin as functions of that which is "in the image," showing how they come to fulfilment as senses and functions of the Body of Christ, a task realized through ascesis, prayer and the sacraments; in other words, with a study of the two themes of the "spiritual senses" and the "indwelling of Christ." In parts two and three of this book I do in fact study these two themes in two specific instances of the tradition. But their comprehensive study throughout the whole of the patristic tradition, in the way that the themes of the image and the garments of skin have been treated, remains still to be done.

[229]Gregory of Nyssa, *Commentary on the Song of Songs* 11, PG 44, 1005A; cf. *Funeral Oration on Placilla*, PG 46, 889C: "She has put on Christ. This is the truly royal and honorable garment." This leads us to the further point that the *correct* use of the "garments of skin" is not enough in itself. What is truly correct is the *full* use, the *full* development of the "garments of skin," since this raises a life which is simply human into one which is theanthropic and leads to the Kingdom of God. The aim of the good things of this life is to lead the way to that which is good in reality. Within this perspective one should note that St John Chrysostom completes his teaching on the technical skills, as outlined above, by marking the limits which set bounds to these skills. This second aspect of Chrysostom's teaching must be taken seriously into consideration (see J. Lappas, *I peri ergasias didaskalia tou Ioannou tou Chrysostomou*, the section on the limits of technical skill), if one is to understand the first aspect correctly.

alienates them, selling them for a mess of potage to corruption and the devil. And thus the works of man, instead of serving him in the realization of his goal, serve the devil in the work of the destruction of man and his world.

At this point is revealed the central meaning which repentance and ascesis have not only for man but also for history and civilization. These spiritual works constitute the warfare by which the faithful put to death within themselves and within their actions the lawless autonomy which alone is the evil element which must be rejected: "for everything created by God is good and nothing is to be rejected if it is received with thanksgiving" (1 Tim 4:4). They establish man and his works in their primeval beauty. They turn the mirror towards the real sun, and what man has created is illuminated and given life.

By the application of this liturgical, ascetico-eucharistic method the Fathers of the Church saved the great cultural institutions of their day. With this method ancient Greek thought, for example, was baptized and Christianized and transformed without being changed externally. The words, such as logos, image, archetype and triad, remained the same, but they became the created clothing of uncreated truth. This means that they have become incorrupt to such a degree that our Church believes dogmas, like the bodies of the saints, to be immutable.

3. THE TASK OF CONTEMPORARY CHRISTIAN THEOLOGY

This last point, which is the natural consequence of a true, that is christocentric, anthropology, leads us to the chief task of contemporary Orthodox theology.

We can safely say that this task does not consist in theologians identifying themselves with scientific research or political action, with the idea of corroborating these things, nor does it consist in their trying to overthrow the achievements of these things on the basis of a supposedly evangelical or patristic teaching. The Gospel teaches that the struggle of the faithful is not "against flesh and blood"—that is, a struggle within the framework created by science, politics and the other dimensions of the "garments of skin," because such a framework is not of its own nature evil—but it is a struggle "against principalities, against powers, against the world rulers of this present darkness" (Eph 6:12), against the devil and sin.

One may go so far as to say that Orthodox theology ought to practise a discernment of spirits. Its aim should be to liberate whatever good exists among the fruits of scientific research, technological development, and so on, from lawless autonomy, which is slavery to corruption and the devil, the ultimate sin, and to assign to this good element an ordered place within its own catholic truth, because that is where it belongs by virtue of its own nature: "for whatever is called good by all men belongs to us Christians."[230] In this way, "taking every thought captive in obedience to Christ" (2 Cor 10:5), we shall fill the good element with the glory of the Image, transforming and saving it. "And we all, with unveiled face, beholding the glory of the Lord, are being changed into His likeness from one degree of glory to another; for this comes from the Lord who is the Spirit" (2 Cor 3:18).

It would in fact be very useful if contemporary Orthodox theology would reflect, for example, on what elements of modern philosophy—the philosophy of matter, of ideas, of life, of essence, of existence, of being—can be accepted by the theology of the incarnate God; if it would reflect on which of the valuable conclusions of the science of psychology may be incorporated into its own synthesis by the experience of the sacramental and ascetic life, and on which of the contemporary sociological currents may be utilized by the ecclesiastical dimension of Orthodox anthropology.[231]

[230]Justin, *Second Apology* 13, *PG* 6, 465C.

[231]My own attempts to comment on specific topics within this perspective may be found in the following studies: "Orthodoxia kai politiki: Treis vivlikes proïpotheseis," *Martyria Orthodoxias* (Athens 1971); "Anthropos kai theanthropos," *Kleronomia* 3 (1971), 111-24; *I neoi kai ta provlimata tis Orthodoxias* (Athens 1971—offprint); "I petra tou Taphou: Scholio stin prosopiki viosi tis Anastaseos tou Sotiros," *Christianikon Symposion* (Athens 1972—offprint); *I Aghia kai Megali Synodos tis Orthodoxou Ekklisias: Skepseis yia mia theologiki theorisi kai proetoimasia tis* (Thessalonike

It is clear, however, that such a task would go beyond the limitations of this study. Here my aim has been on the one hand to show how this work might be accomplished, and on the other, to determine the unique foundation upon which this work should be based. "For no other foundation can anyone lay than that which is already laid, which is Jesus Christ" (1 Cor 3:11).

1972); *I Mitera tou Theou kai o theokentrikos anthropismos* (Thessalonike 1973—offprint); *O thanatos tou Theou kai i anastasi tou anthropou* (Athens 1975—offprint); *Yia ena orthodoxo ikoumenismo,* introduction to the work of that title by D. Staniloae (Peiraeus 1976); *I orthodoxi christianiki didaskalia kai to mathima ton thriskevtikon* (Athens 1977—offprint); "Sacerdoce royal: Essai sur le problème du laicat," *Kleronomia* 8 (1976), 149-62; "Les chrétiens dans un monde en création," *Contacts* 99 (1977), 198-217; "L'Eglise dans un monde en mutation," *Contacts* 103 (1978), 231-6; "Témoignage et service: propositions pour un congrès," *Service Orthodoxe de Presse* 36 (1979), 15-17; "Ta dytika technologika plaisia tis zois kai i Orthodoxi Ekklisia," *Epopteia* 38 (1979), 713-19.

PART TWO

THE SPIRITUAL LIFE
IN CHRIST

A Study of the Christocentric Anthropology
of St Nicolas Kavasilas

The whole corpus of Nicolas Kavasilas's work bears upon the spiritual life. The special interest of this fourteenth-century Byzantine mystic lies not in his being concerned, like most of the ascetic Fathers, with the description of the stages of the spiritual life and the analysis of the means by which that life is lived—repentance, ascesis, purification and the rest—but, while presupposing the knowledge of all this, in his study of its very nature.

In fact, in the course of his inquiry into the sacramental, eucharistic and ascetic life (in *The Life in Christ* and *A Commentary on the Divine Liturgy*), into devotion to the Virgin (in his Marian homilies), and into the lives of some celebrated saints, a few central feasts of the Church, and certain important functions of social life (in the remaining homilies), Kavasilas sets forth the christological and ecclesiological structure of the spiritual life in Christ. From this point of view his contribution to Orthodox theology consists in the notable advance he has made in christological anthropology.

A modern analytical study of Kavasilas's mystical teaching should therefore, in my opinion, be entitled: *The Spiritual Life in Christ According to Nicolas Kavasilas: A Contribution to Orthodox Christological Anthropology*. It would have the following table of contents: 1. The Presuppositions of the Spiritual Life (Salvation in Christ); 2. The Nature of the Spiritual Life (The Life in Christ); 3. The Living of the Spiritual Life (The Christification of Man through Communion with Christ); 4. The Fruits of the Spiritual Life (The Transformation of Creation into an Ecclesial Communion in the Flesh of the Lord). I offer a synoptic sketch of such a study in the essay which follows.[1]

[1] St Nicolas Kavasilas, commemorated in the Orthodox calendar on 20 June, was born in Thessalonike around 1320-3. A member of an aristocratic family, he received an excellent education in secular subjects as well as in

theology; apart from his religious works he also wrote on astronomy. As a young man he entered the imperial service, following a political and diplomatic career. In 1353, although still apparently a layman, he was one of the three candidates proposed by the Holy Synod for the office of Ecumenical Patriarch. He was not in fact chosen, and there is no evidence that he was ever ordained; it is sometimes said that he became a monk at the end of his life, but of this there is no definite proof. Although a friend of St Gregory Palamas, he took no active part in the hesychast controversy of 1338-47; and in his main writings he refrains from discussing the specific problems raised in this controversy concerning the distinction between the essence and energies of God, the divine light of Tabor, and the use of the Jesus Prayer. There is no doubt, however, that he was in sympathy with the hesychast approach. He died soon after 1391.

The Life in Christ is published in Migne, PG 150, 493-726; English translation: The Life in Christ by Nicholas Cabasilas, translated by C.J. deCatanzaro (Crestwood, New York 1974). The Commentary on the Divine Liturgy is also in Migne, PG 150, 368-492, and with a French translation and notes by S. Salaville in Sources chrétiennes No. 4 bis (Paris 1967); English translation: A Commentary on the Divine Liturgy by Nicholas Cabasilas, translated by J.M. Hussey and P.A. McNulty (London 1966). References to these two works will be given simply by the column in Migne. The Homilies on the Mother of God have been edited and translated by M. Jugie in Patrologia Orientalis 19, 3 (Paris 1925), 456-510. They have also been published as the second volume in the series Epi tas Pigas under the title I Theomitor (Athens 1974). References will be given by page number in this edition. For Kavasilas's remaining works and for his life, 14th-century setting and significance, see P. Nellas, Prolegomena eis tin meletin Nikolaou tou Kavasila (Athens 1968). Seven of the homilies have been edited by V. Psevtongas, Nikolaou Kavasila, Epta anekdotoi logoi (Thessalonike 1976).

I

The Presuppositions of the Spiritual Life: Salvation in Christ

Spiritual life, like physical life, needs a progenitor in order to exist. For this reason, Kavasilas maintains, before the "blessed flesh" of the new progenitor of the human race had been conceived in the womb of the Virgin Mary by the Holy Spirit, it was impossible for anybody to live a spiritual life. "It was impossible for anyone at all to live the spiritual life before this blessed flesh had come into being."[2]

Such a power did not even belong to Adam before the fall. For his created nature was different from the nature of God and totally distinct from it. "Our nature was separate from God through being different from Him in everything that it possessed and through having nothing in common with Him." And that was because "God remained Himself alone; our nature was human and nothing more."[3]

Of course Adam was made "in the image" of God. He had thus received, in the measure appropriate to being "in the image," the breath of the Spirit and had truly proved to be a "living soul" (Gen 2:7). But his life was not yet fully spiritual, that is to say, it was not yet the very life of the Holy Spirit, with which the blessed flesh of the Lord lives, and which was given to mankind in the flesh of Christ, the Church, at Pentecost. Unfallen man, as we have already seen in our analysis, had still to be made capable of receiving the hypostatic union, and thereby of finding his true being and full spiritual life.

[2]*Life in Christ*, 596B.
[3]Ibid., 572A.

The distance separating human nature from the divine took on tragic dimensions with the fall. In choosing to live, not with the life given to him by the breath of God, but in an autonomous way, man endowed sin with existence and life, although essentially it has no existence.

The inevitable result of establishing such an autonomy, which is the root of all sin, is the appearance of sinful acts, which according to Kavasilas have within them two elements, the act itself and the "trauma."[4] The act creates the trauma-passion, and this eagerly seeks the consolation of pleasure, which is the fruit of sinful action. In this way the habit (*exis*) of sin is created, which becomes in man a second nature. Sin like a second nature covers man with its darkness, drowns him in the depths of "forgetfulness" (*lithi*)[5] and makes him "disappear."[6] The image is obscured, the "shape" and distinguishing "form" of man perish, and human nature collapses, in Kavasilas's phrase,[7] "like matter without form or shape."[8]

Repeated sinful acts—needs followed by satisfaction of needs through sin; passions followed by satisfaction of passions through sensual pleasure—create a sequence of events in the external world and of emotions in the human person, and thus give the impression of life, although in reality they do nothing but conceal the absence of true life. This is spiritual death. "Accordingly, sin has no end, since habit gives rise to actions and the accumulation of actions aggravates the habit. Thus the evils are mutually reinforced and make continual progress, so that 'sin came to life but I died.' "[9]

Yet the impression of life to which I have referred is not a pure fantasy. The "matter" of humanity continued even after the fall to be organized and alive in itself, endowed with soul and reason, because that is how God created it, and no one can destroy what God creates. Viewed in this way

[4]Ibid., 536A-537B.
[5]Ibid., 413C.
[6]*Theomitor*, 64.
[7]Ibid., 70.
[8]*Life in Christ*, 537D.
[9]Ibid., 563B; cf. "Sin was alive and it was impossible for the true life to rise in us" (513A).

man continues to be real, to live, to move, to create within creation. But his life and movement are henceforth biological functions. The "powers enabling him to live," with which he had been endowed and which were to a degree spiritual, were coarsened, were imprisoned in matter, and instead of being raised into "spiritual senses" lapsed into simple psychosomatic, biological functions, into "garments of skin." Thus when physiological fatigue supervenes and when the biological cycle of the human organism is completed, the body ceases to assimilate the food and air with which life has been maintained in the fact of corruption, is no longer strong enough to sustain the human person, and dies. This is natural death.[10]

It thus becomes clear that there are three things which separate man from God and constitute obstacles to the spiritual life: nature, sin and death.

All these, however, "the Savior removed in succession, the first by partaking of manhood, the second by being put to death on the cross, and the final barrier, the tyranny of death, he eliminated completely from our nature by rising again."[11] And thus "when . . . the barriers have been removed there is nothing which prevents the Holy Spirit from being 'poured out upon all flesh.' "[12]

The manner in which Christ overcame these three obstacles, as well as the significance of this victory for the manifestation of the true nature of humanity, its true life and real dimensions, are studied by Kavasilas in some depth.

With the birth of the "blessed flesh" of the Lord the union was achieved of the two natures, the divine and the human, which until then had been "separated" from one another; the distance between them is abolished, since the common hypostasis, "being a term common to both natures,

[10]There are also other aspects to sin besides its imprisonment in corruption. It is a "sickness" in man, "anarchy" in creation, "enslavement" to the devil, "hubris and enmity" against God. All these, together with the specific ways in which Christ freed humanity on these points, are discussed at length in my book, *I peri dikaioseos tou anthropou didaskalia Nikolaou tou Kavasila*. I have therefore dealt with these matters here merely in a schematic way.

[11]*Life in Christ*, 572CD.
[12]Ibid., 572C.

eliminates the distance between the Godhead and the man-hood";[13] and the difference between the natures is also abro-gated, since through His birth Christ "adapted the whole human race to Himself."[14] The hypostatic union recreates man, making his prelapsarian iconic being whole again. For this reason the conception by the Virgin Mary of the "blessed flesh" of the Lord inaugurates a new human ontology, and Christ constitutes the real progenitor of a new humanity.

Through His holy life, His compassionate works and His supernatural wonders Jesus the God-Man reveals God to the world, since it is God who acts, and at the same time mani-fests the true nature of man, since all His works were achieved through His created human nature.

Through the passion, wounds and sacrifice on the cross of the blessed flesh of the Lord, sin and the authority which the devil had over man are destroyed, human nature is freed from enmity towards God and from enslavement to the devil, and it is healed, restored to its original beauty and justified. The Lord's wounds become the means of healing for human-ity. "It was when He mounted the cross and died and rose again that human freedom was won, that human form and beauty were created."[15]

Through the resurrection of the blessed flesh of the Lord human nature was freed from slavery to corruption and death. Along with His birth the Lord also took on Himself the corruption which began with Adam, and it was precisely for this reason that He died.[16] His death was not only a con-sequence of the cross; it was also the final result of the incar-nation. By descending, however, to death the Logos renewed humanity in general and made it incorrupt along with the human nature which He had assumed and by means of it. Just as on the cross human nature was purified from sin by the blood of the Lord, so in the tomb it was purified in an organic manner from the state of death by laying aside the earthly "garments of skin," that is to say, by laying aside

[13]Ibid., 572B.
[14]Ibid., 681A.
[15]Ibid., 537C.
[16]Ibid., 680B.

mortality. For through His lying in the tomb until the third day the Lord made reparation precisely in the earth for the debt which Adam himself had incurred from the earth through his fall—the debt that takes the form of the "body which casts a shadow,"[17] the "garments of skin," the body's biological composition and structure. And recasting human nature as if it were a shattered and ruined statue,[18] He raised it up new, spiritual and imperishable. The truly human body of Jesus became after the resurrection an immortal[19] and spiritual[20] body, free from the limitations of time and space, naturally endowed with new spiritual senses and functions, and it was manifested as such. "From the beginning our nature has as its aim immortality; but it only achieved this later in the body of the Savior who, when He had risen from the dead to immortal life, became the pioneer of immortality for our race."[21]

Thus the resurrected and blessed flesh of the Lord in which the new theandric spiritual senses function—spiritual vision, spiritual taste, spiritual hearing and so on—becomes the new "type" of humanity. The resurrected blessed flesh of the Lord is the realization and manifestation of the perfect man, the Theanthropos or God-Man. "The Savior was the first and only person to show us the true humanity which is perfect in manner of life and in all other respects.[22]

But the blessed flesh of the Lord is none other than the Church. The "dominical body" in which the Spirit dwells has been manifested as ecclesial communion, and henceforth constitutes the place in which the new spiritual life is lived by the faithful and in which salvation becomes concrete. In this organism of the dominical body the spiritual life of the Head flows down to the members and gives them life. In this sense the creation of the Church constitutes the second presupposition of the spiritual life and the Church itself the second aspect of salvation. Christ is not a simple liberator who

[17]Ibid., 493B.
[18]Ibid., 540C.
[19]Ibid., 645D.
[20]Ibid., 645C.
[21]Ibid., 680C.
[22]Ibid., 680C.

abandons men to their own devices after liberation, after entrusting them with His wise teaching. More radically, He creates a new place for them in which to live. And this place is His body.

Man's coming to know God and the conforming of his will to the divine will constitutes the third presupposition of the spiritual life and the third aspect of salvation. The knowledge of God illumines man and the love of God gives him life. Through correct knowledge and the free exercise of love man can be raised in Christ from being "in the image" to being the Image itself, that is to say, he can arrive at the Likeness.

II

The Nature of the Spiritual Life:
The Life in Christ

In analyzing the nature of the spiritual life, Kavasilas makes at the same time a particularly penetrating study of the true nature of man.

The life of man differs radically from the life of any other animal on earth. From his creation man, made in the image of God, possesses intellect and free will as his inalienable property and can thus create his own world, either a world common to the human race, namely civilized life, or a separate world which gifted individuals create internally for themselves. Life on this level may be "interior," as with the vision of an artist or a philosopher. It may even be called "spiritual," in the sense that it operates through the higher "non-material" functions of the human organism, namely the intellect, the emotions and the imagination. Such an "interior" or "spiritual" life, however, without being narrowly bodily is certainly biological, albeit with all the majesty and wealth which the Creator desired that even the biological limits of man should enclose within them. But, however much the psychic world of man is developed, it cannot while functioning autonomously attain to the reality of God and live with the life of the Spirit. Such a life has no connection with the Christian spiritual life.

But, on the other hand, since man has within him an ineradicable consciousness of his createdness, he also can create a world which takes the existence of God seriously, which is organized with laws and precepts in the sight of

God. Life on this level is called "religious." Since, however, it is merely organized in the sight of God and is not yet united with Him, even this life cannot be called in the true sense "spiritual." The spiritual life is not a life of laws and precepts but a life of participation, affection and love, a life of mingling and mixing with God.

However high, then, the degrees of "interior," "spiritual" or "religious" life may be to which a man has raised himself, he cannot yet be considered a truly spiritual person. St Paul felicitously calls him "psychic" (1 Cor 2:14). Looked at from the ontological point of view, this means that he is not yet a full and true man, and this is precisely because union with God is not some additional element but actually constitutes man. For a man to be a man he must become that which he was created to be.

Kavasilas maintains with clarity that man was formed in the image of Christ. Christ is the real "first-born of all creation" (Col 1:15), the archetype and goal of Adam.[23] Human nature was created in the image of Christ so that the Logos could receive His mother from it and enter as a man into the human world,[24] so that God could become a real God-Man, and man in turn a real god-man too by grace and participation. This is the concrete realization of the true humanity.

Adam was the natural "type" of his descendants. Through their biological birth human beings bear the Adamic form, the Adamic shape and life, which are their biological psychosomatic functions. But the Creator Logos through His incarnation, burial and resurrection melted down and recast the Adamic "type" within Himself and created a new spiritual human "type." He was the new Adam, the new progenitor of the human race, the Father of the age to come.[25] "The former [Adam] introduced an imperfect life which needed countless forms of assistance; the latter [Christ] became the Father of immortal life for men."[26]

[23]Ibid., 680AB.
[24]*Theomitor*, 150-52.
[25]*Life in Christ*, 541A.
[26]Ibid., 680C.

The present life is compared by Kavasilas with the "dark and nocturnal life" which the foetus lives in its mother's womb while being prepared for its birth. "Nature prepares the foetus, all through its dark and nocturnal life, for that life which it will lead in the light, fashioning it as if according to a model for the life which it is about to receive. The saints experience something similar. . . . In actuality this world is in travail with the new inward man, the man created in accordance with God; and when he has been fashioned and formed here, he is thus born as a perfect man into that perfect world which does not grow old . . . This is what the Apostle Paul meant when he wrote to the Galatians, 'My little children, with whom I am again in travail until Christ be formed in you' (Gal 4:19)."[27] "The beginning of the life to come" is experienced in this life. "The provision of the new members and senses" and the "preparation of the heavenly banquet" take place here. And this preparation cannot be accomplished except through our being incorporated into Christ, through our receiving His life and His senses and functions. "It is impossible for us to live our human life if we have not received Adam's senses and the human faculties necessary for this life. Similarly no one can proceed alive to that blessed world if he has not been prepared by the life of Christ and formed in His image."[28]

This line of argument makes it clear that the true human person comes into existence through being born in Christ, that his biological birth constitutes a preparation for the real birth which is in Christ. The latter is by far the higher since it enables a man to be born into a life united with God, and thus renders him a true human person. We have met this teaching in St Maximos the Confessor. Nicolas Kavasilas repeats it, laying particular emphasis on it and explaining it.

In our physical birth, he writes, the progenitor gives the "seed" and "principle" of life to his child. Subsequently, however, the life of each person tends rather to differentiate the

[27]Ibid., 496BC.
[28]Ibid., 541A; cf. "In short, what can these rites do for us? They prepare us for the life to come. For they are 'powers of the age to come,' as Paul says (Heb 6:5)" (688D).

child from his progenitor than to unite it with him, whereas in our spiritual birth Christ gives His life to people and this life of Christ becomes the new and true life of man. In the physical birth the progenitor gives to his child the power to create eyes and members similar to his own, whereas in the spiritual birth Christ actually gives man His own eyes and His own members. The physical birth is a separation of child from mother, the spiritual birth is an enduring union, and if a person is separated from Christ he dies. "The blood by which we now live is Christ's blood, and [our] flesh . . . is Christ's body: . . . we have our members and our life in common with Him."[29] This contemporaneous occupation of our own members and our own life creates a real communion. For there is no certain communion when "both parties possess something, but one at one time and one at another."[30] This "is not so much a sharing as a separation. . . . One does not live with a person merely by living in the same house after he has left."[31] Communion with our physical progenitors is no more than an image of true communion. Real communion is communion with Christ, "since we always possess body, blood, members and all things in common with Him."[32] Christ did not give us life so as to be separated from us afterwards like our parents, "but He is with us at all times and united to us; and by His presence He gives us life and keeps us in being."[33]

A marvellous synthesis thus takes place in which each person is unique and self-determining yet simultaneously an inseparable member of the body of Christ, functioning with the functions of Christ. "There is nothing which the saints need which He does not Himself constitute. He gives them birth, growth and nourishment. He is their light and their breath. He fashions eyes for them Himself, and moreover illuminates them Himself and enables them to see Him. He nourishes and is Himself the food; He provides the bread of life and is Himself what He provides. He is life to those who

[29]Ibid., 600CD.
[30]Ibid., 600D.
[31]Ibid., 600D-601A.
[32]Ibid., 601A.
[33]Ibid., 601B.

live, a fragrance to those who breathe, a garment to those who would be clothed."[34]

Similarly, through physical birth parents give their child an organism capable of living this mortal life, whereas through spiritual birth Christ creates in human beings a new spiritual organism with spiritual eyes and ears by which they live the spiritual life. This organism, which is none other than the new man and which as a spiritual entity is not subject to decay, will survive after death and will keep human life in being in eternity. If we do not possess such an organism with the appropriate senses, how shall we have eyes, asks Kavasilas, with which to see the Sun of righteousness who will shine in the age to come? How shall we communicate at the table which will be prepared? Without such an organism our human existence would be dead: "we would be dead and miserable beings dwelling in that blessed world."[35]

And in order to stress the reality of Christ's union with the believer even more heavily, Kavasilas writes that this union transcends any other union that we could conceive and cannot be represented by any analogy. That is why Scripture uses many analogies simultaneously. The union of Christ with the believer is greater than that of a householder with his home, or of a branch with the vine, or of a man with a woman in marriage, or of a head with the members of the body. This last point was made plain by the martyrs, who preferred to lose their heads rather than Christ. And when the Apostle Paul prays that he should be cursed so that Christ may be glorified, he shows that the true believer is united more closely with Christ than with his own self.[36]

This communion of Christ with man is a communion which delivers the latter from dead life and dead existence, from "formlessness," "obliteration" and "ignorance." This point deserves special attention. Confronting reality from God's point of view, Kavasilas does not hesitate to maintain that God "knows His own," that is to say, the Father knows the Son and whatever belongs to Him.[37] That which does not

[34]Ibid., 500CD.
[35]Ibid., 496A.
[36]Ibid., 500A.
[37]Ibid., 525B.

exist in Christ is "neither manifest to God nor known by Him." But that which is unknown to God is also objectively unknown; it does not exist in reality. "Whatever is not visible to Him by that light is in reality entirely without existence."[38]

By baptism, chrismation, the divine eucharist and the rest of the spiritual life we are incorporated into Christ, we receive a Christian being, that is, a christocentric and christlike being, and the form and life which correspond to it. In this way "the Father . . . finds the very form of the Son in our faces" and "recognizes in us the members of the Only-begotten Son."[39] Thus, "having become known to Him who knows His own,"[40] we emerge from invisibility and oblivion into truth. Man "who was once darkness becomes light; he who once was nothing now has existence. He dwells with God and is adopted by Him; from imprisonment and utmost slavery he is led to the royal throne."[41]

The title of Kavasilas' basic work is not accidental. For our Byzantine theologian spiritual life is precisely the *life in Christ*, or the life of Christ within us. The essence of the spiritual life is represented clearly by St Paul's statement, "It is no longer I who live but Christ who lives in me" (Gal 2:20), provided that we take this statement in a literal sense.

From what has been said about it, it becomes clear that the true nature of man consists in his being like God, or more precisely in his being like Christ and centered on Him. Consequently, Orthodox anthropology must be constructed from within the perspective of christological anthropology, as regards both its essential content and its method and form. Orthodox anthropology is literally "theanthropology."

[38]Ibid., 525BC.
[39]Ibid., 600B.
[40]Ibid., 525B.
[41]Ibid., 532A.

III

The Living of the Spiritual Life

Since a true human being is one who is in Christ, and since the spiritual life is the life in Christ, the living of such a life cannot be realized except by the union and communion of man with Christ, a communion which in its fullness is called in the Orthodox tradition *theosis* or deification, and which, according to Kavasilas, has christification as its real anthropological content. In the five main chapters of *The Life in Christ* Kavasilas explains that the union and communion of man with Christ is realized by man's "being," by the movement which makes this being active, by life, by knowledge and by the will. "Union with Christ, then, belongs to those who have undergone all that the Savior has undergone, and have experienced and become all that He has experienced and become."[42]

1. THE CHRISTIFICATION OF MAN'S BEING

Through baptism man's biological being actually participates in the death and resurrection of Christ. Baptism is literally a new birth in Christ and in this sense a new creation of man. This new creation, however, is not brought into existence *ex nihilo,* nor as in the case of the first man out of pre-existing biological life, but out of the pre-existing biological being of man.

Apart from Christ, the biological being of man—man on the biological level—does not possess, as we have already

[42]Ibid., 521A.

121

seen, either "form" or "name" but is shapeless "matter."
When gold and copper, Kavasilas explains, are put into a
furnace they are purified of extraneous material. When they
are poured into a mould they take on the shape of a piece of
jewelry, or a coin, or a statue, and become that which they
were intended to be. It is precisely then that they take on the
name which shows what each of these things is. Previously
they only had the general name of the matter of which they
were made. In a similar manner man descends into the water
of baptism as "shapeless and formless matter" and rises
"meeting the beautiful form" of Christ.[43] "We are formed
and shaped, and our shapeless and undefined life receives
shape and definition."[44]

Man's nature assumes the form—that is, the structure
and mode of functioning—of the deified human nature of
Christ. For Christ did not limit Himself to bringing light to
the world through His incarnation; He "also provided the
eye." He not only emitted the fragrance of divinity, "but
also gave the means of perceiving it," that is, He created
within the human organism which He assumed those new
dimensions and functions by which man is able to assimilate
the divine life.[45] Through baptism every believer is united
with these new spiritual senses and functions of the body of
Christ and makes them his own. "This sacred washing joins
those who have been washed to these senses and faculties."[46]
Thus "when we come up from the water we bear on our souls,
on our heads, on our eyes in our very inward parts, on all
our members the Savior Himself, free from any taint of sin
and delivered from corruption, just as He was when He rose
again, and appeared to His disciples, and was taken up, and
just as He will be when He comes again to demand the return
of this treasure."[47]

This "union," and the subsequent "change" of the biological dimensions and functions of man into functions of
the body of Christ, does not take place through the destruc-

[43]Ibid., 537D.
[44]Ibid., 525A.
[45]Ibid., 537D.
[46]Ibid., 537D.
[47]Ibid., 517D.

tion of the former but through their transformation. Christ, explains Kavasilas, enters into us in a real manner, a bodily manner, through the biological functions "by which we introduce air and food to assist the life of the body."[48] He makes these functions His own ("assimilates" them). He mixes and mingles Himself with all our psychosomatic faculties, without confusion but nevertheless in a real way,[49] and in the midst of this natural sacramental mixing, under the most effective influence of His resurrected flesh, He transforms, refashions and renews our psychosomatic functions, turning them into functions of His own body. "For when greater powers are brought to bear upon lesser ones, they do not allow them to retain their own characteristics. When iron comes into contact with fire, it does not retain anything of the property of iron; when earth and water are thrown on fire, they exchange their properties for those of fire. If, then, among those things which have similar powers, the stronger affect the weaker in this way, what must we think of that supernatural power? It is therefore clear that Christ infuses Himself into us and mingles Himself with us. He changes and transforms us into Himself as a small drop of water is changed by being poured into a vast sea of perfume."[50] And in another place he writes, "Blending and mingling Himself with us in this way throughout our whole being, He makes us His own body and becomes to us what a head is to the members."[51] "The soul and the body and all the faculties immediately become spiritual, for our soul is mingled with His soul, our body with His body, and our blood with His blood. What conclusions may we draw from this? Greater things are stronger than lesser ones, what is divine prevails over what is human, and as Paul says concerning the resurrection, 'What is mortal is swallowed up by life' (2 Cor 5:4), and: 'It is no longer I who live but Christ who lives in me' (Gal 2:20)."[52]

This last phrase of the Apostle, to which Kavasilas gives

[48]Ibid., 520A.
[49]Ibid., 520A.
[50]Ibid., 593C.
[51]Ibid., 520A.
[52]Ibid., 584D.

special emphasis, shows that the rebirth and refashioning of man in baptism is not only a refashioning of man's nature, of his physical dimensions and functions, but also a rebirth of the human person. Man's being in its entirety, both as nature and as person, is born again and in this sense is created anew. Man is born again spiritually " 'not of blood . . . nor of the will of man, but of God' (John 1:13), of the Holy Spirit."[53] The biological being of man finds through its incorporation into Christ its true spiritual hypostasis.

Created human nature, within which is housed the human person that is incomprehensible without the nature, is enhypostatized in Christ, and finds in Him its truth, its integral wholeness, its health and its correct mode of functioning which stretches out to infinity. By the same act the created human person, within which human nature, which is incomprehensible without the person, becomes concrete, is enhypostatized in Christ and discovers its true eternal "Christian mode of being," which constitutes the unique dignity of man's being.[54] Thus it may be said literally, and not just by way of exaggeration, that Christ truly becomes "another self" to man.[55]

Baptism has a multiple function. It cleanses man from his personal sins, it frees him from the bonds which original sin forged for the human race, but even more fundamentally, it enhypostatizes him in Christ; and it is this that is the cause of all the other blessings which the sacrament bestows. Baptism constitutes for man an ontological event; it refashions and completes his created being. For this reason it constitutes the firm point of departure for every Orthodox approach to the problem of the ontology of man. For this reason, too, it constitutes the "root," the "source" and the "foundation" of the spiritual life.

2. THE CHRISTIFICATION OF MOVEMENT

A person who through baptism has received new being in

[53]Ibid., 601D.
[54]Ibid., 533D.
[55]Ibid., 665A.

Christ acquires the new movement and activation of this being in accordance with Christ through the sacrament of chrismation. "It would therefore be fitting that those who have been spiritually constituted in this way and have been born in such a manner should acquire an activity appropriate to such a birth and a corresponding movement. This can be accomplished for us by the rite of the most divine myrrh."[56]

Kavasilas explains the way in which this activation is realized. He unites the christological and the pneumatological dimensions of the work of the divine economy in an inseparable manner. Before the incarnation of the Logos, he writes, God "was myrrh but remained within Himself."[57] But on the assumption of a human nature by the Logos, the "myrrh" was poured out into it and was thus changed into "chrism." "When the blessed flesh which had received the entire fullness of the Godhead was constituted . . . it was appropriate that the myrrh which had been poured out into it should immediately become chrism and should be called such."[58] By His incarnation the Lord chrismated human nature with the divine nature.

The Holy Spirit thus entered into human nature at this point not as in the first creation but in a personal manner. "In the beginning, Scripture says, 'He breathed into him the breath of life' (Gen 2:7), but now He communicates His Spirit to us (cf. John 20:22)."[59] He is that which moves and vivifies the blessed flesh of the Lord and is poured out over every person who has been created anew and grafted onto Christ. " 'For God,' says Scripture, 'has sent the Spirit of His Son into our hearts, crying, Abba! Father!' (Gal 4:6)."[60] The sacrament of chrismation constitutes the Pentecost of each particular human being.

In this sacrament the Spirit activates and vivifies the new functions which the baptized have acquired in Christ. "He makes the spiritual energies active, one energy in one person, another in someone else, several in a third, according

---

[56]Ibid., 569A.
[57]Ibid., 569C.
[58]Ibid., 569C-572A.
[59]Ibid., 617B.
[60]Ibid., 617B.

to how prepared each person is for the sacrament."[61] Kavasilas refers here to the gifts or charisms of the Spirit, which
in the early years of the Church were given to the baptized
by the imposition of the apostles' hands and are now bestowed
by the holy oil of chrism, and which enable the Church to
organize its life under the inspiration and guidance of God.
He refers, moreover, to the virtues, which are the reflections
of the divine rays, the fruits of the energies of the Spirit,
who comes to dwell in us through the sacrament. Thus the
gifts, and likewise the virtues, can be understood as the new
transformed manner in which our psychosomatic senses and
functions operate when they are grafted onto Christ and are
moved by the Spirit. "Virtues are divine and superior to
human law when God Himself is the mover."[62]

3. THE CHRISTIFICATION OF LIFE

The divine eucharist is life in all its fullness. "After
chrismation we go to the altar. This is the consummation of
life; those who attain it henceforth lack nothing which is
necessary to the blessedness they seek."[63] For here we do not
simply participate in the death and resurrection of the Lord
as newly created persons, nor do we merely receive the movement of our new being. In the divine eucharist all these are
recapitulated and completed since "we receive the Risen One
Himself . . . the very Benefactor Himself, the very Temple
on which the whole cycle of graces is based."[64]

By the "cycle of graces" Kavasilas means the liturgical
and sacramental cycle, the whole structure and life of the
Church as the body of Christ. And it is precisely the body of
Christ, or more correctly the whole Christ, the Logos together
with the flesh which He assumed and with all the works
which He accomplished, who is present and is offered in the
eucharist. "That of which we partake is not something be-

[61]Ibid., 569A.
[62]Ibid., 576B.
[63]Ibid., 581A.
[64]Ibid., 581A.

longing to Him, but is His very Self."[65] For this reason the eucharist "enables the other sacraments to be perfect."[66]

The eucharist is the center of the spiritual life in Christ and its source. Here the union with Christ is complete and full. The whole person in all its dimensions, with all its psychosomatic senses and functions, is joined in a deep union with Christ, is transformed and christified. "This is the celebrated marriage by which the most holy bridegroom takes the Church as His virgin bride . . . by this we become 'flesh of His flesh and bone of His bones' (cf. Gen 2:21)."[67] The divine eucharist makes "Christ our supreme good, superior to everything in us that is naturally good."[68] "O the greatness of the sacraments! . . . What is our mind when dominated by His divine mind! What is our will when overcome by His blessed will! What is our dust when utterly conquered by His fire!"[69]

This christification of man is not just an impression which the believer creates for himself in his own mind. A person does not become a member of Christ merely in a manner of speaking; he becomes it in reality. As an example Kavasilas appeals to Paul, in whom all the human functions were transformed into functions of Christ: " 'We have the mind of Christ' (1 Cor 2:16), [says the Apostle]; and, 'You desire proof that Christ is speaking in me' (2 Cor 13:3); and, 'I yearn for you all with the affection of Christ Jesus' (Phil 1:8). . . . To sum it all up: 'It is no longer I who live but Christ lives in me' (Gal 2:20)."[70]

Kavasilas boldly attempts a physiological description and explanation of this transformation, which he calls *metaskevi*.[71] Commenting on the biblical text, "He who eats me will live because of me" (John 6:57), he refers to the fact that man, as a higher being, can assimilate bread, fish and whatever else he eats. But these foods, he maintains, once again under

[65]Ibid., 584D.
[66]Ibid., 585B.
[67]Ibid., 593D.
[68]Ibid., 616C.
[69]Ibid., 585A.
[70]Ibid., 585A.
[71]Ibid., 716A.

the influence of St Maximos, do not of themselves have life and therefore cannot vivify. They give the impression that they offer life because they sustain the body temporarily, but in reality they offer a mere survival which is subject to decay and oriented towards death. But the bread of the eucharist, which is Christ, he continues, is alive in actuality and is thus able to offer life in a true sense. Of course, absolutely transcendent as He is, He is not Himself transformed when He is offered as food to man but transforms man into what He is Himself. "Our food, whether fish or bread or any other kind of nourishment, is changed into human blood, into the person who consumes it. But in this case quite the opposite happens. The bread of life Himself changes the person who feeds on Him, transforms him and assimilates him to Himself."[72] Thus man is transformed into a real member of the body of Christ, which is nourished and vivified by the head. "For that which belongs to the head must inevitably pass into the body."[73] This analysis makes clear the literal sense in which the Pauline phrases quoted above are to be taken. And these phrases plainly indicate the central axis of Kavasilas's anthropology.[74]

But the divine eucharist also has a more general, a cosmic significance. It reorders not only human life but also the

[72]Ibid., 597AB.

[73]Ibid., 520A.

[74]Kavasilas is much concerned to show that the biblical expressions which speak of the union of man with Christ are not simply metaphorical but possess a real content. He frequently analyzes these phrases at length, especially in the context of the divine eucharist. Here as an example is his analysis of "We are His house" (Heb 3:7) in conjunction with the Johannine statement, "He who eats My flesh and drinks My blood abides in Me and I in him" (Jn 6:56). The divine eucharist, he writes, is that which "makes us dwell in Christ and Christ in us . . . so that we dwell and are dwelt in and become one spirit." And when Christ, he explains, remains within us as His dwelling, what can we need that is lacking? What good can escape us? Or when we dwell in Christ as if in our own house, what can we desire that we do not have? "He dwells in us and He is the house itself. How blessed we are in having such a house! How blessed we are that we have become a house for such an occupant!" What more can we want "when Christ is thus actually with us, and penetrates the whole of our being, and occupies all our inward parts and surrounds us?" No external evil can touch us, for Christ who encloses us like a house wards it off. Similarly He purifies us of every internal evil, since He dwells in us and fills the whole of our being with Himself (*Life in Christ*, 584BC).

whole universe. It constitutes, according to Kavasilas, the final reality, the "end" of all beings, the goal of life on earth, the content of the heavenly life, the transformation of history. The "time" of the eucharist unifies the past, the present and the future; it manifests eternity and activates it in actuality in the midst of everyday life. The "space" of the eucharist is the space of the Kingdom, the real Christian home-land.

As an assembly of the faithful around the altar, the eucharist is a reconstitution of our ancient home in paradise. As a full communion of the faithful with God and with each other, it perfects that home and unites humanity entirely, making it the body of God. As a sacrifice and an offering it creates once again the relationship that man had with creation before the fall and at the same time completes it. The creatures which constitute man's wealth are offered by him with love to God. Thus creation becomes the means by which man is united with God. Matter comes to be filled with the Spirit, and the spiritual life functions within the eucharist unhindered and in its true fullness. All these things take place because the eucharist is Christ, who constitutes the past, present and future of the saints, which is the real past, present and future of the world.

The divine eucharist, as a celebration, as an act of trans-formation of the bread and wine into the body and blood of Christ, and also as a communion of the faithful with this body and blood, re-presents and makes active in the present that which Christ did in the past for the salvation of mankind —His birth, life, passion, death, resurrection, ascension and giving of the Spirit. "This point [of the eucharist] represents that moment in time [of the economy]."[75] Thus the celebration of the eucharist makes present for us events which constitute the past and the future of sacred history, and our participation in this takes us out of the cyclic course of history and brings us into the new time of the Church, in which the eternal enters into time and functions as everlasting present.

The historical body of Christ, as it lived, died and rose again, and as it shines glorified at the right hand of the

[75]*Divine Liturgy* 38, 452B.

Father, is found in reality on the altar and is offered to the faithful as a meal.[76] In consuming it the faithful become members of His body and within this body contemporaries of the historical Jesus, and participate even in this life in the blessings to come. This eucharistic body is the body of the Church, the body of the faithful, the salvation of creation, the glory of God and of men, the freedom, the joy and the food of the saints. This body, as eucharist, as communion, as a meal, as the body of Christ and the body of the faithful, is the true "space" and the true "time" of the Church, for in Him we live and move and have our being.[77]

4. THE CHRISTIFICATION OF THE MIND

In the sacraments God offers everything, and nothing can be added beyond that. It is necessary, however, for a person to appropriate the treasure which he has received in the

[76]When "the whole of the rite has been accomplished and completed ... the great victim and oblation, which was slain for the world, is seen to lie upon the altar. For the bread of the Lord's body is no longer a type ... but the very body of the most holy Master, which actually suffered all those outrages, insults and blows, which was crucified and slain, which in the 'testimony before Pontius Pilate made the good confession' (1 Tim 6:13), which was scourged, maltreated and spat upon, which tasted gall. Similarly the wine is the very blood which gushed from that body when it was slain. It is that body and that blood which was formed by the Holy Spirit, born of the Holy Virgin, was buried, rose on the third day, ascended into heaven, and is seated at the right hand of the Father" (*Divine Liturgy* 27, 425CD).

[77]In such an essay I can naturally only make a summary presentation and interpretation of Kavasilas's teaching. I am obliged to pass over a number of crucial points, such as the fact that the divine eucharist constitutes the real content even of the eschatological Kingdom. We would gain a much deeper understanding of what happens in the divine eucharist, and also of what constitutes the Kingdom of Heaven, if we were to take serious note of, for example, the following passages: "That which brings every delight and bliss to those who have entered into the next world—whether you choose to call it paradise, or Abraham's bosom, or the bright, green and refreshing places free from all sorrow and pain, or the Kingdom itself—is none other than this bread and this cup" (*Divine Liturgy* 43, 461CD). And: "It has been shown that all the refreshment of souls and every reward of virtue, whether great or small, is nothing other than this bread and this cup. ... For that is why the Lord has called the refreshment of the saints in the age to come a banquet, in order to show that there will be nothing there beyond this Table" (*Divine Liturgy* 45, 465AB).

sacraments by his personal co-operation—"just as in worldly affairs it is right and proper . . . once we have received life not to sleep as if we already possess everything, but to seek the means of preserving it."[78]

But man is basically what he thinks and what he desires. It is therefore impossible for him to be considered united with Christ unless these higher functions of his are also united with Him. If he is not so united he is still a "child" and "member" of Christ, since he communicates with Him through the body and the blood, but he is "blameworthy" and "dead."[79] On the other hand, when his thought is united with the thought of Christ and his will is made to conform to the will of Christ, it is natural for the whole man to follow, and the union is then complete.

The manner in which a person can, by appropriating the new birth, movement and life which he finds in the sacraments, work to accomplish the christification of his intellect and will is the subject to which Kavasilas devotes the last two chapters of *The Life in Christ*.

Taking for granted the ascetic method for the purification and unification of the intellect, Kavasilas does not make this his theme but directs all his efforts towards showing that Christ is the only Truth, and that it is consonant with our nature and therefore useful and necessary that we should study Him above all.

More particularly, he writes, the study of the works of the divine economy fills the human intellect with the majesty

[78]*Life in Christ*, 641A. The sacraments are not effective without human co-operation: "There are said to be two ways in which grace operates in the precious gifts; first, the way in which they are sanctified, and secondly, the way in which grace sanctifies us through them. The first operation of grace, the operation in the gifts, cannot be impeded by any human wickedness . . . But the second demands effort from us. For this reason it can also be impeded by our own indolence. For grace sanctifies us through the gifts if it finds us suitably disposed towards sanctification; but if it comes upon us when we are unprepared, not only does it bring us no benefit but it even inflicts serious harm on us" (*Divine Liturgy* 34, 444D-445A). For a detailed discussion of this theme, see P. Nellas, *I peri dikaioseos tou anthropou didaskalia*, esp. 137-58. On human co-operation generally, see the observations of Kavasilas in *I Theomitor*, which are among the finest words ever written on the subject.

[79]*Life in Christ*, 641D.

and beauty of Christ and does not allow it to be attracted by evil. For how could we possibly advance towards evil when we understand the "frenzied love"[80] with which God has loved us, so much so that He came among us, made the miseries of our life His own together with our toil, our death and our sins, emptied Himself, mingled Himself with us, and made us His temples and His members.[81]

The other aspect of the study of what God has done for us is the examination "of the dignity of our nature."[82] Our members, Kavasilas explains, are members of Christ. "The Head of these members is worshipped by the cherubim, while these feet, these hands depend on His heart. . . . What could be more sacred than this body to which Christ cleaves more closely than He could by any physical union? . . . How then could we use it for anything that is not seemly? . . . We shall not move our feet, we shall not stretch out our hands towards anything evil."[83]

It is possible for us to maintain this attitude to life "if we keep the recollection of these things active in our souls, since they are members of Christ and sacred and, so to speak, a vial containing His blood."[84] These words make it clear that Kavasilas does not at this point speak emotionally or metaphorically. Beneath the lyricism of the expressions and images which he uses lies the firm foundation of the new anthropology in Christ. In order to establish his viewpoint more securely, he explains in the same chapter that "it was for the new man [Christ] that human nature was created at the beginning. It was for Him that our intellect and appetitive aspect were prepared. We have received our reason that we might know Christ, our desire that we might run towards Him; we have memory that we might bear Him within us. He is the archetype for all who have been created."[85] It is precisely for this reason that "man hastens towards Christ by his nature, his will and his thoughts, not only because of

[80]Ibid., 648A.
[81]Ibid., 644-645A.
[82]Ibid., 652A.
[83]Ibid., 648B-649A.
[84]Ibid., 648CD.
[85]Ibid., 680A.

His divinity, which is the goal of all things, but because of His other nature as well. He is the fulfilment of human love. He is the delight of our thoughts."[86] Should either our love, he continues, or our thought be turned towards anything that is not in Christ, this would constitute a manifest "turning aside from the original first principles of our nature."[87] And this is because Christ is the "subject of our thoughts."

As I have already mentioned, Kavasilas does not describe any specific form or any specific stage of the spiritual life. He wants to demonstrate the ontological foundation common to all its forms and all its stages. In this way he demonstrates the ontological foundation of the "contemplation" which the hesychasts attain after a long journey of purification and concentration within the self. The purified and unified intellect can see God and can rest in Him because He is the definitive "subject" of all human thoughts.

But at the same time he shows that a purification and transformation of the intellect based on this same ontological principle can be realized gradually—through the concentration of the thoughts on Christ, on whatever builds up the body of Christ, and on the means by which everything can be built up into the body of Christ—by all the faithful living among the cares of the world and can lead all of them to the fullness of the spiritual life. He thus proposes a kind of spiritual life suitable for the people of his own time, yet also especially applicable to conditions today.

There exist, he teaches, different conditions of life and therefore different forms of virtue. The spiritual life is lived in one way by those who "govern the state" and in another by those who "live as private citizens," in one way by those who have not bound themselves to any special obligation after baptism and in another by those who have taken vows of "virginity and poverty" and "live the monastic life." There is, however, one "obligation common to all who are named after Christ."[88] And this, at the specific stage in the dicussion

[86]Ibid., 681AB.
[87]Ibid., 681B.
[88]Ibid., 641B.

we are studying here, is the concentration of the thoughts on Christ, which is made complete in *prayer*.

It is not necessary, he explains, to find oneself in special circumstances in order to pray. "There is no need of special preparation for prayer, no need of special places or of a loud voice. . . . There is no place in which [Christ] is not present; it is impossible for Him not to be near us. For those who seek Him He is closer to them than their very heart."[89] Nor is there need for anyone to have raised himself to the heights of holiness: "For we do not call upon the Master in order that He may crown us."[90] Therefore all have the obligation to pray—even the "wicked," because "He who is called upon is good." The sacraments and prayer are the common highway for all, the common content of all forms of the spiritual life.

Through prayer all human thoughts together with their referents—persons, things, situations, concepts—are offered to Christ, and Christ is entreated to enter among them. Prayer, even if it does not attain to contemplation, leads thoughts and their content to God, illumines the intellect and all that the intellect grasps by the light of God, and thus leads man to truth. For this reason prayer, as the whole patristic tradition teaches, bestows real knowledge, and the art of prayer constitutes the true science and philosophy.

The permanent, uninterrupted communion of the human intellect with the intellect of Christ leads the former to see reality from the point of view of God. to think with an intellect closely attuned to the intellect of Christ.

This communion when fully realized constitutes a genuine transformation and christification of the intellect and bestows supreme knowledge. The Father recognizes in our intellect the intellect of His Son, and we through the mind of the Son attain to the recognition of the Father. According to St John the Evangelist it is this that constitutes the content of eternal life: "And this is eternal life, that they know Thee the only true God, and Jesus Christ whom Thou has sent" (John 17:3).

89Ibid.. 681B.
90Ibid., 681D.

5. THE CHRISTIFICATION OF THE WILL

Parallel to this is a union and communion with Christ which takes place through the will.

The will, explains Kavasilas, is expressed and activated by desire. But human desire is not satisfied with anything created. Whatever good a man succeeds in attaining, his desire always pushes him further, "since all things are inferior to Him and fall below Him. Were anyone to attain to all the good things that exist, he would still look beyond them and seek what he does not have, ignoring what he does have."[91] This does not happen because the desired good is infinite, whereas man's appetitive faculty, his function of wanting and desiring, is finite. If this were so, the finite would not have been able even to seek the infinite. On the contrary, it happens because man's appetitive faculty itself "is in proportion to that infinity and has been prepared accordingly."[92] And this human function "does not know any limit" because the Creator has "fashioned it with a view to Himself . . . so that we may be able to enjoy Him alone with complete delight."[93] Here too we may observe the application of the fundamental principle of the creation of man in the image of God. Man's will tends towards infinite good because that is how it was created from the beginning. This tendency is a constituent element of its being. This is the foundation on which Kavasilas's teaching concerning the christification of the human will is based.

Kavasilas fills out this ontological observation with a second one located, as we would say today, in the field of phenomenological anthropology. The will, he writes, is the central moving power in man. "All that is ours follows the

[91]Ibid., 708B.

[92]Ibid., 708B.

[93]Ibid., 708C. Thus before the advent of Christ no one could be truly happy, "for the object of desire was not present anywhere." Whereas "for those who have tasted of the Savior the object of desire is itself present, the object or person for which human love was prepared from the beginning as if to a model or pattern, like a treasury so huge and so broad that it is able to receive God" (Ibid., 560D).

will and moves where the will directs it."[94] Both the impetus
of the body and the movement of the thoughts are directed
by the will, as indeed is every act and in general everything
human. "In short, it is the will which, as far as we are concerned, leads us and carries us. If it is impeded in some way,
all things seize up at that point."[95]

Yet, so he continues, synthesizing the above two views
and reaching a conclusion, man desires to be happy. He lives
and exists for "well being." All the movements of his soul
press towards a true and happy "being." "We wish to exist
because we wish to be happy."[96] Consequently, because man's
true "being" is found, as we have seen, in Christ, "those
whose will has been captured entirely by the will of Christ,
and who cleave to Him completely, and He is all that they
desire and love and seek,"[97] find in Christ their true completion and their real happiness.

Within this perspective the spiritual life is revealed as a
life directed not by laws external to man but by the radical
existential demand of man for happiness. The spiritual life
is of the highest significance and value to man since it guides
his "being" towards "well being." Its content is not moral,
as the term is generally used today, or sociological or anything else peripheral, but ontological. If this were not so,
Christ would not have been something essential for man,
that "unity in which there is nothing lacking." And the
Christian Church would not have been the catholic truth of
man and of the world, but the religious expression of the
outlook, culture, society and so on of one or another people.

Furthermore, the spiritual life is revealed as the full
development and activation of the faculties and functions of
man. With a full sense of the reality of the matter, Kavasilas
insists that the will has been created in order to seek the
good, the source of which is God. Outside the good, the will,
which is the organ for attaining happiness, is subject to necessity and functions below its capacity or in a distorted way, just

94Ibid., 721C.
95Ibid., 721C.
96Ibid., 709C.
97Ibid., 721C.

as the eye, which is the organ of sight, functions below its capacity when there is no light. The human eye was created for the light, and the human will for the good. The eye without the light and the will without the good are alienated from their nature and function contrary to nature. "For it is impossible for the will itself to be alive and active unless it abides in Christ, because all good resides in Him, just as it is impossible for the eye to function without making use of light."[98] "The eye was designed for light, the ear for sound, and each is adapted to its purpose. And the desire of the soul presses on towards Christ alone. He is its home because He alone is goodness and truth and anything else for which it yearns."[99]

The call of Christ, Kavasilas teaches, touching on another aspect of the theme, is directed to all people regardless of sex, race, age, profession or social position, and regardless of whether one dwells in the "desert" or in the "city with all its tumults." The common invitation issued to all is that they "should not oppose the will of Christ."[100] The response to this call is the content of the spiritual life in its first stage. In the later stages the call is "to participate in the will of God."[101] However, in spite of the difference of degree, in all the stages and all the forms of the spiritual life its content, looked at from the aspect we are considering in this section, is the same: the participation of the human will in the will of Christ.

Since the will plays such a central role in the spiritual life, God seeks to assimilate this human function to Himself before any other. Having created heaven and earth, the sun and all the beauty of the visible and invisible worlds, He displays His wisdom and His goodness to man, in the way that ardent lovers display their finery, "in order to inspire us to love Him."[102] And when man instead of giving his love fled far from Him, God put on human nature and suffered countless evils "that He might attach Himself to the be-

[98]Ibid., 721C.
[99]Ibid., 561A.
[100]Ibid., 641C.
[101]Ibid., 701C.
[102]Ibid., 657C.

loved,"[103] "that He might turn us to Himself and persuade
us to desire Him."[104] And He did not confine Himself to this
alone but offered Himself as a redeemer on the cross, so as
to purchase man's will from him because only from within
his will could He offer him happiness. "In other respects He
was our Master and had control over our whole nature."[105]
But we kept escaping Him through our free will. "And He
did everything He could to win it. Because of the fact that it
was our will which He was seeking He did no violence to it;
He did not seize it but purchased it."[106] Thus for anyone to
accept Christ as Savior is tantamount to offering Him his will
absolutely and completely. The will of those who are saved
does not belong to them but to the Savior. This, explains
Kavasilas, is the sense of Paul's words: "You are not your
own; you were bought with a price" (1 Cor 6:19-20). It is
the transfer of the will from ourselves to Christ that constitutes salvation.[107]

The completion of the participation of the human will in
Christ, the christification of the will, is the content of the
spiritual life at its highest stage; it functions as love and is
called holiness. The saint desires "not his own self but God.
. . . He leaves self behind and goes out to God with all his
will. He forgets his own poverty and looks forward with
eagerness to these riches. . . . The power of love, then, knows
how to make lovers assimilate that which belongs to the
beloved. In the saints all the power of their will and their
desire spends itself wholly on God. They regard Him alone
as their proper good; neither the body can delight them, nor

[103]Ibid., 657D.
[104]Ibid., 688C.
[105]Ibid., 716C.
[106]Ibid., 716CD.
[107]The use of the particularly strong verb "to purchase" (*agorazein*)
by Paul and Kavasilas, the expression "you are not your own," and also
the parallel expression "slaves of Christ," may appear exaggerated and hard
to the modern reader. It is not possible for me to attempt here a deeper
analysis of them. The reader who wishes to see how freedom's highest good
is revealed in these expressions, how the Orthodox understanding of salvation is identical with the restoration within the human person of his freedom,
and how freedom operates in the process of salvation when it is undertsood in
an Orthodox way, should refer to Kavasilas's own writings or to my study,
I peri dikaioseos tou anthropou didaskalia, esp. 117-25 and 137-68.

the soul . . . nor anything else that is akin to nature and proper to it. . . . . It is as if they have gone out of themselves once and for all, and have removed their life and all their desire elsewhere, and have become ignorant of self."[108] The saints thus rejoice in whatever Christ rejoices in and grieve over whatever He grieves over. They express and make active within history the will of Christ. They speak as mouths of Christ and manifest the truth. They operate as hands of Christ and work miracles.

Abiding in love means abiding in God. " 'He who abides in love,' Scripture says, 'abides in God, and God abides in him' (1 John 4:16)."[109] Kavasilas teaches us that the true spiritual life is love. "If life is also the power that moves living things, what is it that moves those who are truly alive, whose god is God, who 'is not God of the dead but of the living' (Mark 12:27)? You will find that it is nothing but love itself. . . . What, then, may life be more fittingly called than love?"[110]

For these reasons, Kavasilas concludes, the blessed life, that is, a stable, permanent and complete happiness, is created through the human will and dwells within it. "If we examine the will of someone who lives in accordance with God, we shall find the blessed life shining within it."[111]

The above reveals clearly that communion with Christ renews man. His new being, his new activity, life, knowledge and will, the whole transformed Christlike organism with the spiritual senses and graces of the Spirit which constitute his new modes of functioning, make up the new man in Christ. All these, in my opinion, are the constituent elements of an Orthodox christological anthropology.

[108]*Life in Christ,* 708D-709A.
[109]Ibid., 721A.
[110]Ibid., 725CD.
[111]Ibid., 689A.

IV

The Fruits of the Spiritual Life

1. THE TRANSFORMATION OF CREATION INTO ECCLESIAL COMMUNION

The vivification and renewal which the Spirit of God grants to man is extended throughout the whole of creation. Kavasilas enriches his christological anthropology with his marvellous teaching on the christocentric character which creation as a whole possesses when it is exalted into Christ's body. We have already examined, in the first part of this book, the teaching of the Fathers on the organic relationship existing between man and the rest of creation. Man is truly "the link uniting all creation";[112] he has "in himself all the parts of the whole."[113]

According to Kavasilas, the portion of creation which the Logos assumed at His incarnation was not only, as we have seen, delivered from corruption, but was also changed in a fundamental way. The purpose for which the world had been created from the beginning was realized within it. What the Logos had created became through the incarnation the body of the Logos; it found outside creation the real "ground of its being."

This assumed matter, the Lord's body, henceforth functions for the rest of creation as "chrism."[114] What happens, explains Kavasilas, is akin to that which occurs in the case of a phial containing perfume. When the sides of the phial

112Cosmas Indicopleustes, *Christian Topography* 5, *PG* 88, 320A.
113Methodios of Olympus, *GCS* 27, p. 351.
114*Life in Christ*, 572A.

are in some way changed into the contents, then instead of separating the perfume from the surrounding atmosphere they enable it to pervade it. "Similarly, when our nature is deified in the Savior's body, there is nothing which separates the human race from God."[115] "Flesh was deified and human nature received God Himself as its hypostasis, the barrier now becoming myrrh."[116] In this way that which used to separate man from God now unites him to Him. Chrismated created nature became a bearer of divinity, body of Christ, anointed nature, ecclesial communion. And that which in consequence is grafted onto the Lord's body is really transformed into the body of Christ, becomes Church or ecclesial communion. The Church is creation grafted onto Christ and vivified by the Spirit.

According to Paul, the primary and highest mystery of our faith is Christ—the incarnation and the divine dispensations by which the Logos saved the world (cf. 1 Tim 3:16). This primary mystery or sacrament which is Christ is refracted, according to Kavasilas, and becomes concrete and active within time through the sacramental mysteries, by which the Church is organized and by which it lives. Kavasilas teaches that an internal identity exists between the historical body of Jesus and the Church, between the energies of the concrete body of the Lord and those of the sacraments. The sacraments truly extend the functions of that body and make its life available in actuality. "The sacred rites which are celebrated belong to the incarnation of the Lord."[117] For this reason the Church is created, is organized and lives within the sacraments. "The Church is represented in the sacraments not in a symbolic way but as limbs are represented in the heart, as branches in the root, and, as the Lord has said, as shoots in the vine. For here is no mere sharing of a name, or analogy by resemblance, but an objective identity."[118]

The movement is two-fold. Christ is extended within time through the energy of the Spirit, and the world is assumed by

[115]Ibid., 572B.
[116]Ibid., 572A.
[117]*Divine Liturgy* 12, 392D.
[118]*Divine Liturgy* 38, 452CD.

Him. Christ is extended in the process of assuming the world. The Church is not a static situation. It is a dynamic, transforming movement. It is the perpetual marriage in space and time of the Creator with His creation, the enduring mingling of the created with the uncreated. Through this unconfused mingling in Christ of created with uncreated nature, the created is subsumed into the flesh of Christ, is rehabilitated sacramentally, is transformed, becomes body of Christ and lives as such.

The manner in which this transformation is effected is through the sacraments, since, precisely in the way we have seen, they constitute an extension of the incarnation and of the saving acts of the Lord. It is on the sacraments that Kavasilas bases his whole ecclesiology, that is to say, his teaching on what might be called christocentric cosmology—in other words, his teaching on the new creation, the world which in its entirety is transformed, is organized and lives as Christ's body.

The teaching of Kavasilas on the sacraments, however, is very different from that which was shaped by scholastic theology, which defined them as the visible rites which communicate invisible divine grace, and fixed their number as seven.

Kavasilas regards the eucharist as the central sacrament which re-presents the economy of the Savior; that is to say, it makes the economy of the Savior actively present once again in each specific place and time, and, moreover, also makes actively present the baptism and chrismation which introduce man to the eucharist. From the eucharist flows a host of sacred rites which embrace the whole of life and all the dimensions of human existence in the world. A new mode of life is thus created together with a new organization of the relationships of human beings with each other, with God and with the world, a new organization in Christ of the communion of mankind with the world. The new life which Christ bestows is called by Kavasilas sacramental life. And those signs of the place and time within which the divine life encounters human life and transforms it—the very fact of the meeting and the transformation as well as the acts, that is, the rites or procedures within which the transformation is realized—he calls sacraments.

By contrast, according to the scholastics there is an external element in the sacraments, which is the visible sign, and distinct from this there is the essence of the sacrament, which is the invisible divine grace. For Kavasilas and for the Orthodox patristic tradition in general this separation does not exist. In baptism the priest first consecrates the water, and in this consecrated water the person is baptized. In the divine eucharist the bread and wine become truly and in actuality the body and blood of Christ. In chrismation the believer is anointed with consecrated oil. The body of man, and consequently man himself, cannot be comprehended except in organic union with the rest of creation.

Within this perspective Kavasilas teaches that the sacraments constitute the "gate" and the "way" by which the life of God enters into creation, liberates it from sin and death, gives it life and sanctifies it. "The Lord opened up this way by coming to us, and unlocked this gate by entering into the world. When He returned to the Father He did not permit the gate to be closed, but comes through it from the Father to sojourn among men, or rather, He is always present, is with us and will be with us for ever. . . . Therefore 'this is none other than the house of God' (Gen 28:17)."[119] "Through these sacred mysteries as if through windows the Sun of Righteousness enters into this dark world. He puts to death the life which is conformed to this world and raises up that which transcends this world. The Light of the world overcomes the world . . . and introduces a life which is enduring and immortal into a body which is mortal and subject to change."[120] The two words which I would stress in the above passages, which demonstrate the understanding which Kavasilas has of the saved world, are "house" and "body" of God. And the sacraments are the "windows" through which the Sun of Righteousness illuminates the "house," the arteries through which the life of the Head vivifies the "body."

The full union of the created with the uncreated within

---

[119]*Life in Christ*, 504CD.
[120]Ibid., 504BC.

the sacraments powerfully "overcomes" the limits of place and time without destroying them, and adds new dimensions to them. Creation, reassembled and restructured sacramentally —which is called Church or ecclesial communion—now has new dimensions, new functions and new life, the dimensions, functions and life of the body of the risen Lord. All things henceforth can be assembled and can live within creation in a new manner which is neither purely human nor exclusively divine but "theanthropic." Liturgical space and liturgical time are created. Within this liturgical space and time the unconfused mingling of earthly with heavenly life, of history with eternity, is realized. "The body of Christ is one . . . the body of the faithful is one . . . and this body is divided neither by time nor by place."[121] "By sojourning among us He has set us among the angels and established us in the heavenly choir."[122]

The union is so fundamental and so complete that it does not merely recall creation to the prelapsarian state of the "home" in paradise, but creates a new home and a new paradise which are much higher than the former ones, namely the Church. The world is no longer merely the house of man but is the house of the living God.[123] God who before the incarnation was "without a house" as far as creation was concerned, now finds a created place in which to sojourn and dwell.[124] Thus not only the altar on which God is worshipped but God Himself is found from now on within creation, and the human race becomes the family of God. The transformation goes even deeper. The Church is not only House and Family but Body of God.

2. THEOCENTRIC HUMANISM

In this new situation human beings live the life of love[125]

[121]John Chrysostom, *Homily on the words, "Know this also ..."* 6, PG 56, 277.
[122]*Divine Liturgy* 20, 413A.
[123]Ibid., 18, 409B.
[124]*Theomitor*, 144.
[125]*Life in Christ*, 725D.

in freedom and joy, sensing the presence of God,[126] contemplating His glory and receiving His radiance.[127] The
saints, these sons of the Father, the members and friends of
the Son, the stewards and heirs of the House, receive the ray
of "the Lord, the Spirit" and reflect it actively. "Would you
like me to demonstrate this?" asks Chrysostom in a passage
cited by Kavasilas. "Consider Paul, whose garments were
efficacious (Acts 19:12), and Peter, whose shadow even had
power (Acts 5:12). . . . . They bore the image of the King
and their radiance was unapproachable."[128] The new mode
of human life, the new Christian ethos, has a Godlike or
Christlike character, or more precisely a theocentric and christocentric character.

Holiness, in fact, has nothing but God as its source. "The
saints come to be holy and blessed in this way because of the
Blessed One who lives with them. . . . They derive not a
single thing from themselves or from human nature or effort
. . . but are holy because of the Holy One, and righteous and
wise because of the Righteous and Wise One who lives with
them."[129] Any human virtue whatsoever has real value only
in so far as it is a virtue of Christ, because only when it is
incorporated into Christ and consequently spiritual ("born
of the Spirit") can it surpass the biological bounds of corruption and death, can it live and have real value, or be
"useful tribute,"[130] in eternity. " 'Be merciful' not with human
mercy 'as your Father is merciful' (Luke 6:36), and 'love
one another even as I have loved you' (John 13:34)."[131]
The faithful are called to love "with the affection of Christ
Jesus with which Paul yearned (Phil 1:8),"[132] and to have
"the peace of Christ" and the love "with which the Father
has loved the Son" (cf John 17:26). For just as the birth
"is a divine and supernatural one, so too the life and regime

[126]Ibid., 561D.
[127]Ibid., 564B.
[128]Ibid., 564C, quoting John Chrysostom, *Homily* 7 *on* 2 *Cor.,* PG
61, 449.
[129]*Life in Christ*, 613A.
[130]Ibid., 616D.
[131]Ibid., 613D.
[132]Ibid., 613D.

and philosophy and all these things are new and spiritual."[133]

The phrase "all these things" refers to the various dimensions and functions of man. These functions are called to be purified and changed, to be filled with the Spirit of God and to function in a new manner closely attuned to the functions of the body of Christ. This will take place, not through the abandoning of these functions, but through a specific process of change and transformation which harnesses the work of man to the grace of God. The "good olive," that is, the new existence and life which Christ bestows, is grafted through the sacraments and the wholly spiritual struggle of man onto the "wild olive," that is, onto man's biological existence and psychosomatic constitution. And the common fruit, the new way of life, is that of the good olive.[134]

The father, for example, who begets his child on the biological level is also called to have it born spiritually in the Church. Spiritual fatherhood leads to its own "end"; it gives eternal value and incorrupt spiritual content to biological fatherhood and in this sense transforms it.

Similarly, the continual process of renewal, thanks to which the human biological organism is kept alive (*i.e.*, the renewal of the cells which keeps the body alive, and of the processes which prevent the whole human psychic world together with its emotional and cognitive aspects from becoming moribund or dead), is completed and radically transformed by the real rebirth of baptism which grants man a spiritual life which is permanent and incorrupt.

The love of two persons which leads them to marriage, yet which, however true it may be, is subject as created love to corruption, is strengthened by the Church's sacrament and broadened to an infinite degree; it is made eternal; it is changed in a radical way; it is transformed without being abolished into a dimension of the love which God has for the world. The union of husband and wife is grafted onto the great mystery of the union of Christ with the world, which raises the world—and the new family which is being created—into ecclesial communion.

133Ibid., 616A.
134Ibid., 592C.

In the same manner, as Kavasilas explains in those of his treatises which have a social content, the justice which governs relations between human beings and organizes their social life, in order to become really effective, is called to be transformed into a Godlike justice, that is, into a justice which reflects the justice of God and activates it within society, for God's justice is that sublime harmony and love in which God originally created the world and now recreates it in Christ.

From the above examples it becomes clear that all the dimensions and functions of life are called to be transformed in Christ and are capable of being so.

Moreover, it becomes clear that the spiritual life is not an escape from the world but a transformation of it. It is not a change of place but a change of manner of existing and living. We live in God, writes Kavasilas, "in this way: . . . we remove our life from this visible world to the unseen world by changing not our place but our life in all its aspects." And he explains the cause of this: "It was not we ourselves who moved towards God or ascended to Him; on the contrary, it was He who came and descended to us. . . . It was He who came down to earth and retrieved the image . . . and lifted it up and stopped it from straying; and this He did, not moving from here but remaining on earth. He made us heavenly beings and established us in a heavenly life, not by leading us up to heaven but by bending heaven and bringing it down to us."[135]

This double truth leads to the conclusion that within the new state of affairs created on earth by the sacraments the faithful can live the fullness of the spiritual life without demanding any special external circumstances in order to do so. The liturgical and sacramental life of the Church is constituted in such a way that it is precisely the circumstances which it itself transforms.

It is not indispensable to the spiritual life that the believer should abandon his profession, writes Kavasilas. "It is no less possible for us to exercize our skills, and there is no obstacle to any occupation whatsoever. The general may command his army, the farmer may till the soil, the artisan

[135]Ibid., 504AB.

may practise his craft."[136] All the dimensions of life—professional, artistic, intellectual—and any other of those functions
which constitute, as we have seen, the "garments of skin,"
can and should be grafted onto the sacramental life. They
then become again not simply "powers which enable life to
be sustained," but more importantly "spiritual senses and
functions," which instead of hindering the spiritual life assist
it and, moreover, become means by which the faithful assume
the world and incorporate it into the Church. Thus our
historical life is grafted onto Christ and becomes His body.
At this point the social mission of Orthodoxy and its great
transforming power become plain.

"One need not undertake extremes of asceticism," Kavasilas continues, "or eat unaccustomed food, or change one's
dress, or ruin one's health, or attempt any extraordinary
feat."[137] For a person to separate himself from human society
and live the monastic life is a noble form of existence; but it
does not constitute an essential precondition of the spiritual
life, and the believer is not inferior if he lives the fullness of
the sacramental life while remaining within society. In spite
of the difference of form, the essential content of the spiritual
life is in both cases the same, namely, a real participation
in the cross and resurrection of Christ, which is the real
death of a person to sin, his rebirth as a member of the body
of Christ, and his entire filling with the Holy Spirit, who
is the provider of the spiritual life.

The concrete and detailed presentation of this truth is
the great contribution of Kavasilas to the ecclesiastical life
and the theology of the fourteenth century and to the history
of Christian theology in general. This teaching of his played
a decisive part in the refutation and the radical rejection of
the accusations made by the intellectual humanists of his day
against the monks. The humanists regarded the attempt of
the monks to attain a union of the body as well as the soul
with God as a gross lapse into materiality. Kavasilas showed
that not only can the body be united with God, when its
functions are rendered healthy through bodily ascesis and it

[136]Ibid., 657D.
[137]Ibid., 657D-660A.

is filled with the Spirit, but that the same is true even of life in the world and of the world itself. "For everything created by God is good, and nothing is to be rejected if it is received with thanksgiving" (1 Tim 4:4): when the world's eucharistic mode of functioning is restored and it is filled through the sacraments with the Spirit, it can be united with God and transformed into His body, thus constituting the Church.

Nicolas Kavasilas is clearly situated in the Orthodox biblical-patristic tradition in general and in the school of St Gregory Palamas in particular. He showed plainly that the created is called to be united with the uncreated God, and that it can do so provided that it continues until death wholly to deny the autonomy which constitutes the kernel and productive cause of sin. By supporting within the specific conditions of the fourteenth century the work of St Gregory Palamas, he thus revealed Orthodox truth and contributed to the condemnation of the heretical humanism of his age.[138] But with the same clarity he showed that the whole of creation and in particular all the forms and functions of life can, when their autonomy is denied, be united through the sacraments with God. Through this last point in his teaching, whereby he absorbed and refashioned as many of the preoccupations of the fourteenth-century humanists as were compatible with Christianity, he laid the theological foundations for a theocentric humanism.

At the same time, by showing that the spiritual life can be lived in its fullness even in the world and by sketching the basic lines of such a way of life, he played a leading part in the vital task of channeling the great hesychastic renaissance of the fourteenth century into the world as a renaissance of liturgical and sacramental life. He thus created the basis for an Orthodox social spirituality. The significance of this work for our age is evident, and it needs to be continued.

But equally valuable is Kavasilas's teaching on the new organization which the world receives when it is transformed into ecclesial communion, and moreover, on the specific and indeed crucial problem of the organization of this same

[138]At the council held in Constantinople in 1351. For details see J. Meyendorff, *A Study of Gregory Palamas* (London 1964), 27.

ecclesial communion. The following points in Kavasilas's teaching should also be noted.

The reconstruction of the world within the Church is successfully accomplished by the liturgical broadening and reorganizing of the basic dimensions which define the world, namely time and space.

The ecclesiastical feasts scattered throughout the year are precisely the focal points which organize time in a new dimension. Easter, Christmas, the fifteenth of August, the Feast of the Apostles and all the other feasts, with their fasts and their services, give time a new direction and dimension. The horizontal movement of time within creation is in this way transcended without being abolished. The daily commemorations of martyrs and saints and also the weekly and daily cycle of the services have the same aim, which is the broadening and reorganization of time. This transformation of time is realized and revealed, as we have seen above in a more detailed way, pre-eminently in the divine eucharist, in which all the services, fasts and feasts culminate.

The new organization of space is achieved in a similar way. This too is realized above all in the divine eucharist, but it is not exhausted by it precisely because the eucharist itself is not exhausted in the two-hour Sunday celebration. The neighborhood within which people pass their conventional daily lives changes when it is organized as a parish around its church, and with it people's lives also change, since in the Church people are not characterized by their sociological attributes (rich, poor, cultured, uneducated, etc.) but are recognized by their baptismal names and are called to live as brothers and sisters. In the same way a province changes when it is organized as an ecclesiastical see and lives as one, and the whole world can change when it desires to live and confront its problems in accordance with the model of the apostolic and ecumenical councils, that is, with a common mind under the inspiration of the Spirit: "It has seemed good to the Holy Spirit and to us" (Acts 15:28). But even the smallest human undertakings, the building of a house, the opening of a shop, the sowing of a field, change when the faithful consciously unite them with the Church's blessing.

The house, the shop, the field are no longer simple portions of our known space; they become cells of the ecclesiastical organism within which human beings, without shedding the specific framework of earthly life, can live the infinite heavenly life. This different content and different organization of the familiar conventions under which human life rolls on is the great gift of the Church to the world. It is the transformation to which Christ calls the world.

3. THE UNITY AND ORGANIZATION
OF THE CHURCH

But the Church, as a specific community of human persons, as a visible organism established in space and time, has in itself certain more specific organizational axes. These specific axes, around which its organization is articulated and its sacramental life develops, are according to Kavasilas three in number.

The first is the sacred *altar* which alone of all creation, except for human beings, is anointed with holy oil. And the holy oil, as Dionysios the Areopagite says and as Kavasilas reiterates, "represents Jesus."[139] Thus there exists within creation a specific sensible sign in which the sacramental presence of the Creator is certain and permanent. For this reason the altar is "the beginning from which every sacred rite proceeds,"[140] the "basis" and "root"[141] of the Church, the "summary of good gifts."[142] This stone has been exalted by the chrism and constitutes henceforth in truth and actuality a hand of Christ holding, performing and providing the sacraments. "The altars imitate the Savior's hand. We receive the bread, the body of Christ, and drink His blood from the anointed table as if from that undefiled hand."[143] In and through the altar, or the antimension which sometimes replaces

139*Life in Christ,* 633C.
140Ibid., 625C.
141Ibid., 628A.
142Ibid., 632A.
143Ibid., 577D-580A.

it, Christ is sacramentally present and active. For this reason the altar is that which "makes the gift sacred."[144]

But the altar is established and consecrated by the *bishop*. The whole rite of the consecration of a church, as analyzed by Kavasilas in the fifth chapter of *The Life in Christ*, is designed to show that the archetype of the altar is the bishop, because "of visible things only human nature is truly capable of being a temple of God and an altar."[145] Just as the craftsman first has in mind that which he creates, so the bishop, the living altar of God, impresses on the stone that which he himself is. Furthermore, "he anoints the altar with wine and oil, which have a sweet smell, the former delighting us . . . the latter being also useful to our life,"[146] so that before the divine chrism is used, which "represents Jesus," "all human things" should be brought to the holy table. For only a really human table can become an altar of God. At this point, too, the anthropological and cosmological dimensions of Kavasilas's ecclesiology become manifest.

The third fundamental dimension of the organization of the world transformed into ecclesial communion is that of the *saints*. This is the reason why in the rite of consecration the central position after the chrism and the bishop is given to the relics of the saints. "Because the chrism is the power of the altar, it was necessary that the matter subject to this power should be appropriate, for it would work better in this way, just as fire and light, I believe, also work better through suitable bodies."[147] But "there is nothing more akin to the sacraments of Christ than the martyrs, since they have body, spirit, manner of death and all other things in common with Christ. He was with them while they were alive, and after they died. . . . He is present and mingled with this mute dust."[148]

It becomes clear from the above that according to Kavasilas there is an interior relationship between the altar, the bishop and holiness. And this relationship is their common center

---

[144]Ibid., 580B.
[145]Ibid., 629C.
[146]Ibid., 633AB.
[147]Ibid., 636A.
[148]Ibid., 636B.

and content, namely Christ. Just as the altar "is Jesus,"[149] so too the real hierarch who celebrates the eucharist is Christ: "And indeed it is said that it is Christ who offers this sacrifice."[150] But the relics of the saints too actually bring Christ among us and in this way constitute further sacraments, since "if it is possible to find the Savior in any visible thing and to contain Him there, it would be in these bones."[151]

These three axes around which the organization and unity of the Church is constituted cannot be separated from each other. The bishop has need of the altar and the saints, the altar of the bishop and the relics, the saints of the bishop and the altar. Each of the three finds its fullness in the other two and is defined by them. All three constitute preconditions for, and attain their culmination in, the divine eucharist, in which the truth and unity of the Church is realized and revealed in its fullness. If one of the three is lacking, the eucharist cannot be celebrated.

A disturbance of the balance, a one-sided emphasis on any one of the three, leads to the shattering of unity and the disorganization of ecclesiastical life, and so inevitably to the shattering and disorganization of the Church as the unified body of Christ. Many of the heresies and schisms which may be observed in the Church are the result of such a disturbance, as also are many of the difficulties which the Orthodox Church faces today in realizing the fullness of its visible unity and organization.

But within the above catholic ecclesiological perspective of Kavasilas, a perspective at once christological, pneumatological and cosmological, it is possible for the solution to these problems to be found, together with the solutions to many other similarly crucial problems which confront the Church today. These other problems relate not only to the Church's unity and organization but also to its pastoral and missionary character, its relationship with the world, and the attempt to define a contemporary asceticism, a contemporary morality and so on. Since, as Kavasilas constantly emphasizes,

[149]Ibid., 580A.
[150]*Divine Liturgy* 49, 477A.
[151]*Life in Christ*, 636B.

the Church is the world transformed into the body of Christ and vivified by the Spirit, the problems of the Church are not the internal concerns of a closed community, but by their very nature are the problems of the structure, unity and life of the world.

It is evident that Kavasilas invites the ecclesiological and theological debates of our time to transcend their historico-philological, narrowly confessional, or merely canonical character, to leave the scholar's study and come out into the broader spaces of the divine economy, that is, of the work which the Father has performed "until now" in order to transform the world—including our own contemporary world —through the Spirit into His Son's body.

V

The Cosmic Body of Christ the Savior: The Eschatological Transformation of the Universe

The ecclesiology of Kavasilas, together with his anthropology and his whole teaching on the spiritual life, is illuminated internally by the expected coming of the Lord.

We have seen that the Logos deified the human nature which He assumed and that the blessed flesh which was conceived from the Holy Spirit and the Virgin Mary is the source and living place of the spiritual life. We have also seen that the bread of the eucharist is truly and in actuality the body of the Lord, and that the world is grafted onto this body by the sacraments and is transformed into the Church. All this teaching of Kavasilas leads finally to the doctrine that this one body, that is, the body of the historical Jesus which is the bread of the eucharist and the body of the Church, will shine forth at the second coming as the great cosmic body of Christ the Savior.

"This bread, this body, to which people in this life draw near in order to carry it away from the altar, is that which in the age to come will appear to all eyes upon the clouds (cf. Matt 24:30) and in one instant of time will display its splendor to the east and to the west like lightning."[152] The radiance of divinity within which the saints live even in this life will not abandon them. On the contrary, when Christ appears, "even this dust [the dead bodies of the saints] will display its proper beauty, when it will appear as a member of

[152]Ibid., 624AB.

157

that lightning (cf. Luke 17:24) and will be made like the sun, and will emit the same radiance."[153] The bodies of the saints will shine with the light of that Body.

Kavasilas, following Paul, describes the general resurrection at the second coming by the phrase "being caught up." For "we shall be caught up together with them in the clouds," says Paul, "to meet the Lord in the air" (1 Thes 4:17). For this reason the Lord called the saints "eagles." For "wherever the body is, there the eagles will be gathered together," says the evangelist (Matt 24:28). When the ropes are cut which keep great weights suspended, explains Kavasilas, they fall heavily to the ground. The same will also happen to the bodies of the saints, which "when freedom appears will rush towards Christ with an irresistible motion so as to find their proper place."[154] The risen body of the incarnate Creator will shine forth as the real center of universal attraction which will draw all things to itself.

Every person will then find his body again. "Bones and parts and members coming together with their head" will make up the human "wholeness." Something similar "will happen to the common Head of all, Christ the Savior." As soon as the Head flashes like lightning in the clouds, "He will receive His own members from every direction," in order that in this way that great Body may be constituted.[155]

But the members of the cosmic body will be persons. For this reason even the Body will be simultaneously Family, Eucharist and Choir. "For when the Master appears the choir of good servants will stand around Him, and when He shines brightly they too will shine. How wonderful will that sight be: to see a countless multitude of luminaries upon the clouds, to be led up as chosen people to a festive celebration beyond any comparison, to be a company of gods surrounding God, of the beautiful surrounding Him who is perfect Beauty, or servants surrounding the Master."[156] The saints in the age to come will be "gods surrounding God, fellow-heirs

[153]Ibid., 624A.
[154]Ibid., 624C.
[155]Ibid., 624B.
[156]Ibid., 649BC.

with Him of the same inheritance, co-rulers with Him of the same Kingdom."[157] The God-man will shine forth as "God in the midst of gods," as the all-beautiful leader who will lead the radiant choir of the saints in the dance: "the beautiful leader of the beautiful choir."[158]

This image is reminiscent of the Apocalypse, that new cosmogony within Christ the Savior: "Christ descends from heaven like lightning to earth, while the earth holds up in turn other suns to the Sun of Righteousness, and all things are filled with light."[159]

[157]Ibid., 520C.
[158]Ibid., 624B.
[159]Ibid., 649D.

PART THREE

THE ANTHROPOLOGICAL AND COSMOLOGICAL CONTEXT OF UNION WITH GOD

A Study of the Service of the Great Canon

I
The Cosmological Context

On Wednesday evening, about the fourth hour of the night, we assemble in church. When the priest has said the blessing, and after the Six Psalms, the Alleluia and the Hymns to the Holy Trinity ... we read the Life of St. Mary of Egypt. Then, after Psalm 50, we begin at once to sing the Canon slowly and with compunction, making the sign of the cross and bowing three times at each troparion, and saying, "Have mercy upon me, O God, have mercy upon me."

These directions from the Triodion[1] on how the Great Canon is to be sung describe not merely the ritual but also the general anthropological and cosmological context in which the service is celebrated. The rubrics define the conditions under which prayer can be real, effective and fruitful, that is, the setting within which a person can concentrate all the as-

[1]English translation: *The Lenten Triodion,* translated by Mother Mary and Archimandrite Kallistos Ware (London & Boston 1978). All the quotations from the Great Canon are cited in this translation, lightly adapted.

The Great Canon by St Andrew, Archbishop of Crete (*c.* 660-740), is sung or read at Matins on Thursday morning (i.e. during the night between Wednesday evening and Thursday morning) in the fifth week of Lent; also in a divided form, at Compline from Monday until Thursday in the first week of Lent. It contains about 260 stanzas, referring to persons and incidents in the Old and New Testaments, with the penitential refrain before each stanza, "Have mercy upon me, O God, have mercy upon me." The *Life* of St Mary of Egypt, by Patriarch Sophronios of Jerusalem (*c.* 560-638), is also read at the service; St Mary herself is commemorated on the fifth Sunday in Lent. After a life of extreme sinfulness in Alexandria, she underwent a dramatic conversion during a visit to Jerusalem, and spent her later life as a solitary in the desert beyond the Jordan. The "Six Psalms," read at the start of Matins, are 3, 37(38), 62(63), 87(88), 102(103) and 142(143).

pects of his existence—intellect, will, conscience, emotions, senses, body—on God and, by adhering to Him constantly and laboriously, can purify them, integrate and illuminate them, and so offer them to God and unite them with Him.

The rising at the fourth hour of the night—about midnight—, the assembly in the church, the blessing of the priest, the singing of the Six Psalms—the time during which they are recited symbolizing the period of the Second Coming, and therefore with darkness and absolute stillness reigning in the church—and immediately afterwards a burst of joy with the hymn of creation in the presence of the Triune God—the Alleluia and the hymns to the Holy Trinity—and then the recitation of the psalter, which like a trumpet-call prepares the faithful for the long nocturnal struggle: all these are the first elements which restructure our prevailing sense of time and space and so create the other, equally real conditions under which prayer, the supreme work of man, can take place.

Thus far the service follows the basic framework of every celebration of Matins. In what follows it assumes a distinctive character because of the special content and specific aim of the service of the Great Canon. The Life of St. Mary of Egypt is read, so that the intellect and will of the believer may be detached from love for the world and, following in the footsteps of the saint, may be guided into the heart of the desert, into the heart of the mystery of repentance.

Thus prepared, the faithful recite the psalm of repentance (Psalm 50) standing, and then immediately afterwards the marathon struggle of the Great Canon begins, in which the whole of the human person is invited to participate.

Come, wretched soul, with thy flesh to the Creator of all. Make confession to Him, and abstain henceforth from thy past brutishness; and offer to God tears of repentance.[2]

The soul draws the body, prepared by fasting and vigils, to a ceaseless veneration—three bows with signs of the cross at each of the 260 troparia of the Canon—and to spiritual tears,

[2]Canticle 1.

so that our prayer may truly become a confession from the depths of the heart, a cry of the human person for his lost rationality.

Another factor which marks out the new and real context within which the service is celebrated, that is to say, the new dimensions which space and time assume when they are reconstituted, consists in the persons who apart from the faithful are actually operative in the act of worship.

First is the Triune God. It is around His throne that the faithful assemble. The night, which through the darkness and the silence stills the senses of the body, the Alleluia, the hymns to the Holy Trinity sung at the beginning of the service, the iconography of the church, all help the human person to turn towards the Triune Deity, to place himself in His presence.

To Thee I raise
the great thrice-holy hymn
that is sung on high.[3]

The aim is that the faithful gathered together in the church should find themselves again in their Father's House, that the world should change through repentance and prayer, and that the ancient Home should be reconstituted in the Church.

Above all, the second person of the Holy Trinity is actively present with an effectiveness which we should call natural, since the created portion of our world which He assumed and rendered infinite by making it His body is the Church, within which our space and time find their new dimensions, those dimensions which allow us to celebrate acts of worship. The assembly of the faithful takes place literally in the body of Christ, Christ being our House.

But the incarnate Logos, the Lord Jesus, is present with an immediate, existential effectiveness. He is the loving Redeemer, the crucified Bridegroom, who wounds the hearts of the faithful with His love and calls them to a mystical erotic union. The interwoven structure of the service of the Great Canon, as we unravel it troparion by troparion, makes it clear

[3]Canticle 4.

that the prayer of the faithful is not a monologue but one side
of a dialogue which takes place in the mystical depths of
human existence.

Next it is the Mother of God who is present in a similarly
effective way. Her own body is the body of the God-man, the
body which is the Church. Mary is the *Theogennitria*, she who
gave birth to God. Within her the great marvel was realized
that one of the Trinity should become that which we are. She
is the Gate and the Ladder which unites earth with heaven,
which causes a saving breach to be made in the boundary en-
closing our time and space, and even now already brings into
the world things which transcend it.

We praise thee, we bless thee,
we venerate thee, O Mother of God:
for thou hast given birth to One of the undivided Trinity,
and thou hast opened the heavenly places
to us on earth.[4]

The Mother of God is moreover the loving consoler of
the faithful in the arid time of fasting, their champion in the
night-long struggle of prayer, the guide leading to Christ, the
intercessor for sins, the conductor of the bride in the mystic
union. She is present from the beginning of the service to its
end. The faithful converse also with her as they do with
Christ.

Furthermore, St Mary of Egypt is likewise present. The
reading of her life does not have as its aim simply to move
the faithful. It plays in the service an organic part which is at
once deeper and more real. The Orthodox faithful know very
well that the feast day of a saint is not a simple honoring of
a holy person or a recollection of his life for didactic reasons.
Rather, it is a real participation in his life, his struggles, his
victory and his glory. The reading of his life takes place in
order to bring the saint amongst us in a true and real manner
with his whole life and all his struggles. For the same reason
his relics are carried in procession and are set in a visible place
in the church, or his icon if there are no relics, and the faith-

4Canticle 7, *Theotokion.*

ful are anointed with the oil of the lamp which burns before
his icon or relics. The reading of the life of the saint is a
liturgical act. It takes place within another form of time,
liturgical time, and together with all the other ritual elements
it creates another form of space, liturgical space.

Within this new space-time continuum the actions which
are performed and the words which are spoken have other
dimensions and other connotations, a different kind of com-
prehensiveness and fruitfulness. Thus the liturgical reading of
the life of St Mary makes the saint present in the assembly of
the faithful in a sacramental manner, so that she can accom-
pany them and struggle with them in the contest of repentance and prayer. For this reason, at the end of each canticle
of the Great Canon there are two troparia in which the faithful address themselves to her:

> *He whom thou hast loved, O Mother,*
> *whom thou hast desired,*
> *in whose footsteps thou hast followed:*
> *He it was who found thee and gave thee repentance,*
> *for He alone is God compassionate.*
> *Pray to Him without ceasing,*
> *that we may be delivered from passions and distress.*[5]

In the same sacramental way St Andrew, the author of the
Canon, is also present. The Church has incorporated into his
Canon at the end of each canticle a troparion which is ad-
dressed to the saint himself. Of course scholars who wish to
make a scientific study of the Canon leave these "later" and
"spurious" troparia to one side. Their aim is to arrive at an
appreciation of the poetry of Andrew of Crete and to assign
it its place within the history of Byzantine literature. In the
same way scientific theologians try to disinter the theological
concepts which lie hidden in the genuine portion of the
Canon. For scholars the confusion of epochs which character-
izes the text of the hymn is strange and impermissible.

But for the Church there is no confusion. In the Synaxary,
which as at every celebration of Matins is read after the sixth

[5]Canticle 7.

canticle and sets out the reason for the liturgical assembly, its content and its aim, the Church explains what the Great Canon is, who its author is, why it is linked with the Life of St Mary of Egypt, which was written in the seventh century by Sophronios, Patriarch of Jerusalem; and generally it gives as much historical information as it deems necessary. But the Church lives and moves in the depths of a dimension cutting across time, which although it contains the monodimensional time which is defined by historical data surpasses it by far. In the depths of this dimension the various moments of historical time are encountered simultaneously, and thus it is not at all strange that St Andrew, the eighth-century archbishop of Crete and author of the Great Canon, should be present each time the Church celebrates this service of his and should himself initiate the faithful into the work of prayer and repentance.[6] In other words, through this as through all the other ecclesiastical acts the faithful enter into a depth of time in which "times are made contemporary," according to the profound expression of the Epistle to Diognetos;[7] and within the Church, which as the body of Christ is a different kind of space from that which we normally experience, they become the contemporaries of St Andrew, St Mary, all the saints, the Mother of God and Christ, and dwellers with them in the same house. In these other dimensions which our familiar space-time acquires, persons are deepened and extended, are made infinite without losing their specific hypostasis, and words and events are likewise deepened and extended, since their significance is enriched to an infinite degree.

We find it difficult today to understand the deeply rational nature of ecclesiastical acts and practices—sacraments, services, festal cycles, prayer, ascesis, repentance—because we are hindered by a monodimensional, pedestrian concept of space and time. But within the Church another cosmology holds sway. This different conception of space-time is expressed by Byzantine architecture and iconography and is also presupposed by Byzantine hymnography. The architectonic whole,

[6]"O Andrew, Bishop of Crete, best of guides, leading us to the mysteries of repentance" (Canticle 3).

[7]*To Diognetos* 12, 9, *PG* 2, 1185.

the icons, the hymns—"Today He hangs upon the cross," "Come, let us be crucified with Him"— are not parables or verbal patterns, the creation of a well-endowed imagination, but express a reality in precisely the same way that the new birth which is granted by baptism, and the communion of the body and blood of Christ which takes place in the divine eucharist, are not metaphors but realities. Unless we take seriously the different cosmological and anthropological settings within which the Church lives and moves, it is impossible for us to understand Byzantine art or biblical, patristic and liturgical texts, and it is equally impossible for us to understand the rationality and reality underlying the specific manner in which the Church's life is constructed as an active, decisive, salvific reorganization and refashioning of the limited dimensions and functions of the created world and the created being of man.

Within this other ecclesiastical perspective, in which creation is raised to the level of a sacrament, that is to say, in which it finds in Christ its deep harmony, its true dimensions and its full mode of functioning, we can understand that the Great Canon, as the author composed it and as the Church celebrates it, is something radically different from a literary text susceptible to analysis by the techniques of modern academic philology, or a treatise in which scientific theology can identify doctrinal concepts. But, more precisely, we can say that taken as a whole the Great Canon is indeed a literary text, since with its deep harmony, its true—infinite—dimensions and its full—theanthropic—mode of functioning, it helps man to enter into that other time and other space, some of the dimensions of which true art hints at and sees and struggles to express. Taken as a whole, it is also a theological treatise, since within it thought, art and historical information, all functioning as prayer, find their true dimensions and their full mode of activity, becoming means which lead man to repentance, that is, to the resolution to change and refashion himself and his environment. Taken as a whole, it is a theological treatise, since it is not a scholarly dissertation but an ecclesiastical liturgical act, that is, an act which changes man and the whole world and saves them.

In this new ecclesiastical space-time a number of different

recollections predominate, recollections of the persons and
events of sacred history. According to the Synaxary, the author
of the Great Canon, "having collected and assembled the
whole history of the Old and New Testaments, composed
the present poem, beginning with Adam and continuing up
to the Ascension of Christ and the preaching of the Apostles."

It is well known that for the Orthodox tradition the line
from Adam to Christ defines the truth of history, the deeper
content and goal of the historical process. Thus the Holy
Scriptures from Genesis to the Apocalypse constitute for the
Church the sacred book of the world, precisely because they
contain the central stages of this deeper historical process.

To this deep river, which leads from the Beginning to the
End, the faithful of every age bring whatever concerns themselves and their world, so that by baptizing these things in it,
by identifying them with the current of this river, they may
transfer them from the ephemeral—from "the flux of time"—
to the permanent, from the narrow limits of daily life or life
in a particular age to that which has its being in Christ and
so contains the eternal and the infinite. This transposition—
the text of the Great Canon calls it *diavasis*, "passing over"—
constitutes the kernel of repentance and is one of the central
aims of the work of reading the Scriptures and praying.

All these things "our holy Father among the saints,
Andrew Archbishop of Crete, skillfully and excellently fitted
together" in his Great Canon.

The recollection of Solomon, who "once did evil in the
sight of heaven and turned away from God,"[8] leads the still
unrepentant sinner to reflect in his conscience that by remaining far from God he keeps his life "conformed" to corruption.

By presenting the door of the Kingdom as wide open
through the incarnation of Christ, and by describing how
thieves and harlots make haste in response to the invitation
of Jesus to "pass through it" into the Kingdom before we do,
"changing their life" through repentance, through a radical
transformation, he encourages the hesistant to lay aside

[8]Canticle 7.

cowardice and to enter into the place where sinners are trans-
figured into saints:

> *Christ became man,*
> *calling to repentance thieves and harlots.*
> *Repent, my soul:*
> *the door of the Kingdom is already open,*
> *and pharisees and publicans and adulterers*
> *pass through it before thee,*
> *changing their life.*[9]

And suddenly he takes the believer, prepared by all that
has gone before, and thrusts him into the choir of the great
suppliants of the Lord, making him cry out too, joining his
voice with theirs:

> *Like the thief I cry to Thee, "Remember me";*
> *like Peter I weep bitterly;*
> *like the publican I call out, "Forgive me, Savior";*
> *like the harlot I shed tears.*
> *Accept my lamentation,*
> *as once Thou hast accepted the entreaties*
> *of the woman of Canaan.*[10]

In this way the recollections of sacred history come to life.
The events of salvation become current events in the lives of
the faithful who are being saved today. And the contempor-
aneity within which the events of salvation are relived is
enlarged; it contains the incontainable, and the barriers of
space and time are shattered, broadened and deepened to
infinity.

This transformation of natural facts, or repentance, or
transfiguration, or whatever else we call it, which leads to
the new man and the new creation in Christ, is salvation. It
is realized fundamentally in the divine eucharist, where the
created, communicating fully with the uncreated, is made
infinited and is deified; and it constitutes the content and aim
of the Church's whole sacramental and ascetical life: of the

[9]Canticle 9.
[10]Canticle 8.

sacraments, the feasts, the services, prayer, fasting and vigils.

This ordered sequence, which has been laid down by the Orthodox apostolic and patristic tradition with its deep knowledge of the psychosomatic make-up of man and of man's relations with the world, presupposes a precise cosmological and anthropological context. It is a context constituted by the beginning and the goal of creation, by man's failure to reach his objective, and by the personal entry of God into created space and time. To these things Holy Scripture refers with the utmost clarity, describing the coming into being of the world and of man, the fall and the providential guiding of humanity, the incarnation of God, the crucifixion, resurrection and ascension of the God-man, the descent of the Spirit, and the expectation of the eschatological Kingdom.

All these are not metaphysical theses, which one must accept in order to escape some punishment or to be granted salvation, but they are facts of history. They determine the co-ordinates within which man and the world were created, experienced the fall, and were recreated in Christ. For this reason they determine the true nature of man and the world, the underlying truth of history. Outside them creation is in conflict with nature; within them it finds the character that naturally belongs to it, and it advances towards its perfection.

Within this cosmological and anthropological context the whole of the Church's life is constructed. This context is presupposed by all the Church's practices, including the Great Canon. Yet, although these things are all of them presupposed, each particular practice stresses certain elements rather than others in accordance with its specific therapeutic and perfective function. The service of the Great Canon, taking place as it does in the middle of Lent, has the aim of helping man to become aware of the tragic nature of the unnatural situation in which he finds himself as a result of sin, and of strengthening him in his resolve and his struggle to return to the prelapsarian life in accordance with nature, as it has been perfected in Christ. For this reason it is the elements corresponding to this aim that are the most evident in the Great Canon. In what follows I shall attempt to describe them.

II
The Prelapsarian Anthropological Context

What is natural to man is determined basically by his state before the fall:

As the potter moulds the clay,
Thou hast fashioned me,
giving me flesh and bones,
breath and life.[11]

In granting existence to man, the Creator constructs ("Thou hast fashioned me") that which pertains to the body ("flesh and bones") and to the soul ("breath and life"). These two dimension of man unite the human person organically with the material and spiritual dimensions of creation, and make him a recapitulator of the universe, a microcosm.

The human person as formed naturally within creation, man in his entirety, has his ontology rooted in God, since he is created in the image of God. His ontology is iconic. It finds its health, harmony, beauty and bliss in God. The grace of God—that is, His love, life and glory, in a word His uncreated energies—is conferred on man together with his God-given existence and is interwoven with it. The human constitution is

the tabernacle fashioned by God ...
the first robe
that the Creator wove for me in the beginning ...

[11]Canticle 1.

the beauty of the image . . .
the beauty which was first created . . .
the first fruits of the original beauty.[12]

Thus man tastes in paradise

the delight of the eternal kingdom.[13]

He possesses

the royal dignity . . .
the diadem and purple robe.[14]

He is

wealthy and righteous . . .
laden with riches and flocks.[15]

We must bear in mind that the Great Canon is not a catechetical text which analyzes and expounds. It is a liturgical
act, and as such it limits itself to recalling that state from
which man fell, so that the believer may have a better aware-
ness of the tragic condition in which he now finds himself,
and may be strengthened for the struggle of repentance. The
lines quoted above, in a comprehensive and wide-ranging
fashion, point to the prelapsarian context like a sharp needle.
Of course a knowledge of the teaching contained more generally in the writings of the Fathers is also presupposed in the
act of worship. Thus the verses cited above succeed in bringing vividly before the believer the familiar teaching of the
Church on the creation of man "in the image of God," which
I have presented analytically as a fundamental theme in the
first part of this book. The Great Canon as a liturgical act
constitutes a specific application of this teaching and a living
out of its implications. But at the same time it is also of
decisive help to us in understanding fully the Church's dogmatic teaching on this point, since knowledge in the Orthodox tradition is fundamentally tied to practical living.

[12]Canticle 2.
[13]Canticle 1.
[14]Canticle 4.
[15]Canticle 4.

III

The Context of Contrition

Adam's transgression, with which the believer identifies his own transgression—"having rivalled in transgression Adam the first-formed man"[16]—is a voluntary change of direction, or more radically, a change of objective.

By making himself his own goal and objective, man "became his own idol."[17] Of his own free will he broke off his iconic relationship with God and impeded his movement towards Him. He made himself autonomous, limited himself to created time and space, to his created nature, with the physiological result that a spiritual famine broke out within him:

A famine of God has seized thee . . .
knowing myself stripped naked of God.[18]

Living not with the life of God but "by his own nature,"[19] he was led physiologically to death. The destruction of his non-created center disorganized his psychosomatic constitution. What was in the image was darkened; what was in the likeness was transformed into unlikeness. Man lost his "robe fashioned by God" and put on the "garments of skin." Originally a theological being, he now became a biological one.

The anthropological context within which this process of disruption and dissolution took place is clearly indicated

[16]Canticle 1.
[17]Canticle 4.
[18]Canticle 1.
[19]The expression is that of Makarios of Egypt, *Spiritual Homilies* 12, 2, *PG* 34, 557B.

175

in the Great Canon and we shall examine it presently below. First, however, the more general context in which sin is situated must be defined.

It is a characteristic that from the beginning of the Great Canon to its end all the verbs which express the operation of sin or define its results refer not to God but to man, and that in the majority of cases they have not a legal but a physical connotation: *I looked upon; my mind was deceived; I have transgressed; I have fallen; I have darkened; I have discoloured; I have stained; I have corrupted; I have destroyed; I am injured; I am smitten; I am wounded; I have contracted leprosy; I have been defiled; I have been stained; I am covered with wounds; I have torn the first garment; I have defiled with filth; I have been covered with mire; thou hast dissolved the essence of thy soul with prodigalities; I have become a murderer of my soul's conscience; I have been dragged away by pleasures; thou hast given life to the flesh; I have clothed myself in the torn coat; I lie naked; I am ashamed; I am famished.*

But even the verbs which have a legal character are immediately qualified. For example:

I have sinned, I have offended,
I have set aside Thy commandments;
for in sins have I progressed
and to my sores I have added wounds.[20]

And:

For this I am condemned in my misery,
for this I am convicted by the verdict of my own
*   conscience.*[21]

The same applies to the nouns: *Deceptive thoughts; irrational appetite; irrational food; poisoned food; defiled life; waves of errors; gluttony of the passions; madness of the passions; darkness of the passions; wounds of the soul and of the flesh; injuries; lacerations; burning; slackening.*

[20]Canticle 7.
[21]Canticle 4.

Influenced by the Western teaching on original sin, we usually place sin in a legal setting. We regard it as disobedience to the commandments of God, and its results as punishments inflicted by God. For the Orthodox biblical and patristic tradition, however, the setting of original sin and of every sin is mainly physical. When man closes his eyes to the light, he finds himself in darkness. When he loses his center, he becomes disorientated. When he distances himself from life, he dies. The commandments of God are not threats about a punishment which will come from a source situated outside man. They describe the healthy state of human existence. The sickness, pain and death which follow offences against the laws of health are not punishments deriving from the laws but the natural consequences of the offences. It is not God but man who is the creator of evil. This truth is of fundamental significance, because it means that the sinner stands before God, not waiting for God to condemn him, but himself taking responsibility for his own actions and so the road to repentance remains open. God in His compassion does not abandon His creatures under any circumstances whatsoever. Man has fled and is called upon to return. This return, this transposition into the realm of God, which goes with the restoration to health, the reconstitution and the transformation of human existence, constitutes the kernel of repentance, the content of the whole spiritual struggle—and of the struggle in which the believer engages in the course of the service of the Great Canon.

The journey which the sinner makes from his disorientated state far from God to eventual contrition is thus situated within the general context of the relationship between God and man. The anthropological setting of contrition is described in the Great Canon with a wonderful sense of the depths of the human soul and the psychosomatic constitution of man's being. I shall present it below, recalling once again that the Great Canon offers not an analysis but the possibility of entering into a living experience. Many of the points mentioned below are discussed analytically in other parts of this book. It is, however, impossible for us to pass over them here without falsifying the picture of the context in which the service of the Great Canon invites us to place ourselves, so that we may live in a spiritual manner. In the Church, the place of true life, there are the inevitable repetitions which are characteristic of life.

Separated from God and deprived of His life, the soul seeks nourishment from the body. In this way the passions of the soul are born. More precisely, the dispassionate faculties of the soul—which constitute within the created human person channels of communication with the uncreated God, and are the means through which the functions of the soul receive the grace of God which nourishes and vivifies the whole human person—are transformed by their subjection to the body into distorted passions, in such a way that the life of the sinful soul becomes a life in pursuit of sensual pleasure. The pleasure-seeking urges devour and exhaust the soul's functions:

> *With my lustful desires*
> *I have formed within myself the deformity of the passions*
> *and disfigured the beauty of my mind.*[22]

The body for its part, not finding life in the soul, turns towards external things, and as is natural becomes enslaved to matter and imprisoned in the cycle of corruption. Thus the pleasure-loving bodily passions appear, whereby man struggles to draw life and joy from material things.[23] A person who lives with the passions, precisely because the bodily passions seek material things in order to be satisfied, ends up by regarding material things as the source of life and replaces God with them. Idolatry is the inevitable consequence of hedonism:

> *Thou hast heaped up crimes, my soul,*
> *setting up passions as idols*
> *and multiplying abominations.*[24]

---

[22]Canticle 2.
[23]"The swine's meat, the flesh-pots and the food of Egypt thou hast preferred, my soul, to the food of heaven" (Canticle 6).
[24]Canticle 7.

In this way the order of nature is reversed. When things are in accordance with nature, matter finds its highest constitution and mode of functioning in the human organism, where through the soul's faculties it is opened up to the uncreated God; but when things are contrary to nature through the rejection of God, the soul subjects itself to the body[25] and the body subjects itself to matter. This reversal of the proper order leads man to the "materialistic and acquisitive life," which constitutes a "heavy chain" for man because it entails an enslavement to the suffocating restrictions of the material creation and an imprisonment within them.[26]

This first reversal goes with another which is equally fundamental. The patristic tradition regards the heart as the center of man's life and psychosomatic constitution, as the organ within which the mystical transition from the psychic to the bodily and from the bodily to the psychic is accomplished. This organ has not only a bodily but a psychic mode of functioning. In the teaching of the Fathers the functions of the soul have their seat in the heart, where they coinhere mutually in one another, and it is from the heart that the operations of the soul flow. The heart is simultaneously the source of the life of the body and the center of the soul. It is therefore within the heart, the deepest center of the conscious, free and rational human person, that according to the Orthodox tradition God meets man.

When man voluntarily rejects God, and instead of being an image of God becomes his own idol, his heart is hardened and "becomes impudent," according to the Great Canon. The unity of his psychosomatic functions "is ruptured" and the integrity of his person is shattered. His bodily functions, no longer nourished by the grace of God, degenerate into mere biological functions. And the functions of the soul, deprived of divine grace, are hardened and coarsened, and function below their true capacity. Nourished as they are by sin, they

[25]"Thy free dignity, O my soul, thou hast subjected to thy body" (Canticle 7).

[26]"I have fallen beneath the painful burden of the passions and the corruption of material things; and I am hard pressed by the enemy" (Canticle 2).

are deflected from their proper function and become totally distorted.

When the will functions in accordance with nature, it activates freedom and love. But when it is turned by sin towards desire, it becomes a slave to this desire and "gives birth to self-will." In the natural man the intellect (*nous*) is the sum total of his cognitive functions and the center of their unity. It is the eye of the soul, the light of man's Godlike reason, which illuminates and directs the human person. But when it is alienated from God, it functions as simple intellectuality. Thus when knowledge functions naturally, it is a full communion in love of the knower with the known. But in its contranatural state it becomes mere observation, that is, a gathering of information for the sake of its objective apprehension and correct exploitation. When the contents of the intellect, the thoughts, abandon their natural center, which is the heart, they wander over the external world and make a person lose touch with reality, go out from himself, and chase outside himself insubstantial idols of his own making.

The bodily and psychic functions of man, from the point of view of their constitution and mode of functioning after the fall, are called "garments of skin" in the patristic tradition. Man's self-limitation to created space has "sewed" these garments of skin onto the human race in place of the dispassionate psychosomatic robe woven by grace:

> Sin has stripped me of the robe
> that God once wove for me,
> and it has sewed for me garments of skin.[27]

This postlapsarian psychosomatic dress of the human person can through ascesis and the spiritual life become once again spiritual; man can live once again with the divine life. But it can also deteriorate and become in the end

> defiled and shamefully bloodstained
> by a life of passion and self-indulgence.[28]

[27]Canticle 2.
[28]Canticle 2; cf. "My mind is wounded, my body has grown feeble, my

In fact, by selling the birthright of its self-determination "to aliens" (that is, to the sinful passions) the will can become in the end "ungovernable," an "irrational impulse," a "pleasure-loving gluttony"; it can be subjected totally to pleasure and be diverted to a life of hedonism.

In an advanced state of sinfulness even the intellect "is mixed with clay," becomes "dust," drowns in materiality, and although it delights in claiming to be "sublime," in reality it ends up, as the Great Canon says, "submerged." When the thoughts co-operate with pleasure-loving passions, they are activated as sinful acts, which wound man severely. Having acquired sin as their content, they become "impassioned" and "murderous"; the believer perceives them as robbers which devastate his life:

> *I am the man who fell among thieves,*
> *even my own thoughts;*
> *they have covered all my body with wounds,*
> *and I lie beaten and bruised.*[29]

When the soul, in which sin always has its origin, is "provoked to frenzy" in this manner, it also corrupts the body. The temple of the Spirit becomes "a refuge of pollutions of the flesh." The charm of the human body, the many powers of communication which the body offers to the human person, are consumed and destroyed by love of pleasure. The body and with it the whole human person "is squandered in unbridled lust."

When man submits wholly to sin, he is led to the furthest bounds of self-destruction. "By his own free choice" he can deaden his conscience, and then "stone his body to death," and finally kill his intellect:

> *By my own free choice I have become a murderer of*
> *my conscience.*[30]

spirit is sick, my speech has lost its power, my life is dead; the end is at the door" (Canticle 9)

[29]Canticle 1.
[30]Canticle 1.

To whom shall I liken thee, O soul of many sins?
Alas! to Cain and to Lamech.
For thou hast stoned thy body to death with thine
    evil deeds,
and killed thy mind with thy disordered longings.[31]

This description of the journey which the sinner follows until he meets with destruction and ruin far from God, situated as it is within the service of the Great Canon, that is, having a practical rather than a theoretical objective, functions organically, so to speak, as a dramatic act. The believer, seeing the context of his life destroyed by sin, becomes conscious of the tragic nature of his sinful state. Standing in the church before the throne of God with the glorious company of the saints around him, he realizes that he does not have a wedding garment, that he is naked. He is ashamed, he draws back, he feels pain and laments his state. The lament which governs all the canticles of the Canon—

Where shall I begin to weep
for the actions of my wretched life?
What first-fruit shall I offer, O Christ,
in this my lamentation?[32]

—reveals the dramatic character of the liturgical act. This act is a drama of the most comprehensive nature in which there are no spectators but only actors, and in which the participants are able through a process of purification to arrive at redemption in the midst of the tragedy.

In the new perspective granted to man by the Church, space is restructured. life is condensed as if on a stage, and on this stage the transition from tragedy to redemption is liturgically enacted. With fresh eyes the believer sees the real depth of sin. He understands that sin involves not just moral darkening but a universal fall. It does not consist in a small or great number of sinful acts but in a wholesale destruction of life. It is, in the true sense of the word, an annihilation

[31]Canticle 2.
[32]Canticle 1.

which is perceived by man as the absence of God, of other persons, of himself, of things, and more generally as the absence of purpose and meaning, and so by extension as hellish loneliness and anguish. Some phrases of the Great Canon are indicative of this: *I am a desert; childless and nomadic; a useless life; a penurious life; without purpose and vain; flood and storm; cataclysmic decline; a bottomless pit; a chasm of the earth; an abyss; flame of unreason; burning; heating of the soul; dizziness; darkening; despair.*

A life of sin is not defined primarily by specific partial transgressions. Its deeper content and real tragedy are made apparent by the general pointlessness, meaninglessness and irrationality which characterize it.

The most penetrating description of the sinner is that given in the parable of the prodigal son. The prodigal is not just guilty of incidental moral deviations. He has distanced himself from his paternal home, vanished from the sight of God, sunk into annihilation and oblivion. He is seen neither by his employer, nor by his friends, nor even by the swine. He is lost even to himself, literally gone to perdition. His re-emergence into existence is characterized in the parable by the deeply significant expression, "he came to himself" (Luke 15:17).

This re-emergence into conscious existence is the first act of salvation, the point of departure. It is to this point above all that the Great Canon itself leads us.

At the same time the liturgical act opens up for the believer the road of return. It calls him and guides him to the specific task of repentance or transformation, that is to say, to the healing, reconstitution and perfection of his own self. The realization of this task constitutes the actual return.

In the section that follows I shall attempt to describe the context in which the service of the Great Canon places this task.

IV

The Context of Return

When the sinner takes conscious stock of his existence, it is likely that he will find nothing within him and around him except the void. But he may also hear the voice of God urging him from deep within himself to remember his forgotten Father and to feel nostalgia for his lost paternal home. One path leads to despair and irrationality, the other begins with a lamentation full of hope, with a joyful sorrow, and reaches its fulfilment in the exultation of union with God. In the first situation is the man who has confined his existence to the limits of creation, who of his own free choice has shut up within narrow limits the various dimensions of his person which of their own nature tended towards God, that is to say, the man who has become autonomous. In the second is the man who has succeeded to a greater or lesser degree—in the last analysis it does not much matter which—in keeping his crushed existence open to God. The source and foundation of man's salvation is his turning towards God.

The sinner who turns towards God experiences first of all the need to call on His mercy and help. He understands that he is unable by himself to advance towards Him. This entreaty is particularly characteristic of the beginning of the journey to repentance and salvation, but it also marks the journey as a whole:

I lie as an outcast before Thy gate, O Savior.
Do not cast me away....[33]

[33]Canticle 1.

> *Do not bring me to justice.*
> *Open Thy door....*[34]

> *I have sinned against Thee; be merciful to me....*
> *I come to Thee; heal me.*[35]

His sins are great:

> *No one among the sons of Adam*
> *has sinned against Thee as I have sinned.*[36]

But the compassion of God is even greater:

> *Let us see, let us behold*
> *the compassion of our God and Master.*[37]

Thus man dares to beseech God with confidence:

> *Take from me the heavy yoke of sin,*
> *and in Thy compassion grant me remission of sins....*[38]

> *Have mercy upon Thy creation, O merciful One,*
> *have compassion on the work of Thy hands....*[39]

> *Thou art the Good Shepherd;*
> *seek me, the lamb that has strayed,*
> *and do not forget me....*[40]

> *Make me a nurseling*
> *in the pasture of Thine own flock....*[41]

> *Thou art my sweet Jesus,*
> *Thou art my Creator;*
> *in Thee I shall be justified.*[42]

[34]Canticle 2.
[35]Canticle 6.
[36]Canticle 2.
[37]Canticle 2.
[38]Canticle 1.
[39]Canticle 6.
[40]Canticle 3.
[41]Canticle 8.
[42]Canticle 3.

But the work of salvation is not accomplished exclusively by the grace of God. The co-operation of man is also required, a co-operation which is undertaken responsibly and is definite and decisive. The sinner who wishes to be saved is invited to bring about within himself, through a progressive healing and reconstitution of his psychosomatic functions, a specific "return" (*anadromi*) to his iconic and Godlike integrity and health, and at the same time to effect a "movement" (*prosagogi*) of his whole being towards God.

This "movement" towards God is indispensable because salvation, that is, the perfection of man with God's help to an infinite degree and the acquisition of a happiness so great that it transcends death, cannot possibly be realized in the place where we have committed apostasy. In this place the sinner is aware of himself as the lost "royal drachma." His value as a person has evaporated. That which he is, does and has is puny, perishable and vapid. He therefore turns his eyes and his footsteps towards the "land of inheritance." He seeks to be "conveyed" to that land, to become like Abraham "a wanderer":

Depart from the land of Haran,
and come to the land which flows with incorruption
and eternal life.[43]

This has nothing, however, to do with a physical move. The flight from "Sodom and Gomorrah" is a flight from "the flame of every brutish appetite." Salvation is gained on earth, in the body. It is a salvation not only of the spirit but of the body, and of the soul too—a salvation of one's life as a whole. In the Great Canon we meet the highly significant expression, "rescue thy life."[44]

The first step of the "return" to our true selves and the "movement" towards God is self-knowledge:

Turn back, repent,
uncover all that thou hast hidden.[45]

43Canticle 3.
44Canticle 6.
45Canticle 7.

It is not only the secret sinful acts, which the sinner confesses in the sacrament of penance in order to receive forgiveness, that must come to light, but also the hidden causes of these acts, the vices, the passions, the sources which give birth to them:

> *The secrets of my heart*
> *have I confessed to Thee, my Judge.*[46]

When the deeply hidden sources of evil have been identified, it is possible for them in consequence to be healed through an appropriate form of therapy. The penances which the sacred canons lay down are not penalties but a kind of therapeutic treatment.

The second step is action. Action signifies basically ascetic discipline, through which the various functions of the human person are purified and healed. Through this the believer tames "the ungovernable urges of sensual pleasure"; he counters "the madness of the passions"; he "battles" against a variety of enemies, hedonism, egoism and the passions; he vanquishes "deceiving thoughts"; he "detaches himself from sin"; he emerges "from his former brutishness"; he attains "manliness" and "firmness of purpose"; he "grows strong"; he becomes "a manly soul." Through poverty of will, fasting, vigils and other ascetic practices, the body breaks its servile dependence on material things, wins a certain independence and freedom from the material world, and at the same time rediscovers its correct relationship with the soul. Thus by means of the body, the physical bond uniting him with the material creation, the human person can again exercise his priestly, prophetic and royal ministry within the world.

Moreover, the good works of love that we do for one another and the keeping of the commandments are also regarded as action:

> *Search and spy out, my soul,*
> *the land of thine inheritance*

[46]Canticle 7.

and take up thy dwelling within it,
through obedience to the law.[47]

"Obedience to the law" is that which leads a person to distance himself from "filthy acts" and to be led towards "acts inspired by God," through which his "leprous life is whitened and cleansed."

The stern effort which is required in order to keep the commandments,[48] and the inevitable failures which ensue, confer on man "an ever-contrite heart" and "poverty of spirit." The believer is aware of his weakness and the great dangers which confront him, "the snares and pits of the deceiver," and "fortifies" his effort step by step with "the fear of God." He dresses himself in "modesty" and "piety," which are the "secure base" of the ladder which reaches us to heaven. This work is a work of the will, which in this way through the keeping of the commandments learns very slowly to harmonize itself with the will of God, who desires nothing other than the salvation of mankind.

The third step, chronologically simultaneous with the second, is knowledge. The work of the will is directed and strengthened by the operation of the mind. The awakening of the intellective functions and their response to the call of God signify the start of the "return" to oneself and the "movement" towards God:

Awaken my mind and turn me back.[49]

The task of purifying the thoughts by which the mind functions, a task which constitutes a fundamental dimension of the return of man to his health and integrity, demands a strenuous effort.

The thoughts must cease to serve the desires. As long as they remain enslaved to the desires their work is to discover ways of satisfying them. And the more subtle, acute and perceptive the thoughts are, the more perfect are the ways of

[47]Canticle 6.
[48]"And without toil, O my soul, neither action nor contemplation will succeed" (Canticle 4).
[49]Canticle 8.

satisfying the desires that they discover; they embellish and perfect evil:

> *Skillfully hast thou planned to build a tower,*
> *O my soul,*
> *and to establish a stronghold for thy lusts.*[50]

The correct relationship of the thoughts to the desires is for the former to direct the latter towards that which is true and consequently good.

Moreover, the thoughts must be liberated from subjection to material things. As long as they are subjected to them they do not discern their meaning and purpose; they minister to a blind process in which man becomes a slave, accepting the poor reward of the satisfaction of his desires. But the true vocation of the thoughts is to illuminate material things, to bring their meaning to light, to develop them and fit them together in harmony with their true nature, in harmony, that is to say, with the purpose which their Creator gave them.

The thoughts are purified and concentrated in the mind to the extent that they are liberated from desires and things. Man returns to himself. The mind henceforth governs a person's life and actions in a reasonable way. Man's psychosomatic functions, having found their center, cease to war among themselves. Man becomes unified and simplified.

Similarly, when the reordered mind is also illuminated by prayer, it can transcend the letter and arrive at the spirit of the law, it can be nourished by the life-giving truth of the divine word:

> *Drink the juice of the law*
> *that flows from their pressing of the letter.*[51]

Man can thus decipher the truth hidden within himself and the world; he can become "a lover of wisdom." The exhortation which the Great Canon gives is "nurture wisdom," that is, take care of it as would a nurse.

[50]Canticle 2.
[51]Canticle 6.

In this way the original healing and transformation of the mind, which is repentance, succeeds in becoming "recognition" (*epignosis*). Man recognizes the truth of existent things, he thinks correctly. He understands, and consequently confronts, reality from God's viewpoint, within the light which shines from Him, with a mind which understands, and in relation to a reality which is understood. This new understanding of reality and confrontation of it is called faith.

Man's psychosomatic functions, when purified by action and illuminated by knowledge, receive the grace of God and function in a new manner. Gradually sensual pleasure is replaced by joy. The more man progresses, the more he discovers that freedom, so far from being an egotistical independence, is in reality love. The passions are delivered from their obsessive infatuation and operate as pure natural functions. According to the degree of union with God that has been achieved, they are raised to the level of virtues; and so, at the more advanced stages of holiness where the union with God attains a certain completeness, they become spiritual senses and functions. Man emerges from the darkness, is revealed again as "a son of the day," acquires a marriage garment, and manifests "the beloved beauty of the bride."

Thus the preconditions have been created for the fourth and highest stage of the spiritual life, which is contemplation and dispassion. The mind, purified and enlightened by divine truth, descends through a laborious effort of concentration into the heart, and there the unified and purified human person sees the unseeable. Contemplation, which is the highest degree of knowledge, advances step by step with dispassion—which is at the opposite pole to inert domination by the passions, since it is now supreme activity, the highest degree of action:

Acquire heavenly dispassion
through the most disciplined way of life on earth.[52]

The entire life of the body is honorable and sanctified:

[52]Canticle 5.

Marriage is honorable,
and the marriage-bed undefiled.
For on both Christ has given His blessing
at the wedding in Cana.[53]

The believer who has received the divine gift of dispassion and contemplation lives a heavenly life without abandoning the earthly life of the body—

Thou hast lived a bodiless life in the body[54]

—which signifies that he leaves behind all preoccupation with whatever is transient and perishable. Like the merchant who discovered the pearl of great price, he sells everything to search "with incomparable love" for that single great pearl which is "the one thing needful" (Luke 10:42):

Be watchful, O my soul, be full of courage ...
that thou mayest acquire action with knowledge,
and be named ... "the mind that sees God";
so shalt thou reach by contemplation the innermost
*   darkness*
and gain great merchandise.[55]

This progressive healing, refashioning and perfecting of man, the specific setting of which we have examined above, is situated within a wider cosmological and anthropological context, that which God has created by His sojourning within creation.

We have seen in the first part of this study how within the Church the dimensions of nature, space and time are reconstituted and renewed, how historical memory functions in a new way, and so on. This transformation is brought about because the Church is the flesh of the God-man, within which Christ has renewed the laws or mode of functioning of nature:

[53]Canticle 9.
[54]Canticle 4.
[55]Canticle 4.

He who is born makes new the laws of nature ...
the natural order is overcome.[56]

But Christ has also renewed within His flesh the specific
mode of functioning of the human person. He has recreated
not only the cosmological but also the anthropological struc-
tures. He has transformed into spiritual functions the powers
whereby man remains alive; He has changed his physical
senses into spiritual ones:

The Creator of the ages
has clothed Himself in human flesh,
uniting to Himself the nature of men.[57]

By this union He channeled the life of God into the human
nature which He assumed, renewed it and spiritualized it.
The faithful are grafted by the sacraments and by ascesis
onto the spiritual human nature of the God-man, take on its
life and mode of functioning, and they are saved. This grafting onto Christ constitutes the real content and the final aim
of the whole sacramental and ascetical life of the Church.
The saint becomes "a likeness of Christ." The Great Canon
calls this grafting onto Christ "forgiveness."

Looked at from the anthropological point of view salvation is called "conversion" or "repentance." But this conversion of man is possible only by virtue of the union or "co-
habitation"[58] with God which is realized within the body of
Christ, the Church. Influenced as we are by the legal understanding of salvation, we regard forgiveness simply as the
remission of sins, whereas in reality it is something much
broader. Even the remission of sins is brought about because
when we "co-habit" with God, the ocean of divine goodness
annihilates human sins. In its full reality forgiveness is
"communion with Christ" and "communion with the Kingdom
of Christ."

[56]Canticle 4, *Theotokion.*
[57]Canticle 5, *Theotokion.*
[58]Greek: *syn-chorisis,* literally a "coming together," and so "acquiescence,"
"indulgence," and eventually "forgiveness." Thus the patristic and modern
Greek word for forgiveness contains within it, through its etymological root,
the idea of meeting and combining.

V

The Denouement of the Drama

As I have emphasized repeatedly, the Great Canon, being a liturgical act, does not embark on abstract analyses. It places the believer within the context of salvation. The realization of this work of salvation extends, however, beyond the specific time during which the service is celebrated. Thus the revelation of what is hidden is to take place in the inner chamber of recollection and confession. The healing and refashioning of the will and the mind is to be brought about by the daily ascesis which transforms the whole of one's life. Contemplation and dispassion are to be attained by ceaseless prayer. The Great Canon sets before us elements of all these things, but I have not thought it right to go beyond the bounds which the writer has placed on his text. The rest is implied and suggested. The chief task that the liturgical service performs is to initiate the participant into that place where all these things can be realised. And that place is Christ.

The service of the Great Canon, situated as it is in the middle of Lent, invites the believer to graft his spiritual life onto Christ's journey to Golgotha and the resurrection, a journey which encapsulates the destiny of the whole of humanity.

I have said above that the Great Canon is a drama. It is well known that in all true dramas the *dénouement* is supplied by future events. In the present instance the *dénouement* comes with the resurrection of Christ, for which the faithful prepare themselves throughout the course of Lent. For the resurrection abolishes corruption and puts death to flight. It brings to human beings and to the whole universe new life and new dimensions open to infinity.

This new reality, however, is already set before the faithful through a messianic vision, the christological prophecy of Isaiah, with which the service of the Great Canon is brought to a close. At the end of the long vigil the voice of God the Father, who sends His Son into the world and proclaims the great things which He will bring to pass, resounds calmly and majestically in the words of the prophet:

"I am the Lord, I have called you in righteousness, I have taken you by the hand and kept you; I have given you as a covenant to the people, a light to the nations, to open the eyes that are blind, to bring out the prisoners from the dungeon, and from the prison those who sit in darkness. . . . Behold, the former things have come to pass, and new things I now declare. . . . Let the desert and its cities lift up their voice, the villages that Kedar inhabits; let the inhabitants of Sela sing for joy, let them shout from the top of the mountains. Let them give glory to the Lord, and declare His praise in the coastlands." The Lord goes forth like a mighty man, like a man of war He stirs up His fury; He cries out, He shouts aloud, He shows Himself mighty against His foes. . . . "And I will lead the blind in a way that they know not, in paths that they have not known I will guide them. I will turn the darkness before them into light, the rough places into level ground. These are the things I will do, and I will not forsake them" (Is 42:6-7, 9, 11-13, 16).[59]

[59]For historical and philological information on the Great Canon the reader may consult the detailed study of P. Christou, *O Megas Kanon Andreou tou Kritis,* Thessaloniki 1952. Cf. the article "Andreas o Kritis" in the *Thriskevtiki kai Ithiki Enkyklopaideia* ii, 647-93, esp. 689-90, and *Le grand Canon de saint André de Crète,* introduction de l'évêque Pierre, présentation de André Fyrillas (Paris 1979).

PART FOUR

PATRISTIC TEXTS

Note on the Choice of Texts

The following texts have been included:

I. A passage from the teaching of St Irenaios (2nd century) on Adam as an "infant," and on the "plan, the arrangements and the sequence" by which man, "created and fashioned by the uncreated God in His image and likeness," was to "make gradual progress and so advance towards perfection." The passage speaks also of the way in which "the Lord came to us in these last days, recapitulating all things in Himself."

II. A highly concentrated summary of the Christian teaching on the human person by St Gregory the Theologian (Gregory of Nazianzus: 4th century). I have made frequent use of this passage, either quoting it directly or using texts from other Fathers who analyze and expound his epigrammatic phrases.

III. One of the basic texts in which St Gregory of Nyssa (4th century) formulates his teaching on the expressions "in the image" and "garments of skin." It could well serve as the best possible summary of the first part of this book. The reader should note how the saint does not treat the content of the expressions "in the image" and "garments of skin" as "theological subjects" in their own right but sets them within the context of the spiritual life as a whole.

IV. 1. The teaching of St Maximos (7th century) on the five divisions and on the way in which man, as the "natural bond" between all things, was intended to unite them; on the manner in which Adam used his "natural power" in a fashion "contrary to nature," and on the fall; also on Christ who, "having fulfilled as man . . . all that He had decreed as God," united the divisions.

2. The fundamental anthropological teaching of St Maximus, which I have presented on pp. 54-6.

3. A reply to a question on the relationship between biological birth and spiritual birth, giving a review of the origin and fall of man, and a synopsis of the divine economy in terms of the way in which man was deified both before and after the fall. It is principally on this text that the section in part one of this book dealing with

marriage is based. It should be studied in conjunction with the quotations from St Maximos contained in the text of St Nikodimos given below.

V. The basic passage of *The Life in Christ* in which St Nicolas Kavasilas (14th century) presents Christ as the archetype of the human person, and deification as union with Christ. Other similar texts may be found in his *Homilies on the Mother of God*.

VI. The "Apology" of St Nikodimos of the Holy Mountain (18th century), the significance of which I have discussed in the Preface.

I

St Irenaios

Against Heresies IV, 38, 1-3, PG 7, 1105A-1108C; *Irénée de Lyon, Contre les Hérésies* IV, 2, ed. A. Rousseau (Sources chrétiennes 100, Paris 1965) 943-57.

1. But if anyone should say, "Could not God have brought man forth as perfect from the beginning?" he should know that as far as God is concerned—who in Himself is always unchanging and unbegotten—all things are possible; but since created things originated subsequently, they must therefore also be inferior to Him who made them. It is an impossibility that things recently created should be at the same time uncreated. Inasmuch as they are not uncreated, it follows that they are inferior to what is perfect. And inasmuch as they are comparatively recent, it follows that they are "infants" and therefore without experience or practice in perfect conduct. Now a mother if she wishes can certainly give solid food to her infant, but as yet he is unable to assimilate this more mature food. Similarly, God could have endowed man with perfection from the beginning, but man was as yet unable to receive it, for he was an infant. For the same reason, when our Lord came to us in these last days, recapitulating all things in Himself, He came not as He could have done but in accordance with our ability to see Him. He was certainly able to come to us in His incorruptible glory, but we would never have been able to endure its intensity. That is why the perfect Bread of the Father offered Himself to us as milk, because we were still infants, coming among us as a man. In this way, being fed as if from the breast of His

flesh, and so becoming accustomed through this milk-feeding to eating and drinking the Logos of God, we are enabled to contain within ourselves the bread of immortality, which is the Spirit of the Father.

2. For this reason Paul says to the Corinthians, "I fed you with milk, not solid food, for you were not ready for it" (1 Cor 3:2); that is, you have been taught about the coming of the Lord as a man, but the Spirit of the Father has not yet rested upon you because of your weakness. . . . Therefore just as the Apostle was able to give solid food . . . but they were unable to receive it . . . so God was able to have endowed man with perfection from the beginning, but as man had only just been created, he was unable to receive it, or having received it to contain it, or having contained it to keep it. That is why, although the Son of God was perfect, He went through a childhood along with every other human being and was restricted in this way, not for His own sake but because of the infancy of mankind, since human beings were not able to contain Him.

3. . . . By this plan, by such arrangements and such a sequence, man came to be created and fashioned by the uncreated God in His image and likeness, the Father being well pleased and giving the command, the Son acting and creating, the Spirit nourishing and giving increase, and man making gradual progress and so advancing towards perfection, coming closer, that is to say, to the Uncreated One. For the Uncreated One is perfect, and it is He who is God. It was necessary for man first to be created, and having been created to grow, and having grown to arrive at manhood, and having arrived at manhood to multiply, and having multiplied to gain strength, and having gained strength to be glorified, and having been glorified to see his own Master. For God is destined to be seen, and the vision of God confers incorruption, and incorruption brings us close to God.

II

St Gregory the Theologian

Oration 45, *On Easter,* 7-9, *PG* 36, 632A-636A. (The same text is also found in *Oration* 38, *On the Epiphany,* 11-13, *PG* 36, 321C-325D.)

7. . . . Having decided to demonstrate this, the Artificer of the universe, the Logos, created man as a single living creature from both elements, that is to say, from the nature of both the visible and the invisible worlds. On the one hand He took the body from already pre-existing matter, on the other He endowed it with breath from Himself, which Scripture terms the intelligent soul and the image of God (Gen 1:27; 2:7). He set man upon the earth as a second world, a great world in a little one, as a new kind of angel, adoring God with both aspects of his twofold being, fully initiated into the visible creation but only partially into the invisible, king of all that exists on earth but subject to the King above, both earthly and heavenly, both transient and immortal, both visible and invisible, situated between greatness and lowliness, at the same time both spirit and flesh; spirit by grace, and flesh that he may be raised on high; spirit, that he may continue in existence and glorify his Benefactor, flesh, that he may suffer, and that through suffering may be reminded and chastened if he grows proud because of his greatness; a living being guided here by divine providence and then translated elsewhere; and, the greatest mystery of all, deified by turning towards God. . . .

8. This human creation He set in paradise (whatever the term "paradise" may mean), and honored him by granting

him self-determination, so that the good might belong to him
by virtue of his own free choice, no less than as the gift of
Him who provided the seeds. He set him in paradise as a
cultivator of immortal plants—perhaps by this is meant divine
concepts, both of the more simple and of the more perfect
kind—naked by virtue of his simplicity and his life without
artifice, and bereft of any covering or protection, for that is
how it was fittting that the original man should be. And He
gave him law as material upon which to exercise his free will.
The law was a commandment concerning the fruits which he
might eat, and which kind he was not to touch. The latter,
the tree of knowledge, was not planted originally with any
evil intent, nor was it forbidden in a spirit of jealousy: let
not the enemies of God make any such suggestion or think
to imitate the serpent. On the contrary, it was good if eaten
at the right time; for, as I understand it, the fruit was contemplation, which is only safely attempted by those who have
attained a more perfect state. But it was not good for those
at a lower stage of development, who have less control over
their desire, just as mature food is not profitable for those of
tender years who still need milk. But afterwards, through the
envy of the devil and the temptation to which the woman
succumbed because she was more vulnerable, and which she
then proposed to the man because she was more persuasive—
alas for my weakness! for mine is the infirmity of my first
parent—he forgot the commandment which had been given
to him and yielded to that bitter food. And so he became an
exile at once from the tree of life and from paradise and
from God through the wrong he had done, and put on the
garments of skin, by which is meant perhaps the grosser
flesh that is mortal and opaque; and thereupon he first experienced shame and hid from God. Yet in consequence he also
made a gain in the form of death, which cuts off sin, and so
prevents evil from becoming immortal. Thus the penalty becomes an act of compassion. For such is the way, I believe,
that God punishes.

9.   Initially man was corrected in many ways on account
of the many sins which the root of evil put forth like shoots,

for various reasons and on various occasions. He was corrected by word, by law, by prophets, by benefactions, by threats, by blows, by floods, by conflagrations, by wars, by victories, by defeats, by signs from the sky, by signs from the air, from the earth, from the sea, by signs performed by men, by cities and by nations, by unforeseen changes of fortune—the purpose of all these things being to extirpate evil. Finally, a stronger medicine was necessary. . . . This was the Logos of God Himself, who exists from all eternity, who is invisible, incomprehensible and incorporeal, who is the principle from the principle, the light from the light, the source of life and immortality, who is the impress of the archetype, the unmoved seal, the exact image, the word and expression of the Father. He came to His own image, put on flesh for the sake of flesh, mingled Himself with a rational soul on account of my soul, purifying like with like, and in all things except sin He became man. He was conceived by the Virgin, who was purified in advance in both soul and body by the Spirit; for it was necessary both that childbearing should be held in honor and that virginity should be held in higher honor still. So God came forth with the humanity He had assumed, a unity from two opposites, flesh and spirit: the second of these conferred deification, the first was deified. O strange mixture! O paradoxical mingling! He who Is becomes, the Uncreated is created, and the Unlimited is limited by means of a rational soul which mediates between the divinity and the grossness of the flesh. He who is rich becomes poor, for He becomes poor through my flesh that I may become rich through His divinity. He who is full is emptied, for He is emptied of His own glory for a little that I may partake of His fullness. What is this wealth of goodness? What is this mystery that concerns me? I partook of the image and did not preserve it; He partakes of my flesh in order that He may both save the image and immortalize the flesh. He communicates a second participation much more amazing than the first: at first He communicated to us what was superior, but now He Himself participates in what is inferior. The second action is more God-like than the first; but for those with understanding it is more sublime.

III

St Gregory of Nyssa

On Virginity 12-13, PG 46, 369-376C; *Gregorii Nysseni Opera,* ed. W. Jaeger, J. P. Cavarnos, V. W. Callahan, vol. VIII/i (Leiden 1952) 297, 24-304, 14; *Grégoire de Nysse, Traité de la virginité,* ed. M. Aubineau (Sources chrétiennes 119, Paris 1966) 398-426.

Since this rational animal endowed with intelligence, which is man, came into being as a product and imitation of the undefiled nature of God . . . he did not have within him either naturally or inherently, as he was first created, anything liable to the passions or to mortality. For it would not have been possible for the essential image to have been preserved if the beauty of the image had contradicted the archetype. On the contrary, passion was added to him later on after the first creation. It was added in the following way. Man was an image and likeness, as I have said, of the sovereign power which rules over all things . . . he was orientated by his own will towards what seemed good to him, and of his own free choice chose what was pleasing to him. But he was led astray by deceit and voluntarily embraced the disaster in which the whole human race is now involved. He himself became the inventor of evil; he did not come across it as something already created by God. For God did not make death; it was man who became, so to speak, the originator and creator of evil.

Now the enjoyment of the light of the sun is common to all who possess the faculty of sight, but one can, should one wish, cut oneself off from the perception of the light by shutting one's eyes. . . . When we shut our eyes the faculty of sight cannot function, and so it necessarily follows that the suspension of the act of seeing becomes an operation of darkness created voluntarily in man through the blocking of vision. Or alternatively, if in building a house one does not allow any openings through which the light can shine on what is inside, one will necessarily live in darkness through having voluntarily prevented the entry of the rays. In the same way, the first earthly man, or rather he who gave birth to evil in man, had the beautiful and the good which was present in nature all around him within his power, yet he deliberately invented by himself what was contrary to nature, and by his own free choice created the experience of evil by turning away from virtue. For evil, regarded as a substance in its own right, has no existence whatsoever in the nature of created things: it exists only in the exercise of free choice. For everything created by God is good and nothing is to be rejected: everything that God made was "very good" (Gen 1:31). But since the whole sequence of sin has intruded perniciously into human life in the way I have described, and from a small starting-point an infinity of evil has been poured into man, even that Godlike beauty of the soul which came into being in imitation of the archetype has been discolored like some iron implement by the rust of evil, and so has no longer preserved the loveliness of its own natural image but has been transformed into the ugliness of sin.

Therefore man, this "great and precious thing" as Scripture calls him (Prov 20:6, LXX), fell away from his own true dignity. Those who slip and fall into the mire find their outward form so plastered over with mud that they become unrecognizable even to their friends. Similarly, when the first man fell into the mire of sin, he not only lost the image of the incorrupt God, but put on the image that is corruptible and made of clay. Scripture urges us to put off this image and wash it away by a pure way of life as if with water (cf. Isa 1:16). When the earthly veil is stripped off, the beauty of the soul stands revealed once more. The rejection of what is alien means the soul's return to the state that is properly and naturally its own. There is no other way for us to attain this except by becoming again as we were when we were first created. . . .

This, therefore, is the meaning of the finding of what was lost: the restoration to its original state of the divine image which is now concealed by the filth of the flesh. We are to become that which the first man was in his first state of life. What, then, was he? He was naked of the covering of dead skins, and saw the face of God with easy familiarity. He did not as yet judge the good by the criteria of taste and sight, but only delighted in the Lord, and it was to this end that he availed himself of the helper that had been given to him, as Holy Scripture indicates when it says that he did not know her at first, before they were exiled from paradise and before she was condemned to the punishment of the pangs of child-birth because of the sin which she was deceived into committing (cf. Gen 2:18; 4:1).

Through this sequence of events, then, we have come to be outside paradise, having been excluded with our ancestor; but now by following the same sequence in reverse it is possible for us to retrace our steps and return to the original state of blessedness. What, then, was this sequence of events? In the beginning it was pleasure, engendered by deception, that began the fall (cf. Gen 3:6). Then shame and fear followed the passion of pleasure, and afterwards Adam and Eve no longer dared to appear in the presence of the Creator but hid themselves in leaves and shadows (cf. Gen 3:7-8). After this they were dressed in dead skins (cf. Gen 3:21). And thus they were sent as exiles into this disease-ridden land that demands such toil, and in which marriage was devised as a consolation for having to die.

If, therefore, we are to be released from this life and to be with Christ (cf. Phil 1:23), it is appropriate that we should begin our return by starting out again from the last stage of our departure. It is the same with those who have been separated from their own people: if they wish to return home, they first leave the place at which they last arrived in their journey. Therefore, since the last stage in our separation from the life of paradise was marriage, our argument suggests to those who wish to be released and to join Christ that they should abandon marriage first, since it is, as it were, their last lodging-place. Then they should withdraw from anxious toil in cultivating the land, to which man was subjected after sinning. Next they should dissociate themselves from the coverings of the flesh by putting off the garments of skin, that is, the will of the flesh, and by renouncing all the hidden deeds of shame. They should no longer be shaded by the fig tree of this bitter life, but should throw away the coverings made of these transient leaves of life and so stand again openly in the sight of the Creator. They should reject the deception of taste and sight, and no longer have the venomous serpent as their counsellor but the commandment of God alone. And the commandment is to touch only what is good and to reject the taste of what is evil, for it was from this that the whole sequence of our evils took its origin—from our not wishing to remain ignorant of evil. That is why it was forbidden to our first parents to acquire knowledge of what is contrary to good as well as of what is good. They were to abstain from "the knowledge of good and evil" (Gen 2:9), and to keep the good fruitful, pure, unmixed and without a share in any evil. This, in my opinion, is nothing other than to be with God alone, and to enjoy this delight continuously and without interruption, and no longer to mingle with this repose anything which draws one in the opposite direction. And if one may dare to say so, perhaps in this way one may be snatched up out of the world, which lies in the power of the devil, and be taken up again to paradise, which is what Paul too experienced when he heard and saw those ineffable and invisible things which it is not permissible for man to utter (cf. 2 Cor 12:4).

IV

St Maximos the Confessor

1. *Ambigua, PG* 91, 1304D-1312B.

The followers and servants of the Logos were initiated directly by Him into the knowledge of existent things, and they in turn imparted this knowledge to those who came after them; and so, in this way, by unbroken succession, the saints have received most of the divine mysteries. They tell us that the whole of created reality is susceptible of five divisions. They say that the first of these is that which divides uncreated nature from the created nature which in its entirety has acquired existence through coming into being. . . . The second is that by which the whole of the nature which has received being through having been created by God is divided into things intelligible and things sensible. The third is that by which sensible nature is divided into heaven and earth. The fourth is that by which the earth is divided into paradise and inhabited land. And the fifth division is that by which man is divided into male and female.

Now man has been set over all things as a kind of worship holding everything together, and has been appropriately placed in creation as a natural mediator in his own person between all the things which are at opposite extremes through any kind of division. Thus man possesses by virtue of his nature full power to bring about union through the mediation between all the extremes that he is able to effect, since in the different aspects of his own nature he is himself related to all these extremes. In this way it is his vocation to make manifest in his own person the great mystery of the divine purpose

211

in bringing into existence things divided—to show how the divided extremes in created beings may be reconciled in harmony, the near with the far, the lower with the higher, so that through gradual ascent all are eventually brought into union with God.

That is why man was introduced last among existent things, as a natural bond mediating between the extremes of the whole through his own parts, and bringing into unity in his own person those things which by nature are far distant from each other. Drawing all things out of their former division and bringing them united to God as their cause, and so advancing into God by the means available in the right sequence and order, he finally reaches the goal of the sublime ascent which is achieved through the union of all things, attaining God in whom there is no division.

First, through his utterly dispassionate relationship to divine virtue he frees the whole of nature from the attributes of male and female, which are in no way dependent, as we have already shown, on the divine purpose concerning the generation of man. It thus becomes clear that, according to this divine purpose, man was not intended to be divided into the categories of male and female, as is now the case; and that by acquiring perfect knowledge of the inner principles according to which he exists he may transcend this division.

Next, by uniting paradise with the inhabited land through holiness of life, he makes a single earth, not divided into its different parts, but rather brought together, since he is not dominated by any passionate attraction towards any of its parts.

Next, uniting heaven and earth through a life utterly identical with that of the angels in respect of virtue, as far as this is humanly possible, he makes the sensible creation in every way a single undivided whole, not separated locally from him at all in any of its dimensions. For he has become weightless through the spirit and is not drawn down to the earth by any bodily heaviness; he is not prevented from ascending to the heavens, for his mind is totally unaware of any of the things which might hold it back, but with full integrity it presses onwards to God and wisely forges ahead, as though upon a highway, a continuously straining forward with all its natural powers towards what lies ahead.

Next, by attaining equality with the angels in respect of knowledge, he unites things sensible and things intelligible, making him in terms of knowledge or ignorance. For his contemplative knowledge of the inward essences of created beings has become equal to that of the angels without falling short in any way. When he has attained this knowledge, true wisdom is poured out upon him with its infinite riches in so far as this is permissible, and henceforth fully and without intermediary it bestows on those who are worthy the unsearchable and inexpressible understanding of God.

And finally, in addition to all this, through love he also unites created nature with uncreated nature—how wonderful is God's lovingkindness towards us!—and manifests them as one and identical with each other by virtue of the habitual state of grace that he has attained. The whole of him then coinheres wholly in the whole of God, and he becomes everything that God is except for identity of essence. He receives the whole of God in place of himself, and as the prize for his ascent to God he comes to possess God Himself alone. For God is the end of the movement of all that moves, the firm and immovable ground of all that is drawn towards Him, the invisible and infinite term and goal of every definition, rule and law, whether of reason, mind or nature.

But man did not move around the unmoved—I mean God —as his own principle in the way that he was naturally created to do; but of his own free will, senselessly and in a manner contrary to nature, he moved around the things below him, over which he had been appointed by God to rule. And he abused the natural power given to him for the union of what was divided, using it instead to create divisions, and was thus pitiably in danger almost of lapsing into non-being. For this reason new forms of nature were devised, and, in a paradoxical way beyond nature, that which is utterly immovable by nature moved without moving, if one may so express it, around that which naturally moves. God, that is to say, became man in order to save man who was perishing: uniting in Himself the natural divisions throughout the whole

nature of the universe, and revealing the totality of the inward
essences which are expressed in all particular things, and
through which the union of what has been divided naturally
takes place, He fulfilled the great will of God the Father by
recapitulating all things in Himself, in whom they had also
been created.

In effecting this all-embracing union of all things in Himself, He began with our own division: He became perfect
man, from us, for us, and in conformity with us, possessing
everything that is ours without omitting anything except sin,
and in no way needing the addition of anything that is naturally connected with marriage. At the same time and by the
same token He revealed, in my opinion, that there also happened to be another method of increasing the human race, a
method foreknown to God, which would have prevailed if
the first man had kept the commandment and had not descended to the level of the beasts by abusing his own faculties, thus bringing about the distinction between male and
female and the division of nature. Man, as I have said, had no
need at all of this division in order to come into being, and
it is possible for him to be without it in the future, there
being no need for these things to endure permanently. For
in Christ Jesus, says the divine Apostle, there is "neither
male nor female" (Gal 3:28).

Then, when He had sanctified our inhabited land through
dwelling in it in a way befitting man, He proceeded after
death to paradise without encountering any obstacle, just as
He promised with complete truth to the thief. . . .

Thereafter. since henceforth there is no difference for Him
between paradise and our inhabited land, He appeared again
in our land and ate with His disciples after His resurrection
from the dead, proving that the earth is a single and undivided whole and keeps its inward essence free from the distinctions caused by division.

Next, through His ascension into heaven He clearly united
heaven and earth, and when He had proceeded into heaven
with this earthly body of the same nature and substance as
ours, He proved that the whole of sensible nature is one in

its more universal inward essence, abolishing in Himself the characteristic division that cuts it in two.

Then, in addition to this, He immediately afterwards united things sensible and intelligible by passing successively through all the divine and intelligible orders of heaven in both His soul and His body, that is, in our complete nature. So in His own person He made manifest the convergence of the whole of creation into a unity, by virtue of its highest and most universal inward essence which is entirely without division or conflict.

And, last of all, He came to God Himself, bringing the true revelation of humanity with Him. On our behalf, as it is written, He appeared as man in the sight of God the Father, He who as Logos cannot be separated from the Father in any way whatsoever. As man He had fulfilled in deed and in truth with faultless obedience all that He Himself as God had decreed should be done. He accomplished perfectly everything that God the Father had willed for us, whereas we through misuse had ruined the faculty given to us naturally from the beginning for this purpose.

He first united us to ourselves in His own person through the abolition of the distinction between male and female. He demonstrated that, instead of being men and women, clearly divided by sexual distinctions, we are properly and truly only human beings, called to total transfiguration in accordance with Him, and bearing safe and altogether unimpaired His image, which is in no way affected by any of the marks of corruption. For our sake and in union with us He embraced the whole of creation along with all its extremes, mediating between them by means of His own parts. He drew together both paradise and the inhabited land, both heaven and earth, both things sensible and things intelligible tightly and indissolubly around Himself, uniting them with each other, since He has body and senses and soul and mind like ours, through which, as being parts of Himself, He has reconciled each extreme with the other that is related to it. In this way He has recapitulated all things in Himself in a manner befitting God, as I have already described, and has proved the whole of creation to be a unity, as if it were one vast human being.

Through the coming together of its parts with one another it is brought to completion and inwardly reconciled throughout the whole of its existence. It is united by virtue of the one, simple, unlimited and undifferentiated concept of creation *ex nihilo*: this shows that the whole of created being has the same single and entirely undifferentiated inward essence, since non-existence preceded its existence.

2. *Ambigua, PG* 91, 1248A-1249C.

The sensible world is naturally fitted to provide the five senses with information, since it falls within their scope and draws them to an apprehension of itself. In a similar way, the intellectual world of the virtues falls within the scope of the faculties of the soul and guides them towards the spirit, rendering them uniform through their unvarying movement around the spirit alone and through their apprehension of it. And the bodily senses themselves, in accordance with the more divine inward essences befitting them, may be said to provide the faculties of the soul with information, since they gently activate these faculties through their own apprehension of the inward essences (*logoi*) of created things; and through this apprehension the divine Logos is recognized, as if in a written text, by those clear-sighted enough to perceive truth.

Thus the senses have been called exemplary images of the faculties of the soul, since each sense with its organ, that is, its organ of perception, has naturally been assigned beforehand to each of the soul's faculties in an analogous manner and by a certain hidden principle. It is said that the sense of sight belongs to the intellective faculty, that is, to the mind, the sense of hearing to the rational faculty, that is, to reason, the sense of smell to the incensive faculty, the sense of taste to the appetitive faculty, and the sense of touch to the vivifying faculty. Or to put it more plainly, the organ of sight, that is, the eye, is simply an image of the mind; the organ of hearing, that is, the ear, is an image of reason; the organ of smell, that is, the nose, is an image of the incensive faculty;

taste is an image of the appetitive faculty; and touch an image of life.

The soul, then, according to the law of God who has wisely created all things, naturally makes use of these senses through its own faculties, and in various ways reaches out through them to sensible things. If it uses the senses properly, discerning by means of its own faculties the manifold inner essences of created beings, and if it succeeds in wisely transmitting to itself all the visible things in which God is hidden and proclaimed in silence, then by the use of its own free choice it creates a world of spiritual beauty within the understanding. This it does by combining the four general virtues with each other as if they were physical elements, so as to form from them a world completely constructed in a spiritual and intellectual way; taking each virtue as foundation, it interweaves the activity of its faculties with the senses. The four general virtues are moral judgment, formed from the interweaving of the contemplative and epistemic activity belonging to the intellective and rational faculty with the senses of seeing and hearing, which are directed towards the sensible objects appropriate to them; courage, formed from the interweaving of the incensive aspect with the sense of smell, that is, with the nostril, in which the incensive aspect is said to dwell as breath, this aspect being directed in a highly controlled way towards the appropriate sensible objects; self-restraint, formed from the interweaving of the appetitive faculty with the sense of taste, directed in a moderate way towards its own sensible object; and justice, formed from the even and well-ordered and harmonious application of the activity of the vivifying faculty through the sense of touch to virtually all sensible objects.

Moreover, from these four general virtues two yet more general virtues are said to be formed by a process of synthesis, namely wisdom and meekness, wisdom being the goal of contemplatives, and meekness that of those leading the active life. Thus from moral judgement and justice is formed wisdom, as the all-inclusive cause of the knowledge exercised in the science of moral judgment and justice; that is why, as I have said, it is the goal of contemplatives. From courage and self-restraint is formed meekness, which is nothing other than the complete immovability of the incensive and appetitive aspects with regard to what is contrary to nature. Some have called this immovability dispassion, and for this reason it is the goal of those engaged in the active life.

These in turn lead to the most general virtue of all, love. In beginners it is productive of ecstasy, in those moved under its influence it is productive of progress, and in those who have arrived at its goal it is productive of union. In contrast to all the other virtues it is productive of deification. Thus the soul, moving in a wise manner and operating in accordance with the divinely perfect principle of its origin and existence, apprehends sensible things in a profitable way through the senses, since it has assimilated the spiritual essences that are in them, and appropriates the senses themselves, now endowed with reason through the abundance of rationality (*logos*) which they contain, using them as intelligent vehicles of its own faculties. It joins these faculties to the virtues, and itself through the virtues to the more divine essences within these virtues. The more divine essences of the virtues are united with the spiritual mind hidden invisibly within them, and the spiritual mind of the more divine essences in the virtues, rejecting entirely the natural and voluntary relationship which the soul has with present things, brings the soul, once it has been rendered simple and whole, as an offering to the whole of God. And God embraces the whole of the soul, together with the body natural to it, and renders them like Him in due proportion, so that He who by nature can in no way be manifested to any being whatsoever as He is in Himself is able to be manifested wholly throughout the whole of the soul in a manner beyond all description.

3. *Ambigua, PG* 91, 1345C-1349A.

To what end and for whose sake did the Teacher unite the birth of baptism with the incarnation? . . . I shall briefly explain what I have learned as best I can. Those who have treated the divine sayings in a mystical way and have invested them, as is fitting, with more sublime interpretations say that in the beginning man was created in the image of God for the undoubted purpose of being born of the Spirit by free choice, and of acquiring what was in the likeness of God through keeping the divine commandment which had been laid upon him. In this way the same man would be on the one hand a creature of God by nature, and on the other a son of God and a god through the Spirit by grace. For it was not possible in any other way for man after his creation to be proved a son of God and a god through deification by grace, unless first by free choice he had been born of the Spirit through the self-moving and sovereign power which naturally unites him with God.

When this deifying, divine and incorporeal birth was abandoned by the first man, because he chose what is pleasant and manifest to the senses in preference to the intellectual blessings that until then were invisible to him, he was condemned appropriately to be subject to a bodily birth which is involuntary, material and perishable. For since he had deliberately chosen the inferior instead of the superior, God decided in His just judgement that man should exchange a birth which was free, dispassionate, sovereign and pure for one which is impassioned, servile and subject to necessity in the likeness of the dumb beasts of the earth, which are devoid of intelligence; and so instead of divine and ineffable honor close to God, he was condemned to a life of dishonor on the same material level as the dumb beasts.

But since the Logos, who had created human nature, wished to free man from this state and restore him to his divine inheritance, He truly became a man from human stock and was born in a bodily way without sin for man's sake, and was baptized, voluntarily undergoing a spiritual birth of adoption on our behalf, although He was God by essence and Son of God by nature. This He did in order to annul physical birth. Therefore since the Son and Logos who made us, and who alone with the Holy Spirit is equal in Godhead and glory to the Father, truly became man for us and from us, and was born in a bodily way without sin, and though God by nature condescended to undergo on our behalf the spiritual birth of adoption through baptism, it was for this reason that the Teacher, in my opinion, joined the birth of baptism to the incarnation, so that it may be understood as a setting aside and superseding of physical birth.

When Adam voluntarily abandoned this spiritual birth which leads to deification, he was condemned to the bodily birth which leads to corruption. He who alone is free and sinless then chose of His own accord, because He is good and compassionate, to enter into our transgression and to become man. He condemned Himself voluntarily along with us; condescending to undergo physical birth, in which existed the power of our condemnation, He mystically restored spiritual birth. And when He had loosed the bonds of bodily birth on our behalf within His own person, He gave to us who believe in His name power through the birth which is spiritual and freely chosen to become children of God instead of children of flesh and blood.

Therefore on account of our condemnation the incarnation and bodily birth of the Lord came first, and then the birth received spiritually through baptism followed next for the sake of our salvation and restoration by grace, or to put it more plainly, for the sake of our refashioning. In other words, God united the principle of my being with the principle of my well being, and healed the separation and division between these which I had caused. Then through these two things He wisely drew me towards the principle of eternal being, in which man is no longer subject to change and alteration, since through the great and general resurrection an end has been brought within the dispensation of the visible world to all such change, and man is born into the immortal life, in which his existence is unchanging. For it was on man's account that the nature of visible things received its being by creation, and it is in union with man that it will receive by grace that which is in essence incorruptible.

Let me briefly recall and summarize the main point of what I have been saying. Conceptually we may distinguish, in the bodily birth of our Savior, between His state preceding His human nature and His present state as a man like us, in which He died. Again, we may distinguish between the natural manner of generation and the manner in which He was born, and furthermore, between the various forms of the substantial generation of the soul and of the body, and in addition, between conception without seed and birth without corruption. It therefore depends on us, as good judges of the various ideas which have been put forward, to choose which is the best.

V

St Nicolas Kavasilas

The Life in Christ 6, *PG* 150, 680A-684B.

It was for the new man that human nature was created at the beginning. It was for Him that our intellect and appetitive aspect were prepared. We have received our reason that we might know Christ, our desire that we might run towards Him; we have memory that we might bear Him within us. He is the archetype for all who have been created. It was not the old Adam who was the model for the new, but the new who was the model for the old. For if it is said that the new Adam was made in the likeness of the old (cf. Rom 8:3), this is because of the corruption which the one initiated and the other inherited, so that He might heal the sickness of our nature with the medicines which He brings and, as Paul says, "so that what is mortal may be swallowed up by life" (1 Cor 5:4).

Therefore to us who have known him first the old Adam seems to be the archetype of our nature. But to Him who has all things before His eyes prior to their existence the first Adam is an imitation of the second and was fashioned in accordance with His form and image. But he did not remain in that state. Instead, he set off towards it but failed to attain it. Therefore it was the former who received the law but the latter who kept it. It was the old Adam who was required to be obedient but the new who actually performed what was demanded. . . . The former Adam introduced an imperfect life which needed countless forms of assistance; the latter became the father of immortal life for men. Our nature from the

beginning had immortality as its aim, but only achieved it
later in the body of the Savior, who, by rising from the dead
to immortal life, became the pioneer of immortality for our
race. To sum up, the Savior was the first and only person to
show us the true humanity which is perfect in manner of life
and in all other respects as well.

Such is man's true goal, and it was with a view to this
final end that God fashioned him. By his final end I mean
a life without defilement, when his body has been purified of
corruption and his will delivered from all sin. Perfection consists in this, that the craftsman makes everything exactly as
he thinks it ought to be, as when a statue is rendered beautiful
by the final touch of the sculptor's hand. Whereas the first
Adam fell far short of perfection, the second was perfect in
all respects, and enabled men to share in perfection, and
adapted the whole race to Himself. How, then, should one
not inevitably conclude that the latter is the model of the
former, and that the second Adam is the archetype from
whom the first has been derived? For it is altogether absurd
to think that what is the most perfect of all strives to attain
the level of the imperfect, and that the blind lead those who
see. It is not surprising that the inferior is chronologically
earlier; yet it is also reasonable to suppose that the perfect is
the source of the imperfect, when we bear in mind that many
things were prepared for human use even before the appearance of man, and that man who is the measure of all these
things emerged from the earth last of all.

So then, for all these reasons man hastens towards Christ
by his nature, his will and his thoughts, not only because of
His divinity, which is the goal of all things, but because of
His other, human nature as well. He is the fulfilment of
human love. He is the delight of our thoughts. To love anything or to think about it apart from Him is a manifest
failure to do what is right, a turning aside from the original
first principles of our nature. So that we may be able to have
our full attention fixed always upon Him, and that we may
remain thus attentive to Him at all times, let us make Him
every hour of the day the subject of our thoughts. There is
certainly no need of special preparation for prayer, no need

of special places or of a loud voice for those who call upon Him. There is no place in which He is not present; it is impossible for Him not to be near us. For those who seek Him He is closer to them than their very heart. And it follows that we should believe strongly that our prayers will be answered, and not give way to doubt because our ways are wicked but take courage because He upon whom we call is good. . . . For we do not call upon the Master that He may crown us . . . but that He may have mercy. . . . Let us call upon God with our voice, with our will and with our thoughts, that we may apply the only saving remedy for all the sins we have committed, "for there is no other name," says Scripture, "by which we must be saved" (Acts 4:12).

The true bread that "strengthens man's heart" (Ps 104:15), that came down from heaven bringing us life, will be sufficient for all these things, will give us the resilience to apply ourselves zealously, and will draw out the innate indolence from our souls. This is the bread that we must seek in every way as our food, let us feed always at this banquet so as to ward off our hunger. And let us not weaken and harm our souls by abstaining from this table more than we should on the grounds that we are deeply unworthy of the sacraments. Instead, we should approach the priests about our sins and so drink the cleansing blood. In any case, if we keep these thoughts before us, we will not become guilty of such grave matters as would exclude us from the sacred altar. To dare to approach the holy gifts after committing mortal sins would be an act of wickedness; but those who are not sick with such diseases should not in an untimely fashion abstain from the bread.

VI

St Nikodimos of the Holy Mountain

"An Apology for my note on our Lady the Theotokos in the book
Unseen Warfare," from *A Handbook of Spiritual Counsel, or
On the Custody of the Five Senses,* published by S. Schoinas
(Volos 1969), 207-16.

Certain learned men, who occupy themselves particularly
with sacred theology, have read the note which I have written
on our Lady the Theotokos in the recently published book,
Unseen Warfare,[1] and have taken issue with me: (a) because
I said that if, for the sake of argument, all men and the rest
of creation chose to become evil, our Lady the Theotokos
would by herself have been sufficient to render thanks to God;
and (b) because I said that the whole of the intelligible and
sensible world was created for this end, namely for our Lady
the Theotokos, and that our Lady the Theotokos was created
in turn for our Lord Jesus Christ. Because some have expressed doubts about these statements, I shall defend myself
briefly here in order to resolve their difficulties.

. . . With regard to the second point I reply that the
whole of the world, both intelligible and sensible, was created
for this end, namely for our Lady the Theotokos, and our
Lady the Theotokos was created in turn for our Lord Jesus
Christ, as the wise and most learned Joseph Vryennios[2] has
expressly stated with great clarity in the following words:
"And to sum up, the entire goal of this world and of every
element and every species in the whole of creation, and of

---

[1] A translation and adaptation of a 16th-century spiritual classic, Lorenzo
Scupoli's *Combattimento spirituale,* made by Nikodimos for Orthodox readers.
[2] Byzantine theologian (early 15th century).

every race and tribe of men in all ages and at all times, has as
its flower our Lady the Theotokos and as its most beautiful
fruit—I speak in a human fashion—her only begotten Son"
(*Second Homily on the Annunciation*, vol. 2, p. 143). Nor
is this all. It is also true that the whole of the intelligible and
sensible world was foreknown and preordained precisely for
this end. How is this evident? From the following. The Holy
Scriptures bear witness that the mystery of the incarnate dispensation of the divine Logos is the beginning of all the ways
of the Lord, and that it comes before all creation, and that
it was preordained before the preordaining of the salvation
of all who are being saved. The Scriptural texts which witness
to this are these: "The Lord created me as the beginning of
His ways, for His works. Before the ages He established me"
(Prov 8:22-3. LXX); "He is the image of the invisible God,
the first-born of all creation" (Col 1:15—notice here that the
Apostle did not say simply "of creation" but "of all creation,"
that is, of both the intelligible and the sensible parts of
creation); and, "Those whom He foreknew He also predestined to be conformed to the image of his Son, so that He
might be the first-born among many brethren" (Rom 8:29).
Such, then, are the words of the divine Paul.

And many of the holy Fathers agree here with the divine
Scriptures. In their interpretation of the above texts they say
that the phrases "the Lord created me as the beginning of
His ways" and "the first-born of all creation" are to be understood as referring to Jesus Christ, but not with regard to His
divinity, because as God He is of one substance with the
Father and coeternal with Him, and He was not created by
God, nor is He the first of creatures, as Arius blasphemously
says. On the contrary, they are to be understood as referring
to His humanity, which God foresaw before any other thing
as the beginning of His divine and eternal decrees, the first
of all created things. The Fathers who affirm this are Athanasios the Great, *Against the Arians* iii and iv; Cyril of Alexandria, *Treasury* iv, 4, 6 and 8; and the divine Augustine, *On
the Trinity*.

That the foreordaining of Christ is the beginning and
source of the foreordaining of all who are being saved, the

Apostle witnesses when he says, "Those whom He foreknew He also predestined to be conformed to the image of His Son" (Rom 8:29). And Oikoumenios also confesses the same doctrine in his interpretation of this text: "That which the Son of God is by nature in the incarnation," he says (namely holy and sinless), "is what they too will be by grace. And he calls the dispensation an image of the Son, and therefore His body." This image, a life lived in holiness, utterly blameless in every way, was also interpreted by Cyril of Alexandria in the same way as by Oikoumenios. And Koressios[3] in his work on predestination sets out this teaching in greater detail.

In the sixtieth solution of the *Questions* on the divine incarnation, the Godbearing Maximos says the following: "This is the great and hidden mystery. This is the blessed end for which all things were created. This is the divine purpose that underlies the beginning of existent things, the purpose formed by God before ever they existed, on account of which all things exist, whereas it does not itself exist on account of anything. With a view to this end God brought forth the essences of existent things. This is properly the fulfilment of providence and of all that has been planned, by virtue of which all the things made by God are recapitulated in Him. It is this that circumscribes all the ages and manifests as a mystery the great will of God that is infinitely transcendent, that is beyond infinity and exists before all ages. It was a Messenger of this that He who is by essence the Logos of God became man and, if it is permissible to speak thus, rendered visible the very inmost depths of the Father's goodness, and in His own person showed the end for which created things wisely received the beginning of their existence." Do you see how it was for the sake of this mystery that all things were foreknown and preordained and brought into being, but the mystery itself was not foreknown or preordained or brought into being for the sake of any other end?

Gregory of Thessaloniki[4] says almost the same as the

---

[3]George Koressios of Chios: Greek lay theologian and physician (17th century).
[4]St Gregory Palamas.

Godbearing Maximos in his sermon on the Epiphany in the following words: "When the Father said about Him who was baptized in the flesh, 'This is my beloved Son in whom I am well pleased' (Matt 3:17), He showed that all the other things which had earlier been proclaimed through the prophets—the lawgivings, the promises and the adoptions— were incomplete and were not spoken and performed in accordance with the antecedent will of God, but looked to this present end and were brought to fulfilment through what is now being accomplished. And why do I mention the law- givings and promises and adoptions which came to us through the prophets? Even the original creation of the world was established for Him who is baptized here below as son of man but is acknowledged by God from above as the only beloved Son, through whom are all things and for whom all things exist, as the Apostle says (cf. 1 Cor 8:6). Therefore even the original creation of man, when he was fashioned in the image of God, took place on His account, that man might be able some day to accommodate the Archetype. And the law decreed by God in paradise was on His account. For the Legislator would not have made a decree if it was intended that it should remain unfulfilled for ever. And the things subsequently spoken and performed by God were nearly all on His account. Nor is this all. Everything beyond this world, the angelic natures and orders and the heavenly degrees, have also from the beginning had as their final end the dispensa- tion of the incarnation, and to this they have ministered from start to finish. For the good pleasure of the Father is the prevenient and good and perfect will of God. And He is the One alone in whom the Father is well pleased and rejoices and takes pleasure; One alone is His wonderful Counsellor, the Angel of His great will; One alone listens to His Father and speaks and bestows eternal life on those who obey Him."

Do you see that God made man in His own image for this reason, that man might be able to accommodate the Archetype through the incarnation? Therefore God created man as a link between the intelligible and the sensible worlds and as a recapitulation and summary of all creatures for this purpose, that by being united with man He might be united with all creatures, and that everything in heaven and on earth might be recapitulated in Christ, as Paul says (cf. Eph 1:9-10), and that Creator and creation might be one by hypostatic union, in the words of the Godbearing Maximos. Therefore the incarnation of God was necessary, as the divine Cyril of Alexandria testifies (in chapter 17 of his *Commentary on Matthew*). . . . Furthermore the holy Augustine also says in his *Enchiridion* (chapter 26) that it was for this reason that God assumed a human body, that both the soul and the body of man might be sanctified, the soul through His divinity and the body through his humanity.

I will not dwell on the fact that the angelic orders also had need of the dispensation of the incarnation, not only that they might receive immutability through it—for before the incarnation they did not possess this attribute, in the opinion of many theologians—but also that they might become more receptive and consequently enjoy the illuminations and mysteries of God with much greater clarity. That is why the wise Theodoret said that the angels after the incarnation see God not in the likeness of His glory as they did previously, but in the true and living covering of His flesh. And for the same reason Paul called Christ (that is, as man) "the head over all things" (Eph 1:22), or as the divine Jerome says, "over all the Church, that is, over angels as well as men." Dionysios the Areopagite also says the following on the subject of angels: "They were counted worthy to enter into communion with Jesus in a similar way, not through divinely formed images representing the theurgic likeness of God but by approaching Him in very truth through direct participation in the knowledge of His theurgic illuminations" (*Celestial Hierarchy*, chapter vii, 2). And St Isaac said: "Before the sojourning of Christ in the body it did not lie in the angels' power to approach these divine mysteries, but when the Logos became incarnate, He opened the doors to them through Jesus" (*Homily* 84).

Miniatis[5] says the same most clearly in his sermon for the Sunday before the Nativity of Christ: "Since the great mystery

[5]Elias Miniatis, Bishop of Kernitsa and Kalavryta (d. 1714): the most celebrated Greek preacher in the period of the Turkocratia.

of the incarnate dispensation is the most sublime, the most noble and the most perfect work of the divine wisdom and power of the Creator, it was accordingly predetermined and foreknown before anything else by the omniscient mind of God. Before God preordained the creation either of angels or of men or of any other creature, He preordained in His eternal will the incarnation of the divine Logos. Therefore the incarnation of the divine Logos is called in the sacred Scriptures 'the beginning of the ways of the Lord' (Prov 8:22, LXX), and the incarnate divine Logos Himself, 'the first-born of all creation' (Col 1:15)." He then continues: "And it was fitting that the incarnate dispensation should have been pre-ordained by God before any other work. For the sacred theologians say that the incarnate dispensation more than any other of God's works renders the greatest glory to God. All human beings as a whole and all the angels as a whole cannot aspire to rendering as much glory to God as the God-man, the Logos, renders on His own. It is for this reason that in speaking to the unoriginate Father He says, 'I glorified Thee on earth' (John 17:4)." If then according to this wise teacher the mystery of the incarnation was foreknown and preordained before any other creature, it follows that this must be the end for which all creatures were foreknown and preordained, since they were foreknown and preordained after it.

Moreover, George Koressios says in his *Difficulties Relating to the Incarnate Dispensation* that Christ is named last of God's works according to Cyril of Alexandria and other doctors. If, then, Christ is called the end of God's works as regards His humanity, and the end of each thing is prior in contemplation and knowledge, although subsequent in action and coming forth, according to Aristotle (*Metaphysics*, Book 7) and all the ancient and modern metaphysicians, it follows that Christ too as regards His humanity, by virtue of which He is the end of God's works, was contemplated and fore-known and preordained by God before anything else, even though He was later in terms of coming forth, since according to the philosophers all intermediate stages are formed in the mind in dependence on a pre-existing end. Furthermore, the mystery of the incarnate dispensation is called by Isaiah "the ancient plan" of God: "O Lord, Thou art my God," he says, "I will exalt Thee, I will praise Thy name; for Thou hast done wonderful things, an ancient and true plan" (Isa 25:1). It was called the ancient plan because it was the original and first of all God's plans. If another plan had been foreknown before this one, this plan would not have been called ancient but rather later and more recent.

I will add something at once more sublime and more profound. There are three things in God, namely essence, hypostasis and energy. The energy is more exterior, the hypostasis more interior, and the essence the most interior of the three. For Basil the Great said, "The energies of God descend to us, but His essence remains unapproachable." In accordance with these three, God possesses from all eternity three general relationships. First, the Father possesses the relationship of communicating in His essence with His consubstantial Son and His Holy Spirit, the former begotten and the latter proceeding from all eternity. For if God had remained utterly and absolutely without relationships, He would have had neither a Son nor a Holy Spirit, and He would not have communicated His essence to them. Instead, the three would have been a single essence. Secondly, the Son possesses the relationship of communicating in His hypostasis with His humanity; through this relationship He foreknew and preordained His actual union with His humanity in time. For the humanity, not having its own hypostasis, communicated in the hypostasis of the Son and received its being through it. Thirdly, from all eternity God—and especially the Holy Spirit, in whom all the common energy of the Blessed Trinity resides in a special way, according to Koressios and other theologians—possesses the relationship of communicating in His energy with all creatures. Through this relationship He foreknew all intelligible and sensible creatures and preordained their existence. For creatures participated only in the energy and power of God, and not in His hypostasis or essence and nature, since they receive their being through the divine power and energy. Thus as regards the things that were foreknown, it follows that since the hypostasis is more interior than the energy, the relationship according to hypostasis is more interior than the relationship according to energy. If this is so, the foreknowledge and predetermination of the humanity of the divine Logos will consequently be more interior than the foreknowledge and predetermination, according to the relationship of the energy, of all other creatures. And if the foreknowledge of the humanity of the Lord is more interior, it is clear that it is also prior in order and the cause of the foreknowledge of creatures. For the divine hypostasis, on which the relationship and foreknowledge of the humanity is based, is the cause of the divine energy, as all theologians admit. And it is on this energy that the relationship and foreknowledge of all creatures depend.

To what has been said I would also add the following. Using almost the same sublime and God-befitting terms as those in which the Godbearing Maximos, as mentioned above, honors and discusses the mystery of the incarnate dispensation, Andrew of Crete, that divine hymn-writer and most penetrating of theologians, also celebrates the life-giving and God-receiving substance of the Theotokos as the instrument and direct means and most necessary because without which such a mystery would not have been possible. And what else should we expect, seeing that she is the mother of the incarnate divine Logos? And so it is that he says of her in the second of his three homilies on the Dormition: "The body of the Theotokos is therefore life-giving, since it received the life-giving fullness of the Godhead itself. It is the exact copy of the original beauty. It is matter totally consonant with the divine incarnation. It is the macrocosm in miniature, bringing the world that does not exist into existence. This is the consummation of the covenants which God has made with us. This is the revelation of the hidden depths of divine incomprehensibility. This is the objective which was planned before all ages by the Creator of the ages. This is the fulfilment of all the divine oracles. This is the ineffable design, transcending all knowledge, of God's pre-eternal solicitude for man." If the Theotokos is called by this theologian the "objective" planned by God "before all ages," and if the Godbearing Maximos in referring to this divine objective said that it is the purpose and end formed by God before all things existed,

it follows that the Theotokos may not inappropriately be herself called the purpose and end, with a view to which God
has produced the essences of created beings, that is, the intelligible and sensible worlds. . . . And this is proved by the
outcome. For the intelligible world of the angels and the
sensible world of men were through the Theotokos counted
worthy, the one of immutability, the other of the knowledge
of God, as the famous theologian and teacher Joseph Vryennios testifies when he says that God "created another heaven
endowed with a soul and with reason, so that through this
men could attain knowledge of Him and those angels which
had not yet fallen could attain immutability" (*Second Homily
on the Nativity of the Theotokos,* vol. iii, p. 15). And now,
since our Lady the Theotokos as the Mother of God is in the
immediate presence of God and incomparably surpasses not
only men but even the first and highest ranks of the angels,
the cherubim and the seraphim, she distributes in her own
person the wealth of all the graces and divine illuminations
that come from God to all, to angels as well as men, just as
the Church of Christ as a whole generally believes.

    . . . Why did the Godbearing Maximos say above that all
creatures were made for the mystery of the divine incarnation,
but the latter was not made for any other end, whereas the
divine Scriptures and the other Godbearing Fathers manifestly proclaim that this mystery was brought about for the
refashioning and salvation of man? It seems to be that since,
as the metaphysicians say, some things are only intermediate
terms and not ends, others are both intermediate terms and
ends at the same time, that is, ends in relation to what is
inferior to them and intermediate terms in relation to what
is superior, and others are only ends and not intermediate
terms—these are also called ends of ends since they are
superior to everything else—this is why the Godbearing Maximos teaches here that the mystery of the incarnation of the
divine Logos is only an end and not an intermediate term.
For it is the highest and most sublime of all the works of the
Holy Trinity and the supreme end of ends, on account of
which all things exist, while it does not itself exist on account
of anything. For what else is higher than the hypostatic union

of the Creator with the creature? Yet if it is viewed in a
different light, it may be said to have taken place for the
refashioning and salvation of man.

Broadly speaking, the mystery of the divine incarnation is
a beginning and an intermediate stage and an end of all
creatures because the foreknowledge and predetermination
of this mystery was the beginning and cause of the foreknowledge and predetermination and creation of all creatures, according to the texts, "The Lord created me as the beginning
of His ways, for His works" (Prov 8:22, LXX), and, "the
first-born of all creation" (Col 1:15), which, as I have already
stated, refer to the Son and Logos as man. And the Godbearing Maximos says in the sixtieth solution of the *Questions*:
"For the sake of Christ, that is, in accordance with Christ, all
the ages and whatever exists in the ages received the beginning and the end of their being in Christ. For before all ages
there was planned the union of finite and infinite, measured
and unmeasured, limited and unlimited, created and uncreated, motionlessness and movement; and in these last days
this union has come to pass, revealed in Christ, thus fulfilling
the foreknowledge of God."

This mystery also became an intermediate stage because it
brought to fulfilment the foreknowledge of God, as the divine
Maximos has just said. It gave immutability to the angels and
motionlessness to evil, as was stated above in quotations from
the divine Gregory of Thessaloniki, Joseph Vryennios and
Nikitas. This immutability of the angels was called the salvation of the invisible world by Gregory the Theologian in his
Oration on Easter. The divine Maximos also said that the
mystery of the incarnation was foreknown for the following
reason: "that those things which move by nature might stand
around that which is by essence utterly immovable, having
transcended movement towards themselves and towards each
other;" and Maximos's scholiast adds: "by the union with God
of all that has been transformed and made immutable." It
granted to men the dissolution of original sin, the gift of
divine grace, incorruptibility, immortality, immutability, salvation and a thousand other blessings.

This mystery is also an end because for both angels and

men and for the whole of creation it became their perfection and deification and glory and blessedness, and because it became the recapitulation of things heavenly and earthly, the hypostatic union of Creator with creatures, and the glory of the unoriginate Father, who is glorified not by mere creatures but by His own essential Son and Logos, who put on human nature. This is the final end of all things beyond which there is no higher end, "on account of which all things exist but which does not itself exist on account of anything," to quote the divine Maximos again, so that, as the Apostle says, "at the name of Jesus every knee should bow, in heaven and on earth and under the earth, and every tongue confess that Jesus Christ is Lord" (Phil 2:10-11). Why and for what purpose? In order to glorify the Father—"to the glory of God the Father" (Phil 2:11).

From what has been said, then, anyone can conclude that unquestionably the mystery of the incarnation had to take place, for the chief and supreme and essential reason that this mystery was the preordained will of God, as I have said following Gregory of Thessaloniki, and has as its supreme moving cause the infinite and essential and supremely good goodness of God, or rather, "the very inmost depths of the Father's goodness," as the Godbearing Maximos said; and secondly because it was necessary for all creatures, both intelligible and sensible, as their beginning, middle and end, as I have shown.

These few points are sufficient, I think, as an apology to fair-minded arbiters and readers of my note on our Lady the Theotokos which I have mentioned. I beg them not to calumniate me unreasonably. For I have not written on this matter in accordance with my own opinion and teaching but have followed the teaching of the theologians I have mentioned. But if some people are perhaps moved by passion to condemn me (and I pray that this may not be the case), they would be condemning rather the Godbearing Maximos, Gregory of Thessaloniki, Andrew the Great and the others, from whom I have drawn this teaching.

Bibliography

AGOURIDES, S., *Philon o Ioudaios* (Offprint from *Grigorios Palamas*), Thessaloniki 1967.

AUBIN, P., "L'image dans l'œuvre de Plotin," *Recherches de science religieuse* 41 (1953) 348-79.

BENOIT, A., *Saint Irenée, Introduction à l'étude de sa théologie*, Paris 1960.

BERNARD, R., *L'image de Dieu d'après saint Athanase*, Paris 1952.

BRATSIOTIS, P., "To Gen. 1, 26 en ti orthodoxo theologia," *Orthodoxia* 27 (1952) 359-75.

_____ *Anthropologia tis P. Diathikis*, I. *O anthropos os theion dimiourgima*, Athens 1967.

BURGHARDT, W., "Cyril of Alexandria on Wool and Linen," *Traditio* 2 (1944) 484-6.

CAMELOT, P., "La théologie de l'image de Dieu," *Revue des sciences philosophiques et théologiques* 40 (1956) 443-71.

CHRISTOU, P., "To anthropinon pliroma kata tin didaskalian tou Grigoriou Nyssis," *Kleronomia* 4, 1 (1972) 41-62.

CORSINI, E., "Plérôme cosmique chez Grégoire de Nysse," *Ecriture et culture philosophique dans la pensée de Grégoire de Nysse*, ed. M. Harl, Leiden 1971, 111-26.

CROUZEL, H., *Théologie de l'image de Dieu chez Origène*, Paris 1956.

DALMAIS, I.-H., "Divinisation, Patristique grecque," *Dictionnaire de spiritualité* 3, 1376-89.

DANIÉLOU, J., "L'apocatastase chez saint Grégoire de Nysse," *Recherches de science religieuse* 30 (1940) 328-47.

_____ *Platonisme et théologie mystique. Doctrine spirituelle de saint Grégoire de Nysse*, nouvelle ed., Paris 1954.

_____ "Les tuniques de peau chez Grégoire de Nysse," *Glaube Geschichte. Festschrift für Ernst Benz*, Leyden 1967.

DIMITROPOULOS, P., *I anthropologia tou M. Athanasiou*, Athens 1954.

ELTESTER, F., *Eikôn in Neuen Testament*, Berlin 1958.

FLOERI, F., "Le sens de la 'division des sexes' chez Grégoire de Nysse," *Revue des sciences religieuses* 27 (1953) 105-11.

GAITH, J., *La conception de la liberté chez Grégoire de Nysse*, Paris 1953.

GIBLET, J., "L'homme image de Dieu dans les commentaires littéraux de Philon d'Alexandrie," *Studia Hellenistica* 5 (1948) 93-118.

GILLET, R., "L'homme divinisateur cosmique dans la pensée de Grégoire de Nysse," *Studia Patristica* 6, Berlin 1962, 62-83.

GRAEF, H., "L'image de Dieu et la structure de l'âme chez les Pères grecs," *La vie spirituelle* (supplément) 22 (1952) 331-9.

JERVELL, J., *Imago Dei. Gen. 1, 26 im Spätjudentum, in der Gnosis und in den paulinischen Briefen*, Göttingen 1960.

KARAVIDOPOULOS, I., *"Eikon Theou" kai "kat' eikona" Theou para to Apostolo Pavlo. Ai Christologikai vaseis tis Pavleiou anthropologias*, Thessaloniki 1964.

_____ *I peri Theou kai anthropou didaskali Philonos tou Alexandreos* (Offprint from *Theologia*, Athens 1966, 33-53).

_____ "Erminevtikon ipomnima eis tin pros Kolossaeis epistolin tou Apostolou Pavlou," *Epistimoniki Epetiris Theologikis Scholis Panepistimiou Thessalonikis* 13 (1969) 383-492.

KITTEL, G., *Theologisches Wörterbuch zum Neuen Testament* 2, 386-7, 393-6.

KOHLER, L., "Die Grundstelle der Imago-Dei-Lehre Gn. 1, 26," *Theologische Zeitschrift* 4 (1948) 16-22.

KORNITSESKOU, K., *O anthropismos kata ton ieron Chrysostomon*, Thessaloniki 1971.

LADNER, B. G., "The Philosophical Anthropology of Saint Gregory of Nyssa," *Dumbarton Oaks Papers* 12 (1958) 59-94.

LASSIAT, H., *Promotion de l'homme en Jésus-Christ d'après Irénée de Lyon*, Paris 1977.

_____ "L'anthropologie d'Irénée," *Nouvelle revue théologique* 100, 3 (1978) 399-417.

LEYS, R., *L'image de Dieu chez Saint Grégoire de Nysse. Esquisse d'une doctrine*, Bruxelles-Paris 1951.

LIESKE, A., "Die Theologie der Christus-mystik Gregors von Nyssa," *Zeitschrift für Katholische Theologie* 70 (1948) 49-93, 128-68, 315-40.

LOSSKY, V., *The Mystical Theology of the Eastern Church*, Cambridge & London 1957.

_____ *The Image and Likeness of God*, Crestwood, N.Y., & Oxford 1975.

MCGARRY, W., "St Gregory of Nyssa and Adam's Body," *Thought* 10 (1935-6) 81-94.

MAVER, A., *Das Bild Gottes im Menschen nach Clemens von Alexandrien*, Rome 1942.

MERKI, H., *Omoiosis Theo, Von der platonischen Angleichung an Gott zur Gottähnlichkeit bei Gregor von Nyssa*, Freiburg im B. 1952.

_____ "Ebenbildlichkeit," *Reallexikon für Antike und Christentum* 4 (1959) 459-79.

MOUTSOULAS, I., *I sarkosis tou Logou kai i theosis tou anthropou kata tin didaskalian Grigoriou tou Nyssis*, Athens 1965.

NELLAS, P., *Prolegomena eis tin meletin Nikolaou tou Kavasila*, Athens 1968.

_____ *I peri dikaioseos tou anthropou didaskalia Nikolaou tou Kavasila*, Peiraeus 1975.

ORBE, A., *Antropologia de San Ireneo*, Madrid 1969.

ORPHANOS, M., *I psychi kai to soma tou anthropou kata Didymon Alexandrea (ton typhlon)*, Thessaloniki 1974.

PETERSON, E. *Pour une théologie du vêtement*, Lyon 1944.

_____ "L'homme image de Dieu chez saint Irénée," *La vie spirituelle* 100 (1959) 584-94.

PHILLIPS, A., *The Eschatology of St Gregory of Nyssa*, Oxford 1963.

QUASTEN, J., "A Pythagorean idea in Jerome," *American Journal of Philology* 73, 2 (1942) 207-15.

_____ "Theodore of Mopsuestia on the Exorcism of the Cilicium," *Harvard Theological Review* 35 (1942) 209-19.

RADOSALIEVITS, A., *To mistirion tis sotirias kata ton aghion Maximon ton Omologitin*, Athens 1975.

ROLDANUS, J., *Le Christ et l'homme dans la théologie d'Athanase d'Alexandrie. Etude de la conjonction de sa conception de l'homme avec sa christologie*, Leiden 1968.

ROMANIDES, J., *To propatorikon amartima*, Athens 1957.

SCHMIDT, K. L., "Homo Imago Dei im Alten und Neuen Testament," *Eranos-Jahrbuch* 15 (1947) 149-95.

SKOUTERIS, K., *Synepeiai tis ptoseos kai loutron palingenesias*, Athens 1973.

STAMM, J. J., *Die Gottebenbildlichkeit des Menschen im A.T.*, Zurich 1959.

STEPHANOU, E., "La coexistence initiale du corps et de l'âme d'après saint Grégoire de Nysse et saint Maxime l'Homologète," *Echos d'Orient* 31 (1932) 304-15.

THEODOROU, A., *I peri anakephalaioseos didaskalia tou Eirinaiou*, Athens 1972.

THUNBERG, L., *Microcosm and Mediator. The Theological Anthropology of Maximos the Confessor*, Lund 1965.

VELLAS, V., *O anthropos kata tin Palaian Diathikin*, Athens 1966.
WILLMS, H., *Eikon. Eine begriffsgeschichtliche Untersuchung zum
    Platonismus, 1.* Teil, *Philo von Alexandreia. Mit einer Einleitung
    über Platon und die Zwischenzeit*, Münster 1935.
ZISSIS, Th., *O anthropos kai o kosmos en ti oikonomia tou Theou
    kata ton ieron Chrysostomon*, Thessaloniki 1971.

Glossary

Antimension (literally "instead of the table," *anti* + *mensa*): a cloth of silk or linen, containing relics, and usually decorated with a representation of the entombment of Christ. Used for the celebration of the Liturgy where there is no consecrated altar; also used, even on a consecrated altar, in the manner of a Western corporal.

Apocatastasis: The Origenistic teaching that all creatures endowed with reason will be saved on the consummation of God's plan for the universe, divine punishment being educative rather than retributive. This doctrine was condemned by the Second Council of Constantinople in 553.

Apophatic: The approach characteristic of many of the Greek Fathers in which God is discussed in terms of what He is not rather than of what He is, most positive terms being considered finite and therefore in some way misleading.

Canon: a hymnological composition, consisting of nine (in practice, except in the Great Canon of St Andrew of Crete, usually eight) "odes" or canticles, each containing several toparia or stanzas; read or sung chiefly at the service of Matins or Orthros.

Euchologion (literally "Book of Prayers"): contains in particular church services for specific occasions (baptism, marriage, visitation of the sick, funerals, etc.), together with prayers and blessings for special objects or needs (blessing of crops, vineyards, flocks and cattle, of a new home, a car, etc.). Sometimes entitled *Hagiasmatarion* (literally "[Book of] Sanctification").

Hagiasmatarion: see *Euchologion.*

Orthros (literally "[Service for] Dawn"): the morning office corresponding to Matins and Lauds in the West.

Pneumatohylic: with spirit (*pneuma*) and matter (*hyle*) operating in perfect unison.

Prelapsarian/postlapsarian: refers to the human situation before/after the fall.

Synaxary: a short account of the saint (or saints) for the feast or other commemoration appointed daily in the Church calendar; read at Orthros after the sixth canticle of the canon.

Theandric: refers to the operation of Jesus Christ who is simultaneously both fully God (*Theos*) and fully man (*anir*).

Triodion: the liturgical book containing the special services for the four preparatory Sundays before Lent, for Lent itself, and for Holy Week.

Troparion: a stanza of religious poetry, sung either on its own or as part of the canticles that make up the canon.

Index of Patristic Texts

Index of Subjects

ADAM, created in image of Christ, 35, 223; as type of his descendants, 116; his prelapsarian life, 52, 72, 109; his fall, 57, 58-9, 61, 175, 208-9, 219-20; his transmission of pleasure and death, 47-8, 76-7, 81. *See also* ANTHROPOLOGY.

ALTAR, 152-3, 154

ANASTASIOS OF SINAI, ST, 27

ANDREW OF CRETE, ST, 163n, 167, 170, 234

ANGELS, 231

ANSELM OF CANTERBURY, 62n

ANTHROPOLOGY, and apophatic method, 73; and Orthodox theology, 103, 120. Man as created for Christ, 35, 38, 40, 135-6, 223, 224; as midway point of creation, 26-7, 211-12; as called to transcend his nature, 28-9; as a microcosm, 29-30, 141, 203; as a "deified animal," 12, 30; as a theological being, 30, 34, 73, 83; as iconic in his ontology, 33-4, 37, 75; as lacking autonomy, 42; as containing an element of the divine, 30-1, 34; as different in nature from God, 109; his prelapsarian life, 52, 73, 86-9, 173-4, 203-4; his experience of the results of the fall, 53, 57, 85, 86, 87-91; his enhypostatization in the Logos 36-7; his renewal by Christ, 112-13, 116-18, 119, 122-3, 139, 193. *See also* ADAM, AUTONOMY, DEIFICATION, FALL, GARMENTS OF SKIN *and* IMAGE.

ANTIMENSION, 152

ARIANISM, 39-40, 228

ARISTOTLE, 59, 232

ASCENSION, 214-15

ASCESIS, 101n, 102, 149, 188-9

ATHANASIOS OF ALEXANDRIA, ST, 24, 25, 28, 228

AUGUSTINE, ST, 94, 228, 231

AUTONOMY, 42, 93, 95, 96, 102, 103, 110

BAPTISM, 82, 83, 84, 120, 121-2, 124, 147, 169, 219-20

BASIL THE GREAT, ST, 38, 233

BISHOP, 153, 154

BODY, 52-3, 158-9

CANON, GREAT, 163, 167, 169, 172, 174, 176, 177, 195, 196n

CHRISMATION, 120, 125-6, 142

251